DIALOGUE AMONG THE FAITH COMMUNITIES

Lucien F. Cosijns

Foreword by Marcus Braybrooke

Hamilton Books
A member of
The Rowman & Littlefield Publishing Group
Lanham · Boulder · New York · Toronto · Plymouth, UK

Copyright © 2008 by
Hamilton Books
4501 Forbes Boulevard
Suite 200
Lanham, Maryland 20706
Hamilton Books Acquisitions Department (301) 459-3366

Estover Road
Plymouth PL6 7PY
United Kingdom

Library of Congress Control Number: 2008925247
ISBN-13: 978-0-7618-4085-5 (paperback : alk. paper)
ISBN-10: 0-7618-4085-0 (paperback : alk. paper)

Table of Contents

Foreword

by Marcus Braybrooke

Lucien F. Cosijns' story could almost serve as evidence for reincarnation, except that his three incarnations have all taken place in one remarkable and varied life.

Born in Belgium, Lucien trained as a priest of the Belgian Scheut Congregation and served for fourteen years in Japan. There he learned a deep appreciation of Japanese values and way of life. His second life, as a married man, was in business – at first in Japan and then back in Belgium. Since 1993, in his third life, Lucien, whom I am glad to call a friend, has devoted himself tirelessly to promoting interfaith dialogue. To such dialogue, which has often been a largely Western activity, Lucien has brought his appreciation of Eastern values and especially the Japanese spirit of harmony or 'WA'.

With a business man's concern for results and deeply conscious of the gravity of the evils of poverty and violence, Lucien has tried, with some success, to spur interfaith organisations into working more closely together. In 1993, when he became involved in interfaith work, many interfaith organisations held events to commemorate the centenary of the first Parliament of Religions, which was held in Chicago. But, as Lucien recognised, the impact of the interfaith movement is limited because it is fragmented.

Lucien has been one of the prophetic voices calling for 'a global world organization like a United Religions Organization, next to the United Nations, which could become a one-voice moral forum of the world faith communities.' Such a world spiritual body would make the politicians of all governments mindful of their duty to take efficient measures on a local and global scale to stop the proliferation of poverty and violence.' At present, as he says, the activities of interfaith organisations are largely confined to providing local remedies, without really changing the overall dramatic situation, and the socio-economic and political systems which are at its roots.

Lucien has also produced important interfaith guidelines, which he explains in some detail, for all engaged in interfaith activity. They will be of special value to those new to this area of work

Lucien's personal story is fascinating, but his book also includes a wealth of information. It is a challenge to those already engaged in interfaith work to redouble their efforts and a call to others to engage in a task which is vital for the future of the world.

Reverend Marcus Braybrooke was born on 16th November 1938, is a retired clergyman, priest of the Church of England and has been a vicar of parishes in Kent and Bath near Oxford as well as a Prebendary of Wells Cathedral. Some of his more than thirty books are taken up in the bibliography at the end of this book. He has played an active role in several interfaith organizations, such as:

- Executive Director, Council of Christians & Jews (UK)1984-87
- Chairman, World Congress of Faiths 1978-83 & 1992-99,
- VP 1986 - 97; Co-President 1997-2000; President 2000-
- Chairman International Interfaith Organisations Committee 1988-93
- Trustee: International Interfaith Centre 1993-2000
- Patron: International Interfaith Centre 2000-
- Trustee: International Peace Council 1995-2000; Peace Councillor 2000-
- Member of the International Advisory Committee of the Council for Parliament of World Religions 2002-
- Editor: World Faiths Insight 1976-91
- Co-Founder of the Three Faiths Forum.

Introduction

After 25 centuries of an ever faster-going evolution of humankind, *DIALOGUE* has now come to be a word and a concept of daily use in the media and a theme of discussion all over the world. In the current period of our human history, the centuries long struggle for life and of belligerent confrontation is at last being replaced by a new era of collaboration in dialogue with each other. The most eye-catching aspect of this dialogue is the worldwide interfaith dialogue movement which has in de past 15 years spread out all over the world and which has resulted in efforts towards a corroborative dialogue between the world of faiths and the political world. This book's aim is a sketching of this movement in its philosophical and religious evolution and expression.

The background from which this book has been formed needs some explanation.

According to our current knowledge of the universe, after 15 billion years of evolution it has taken two billion years for primitive cells to incorporate a nucleus as one of the first steps towards complexity. About 4 billion years ago, the solar system was formed and it took only 200 million years to evolve multicellular animals. It took only a short period of time of four million years to go from small-brained apes with crude bone tools to modern man and genetic engineering. This shows how small we are as human beings in this vast universe and how fast the pace of development has increased since the human being has come to a rather mature intellectual existence in the course of it evolution. The creativity of the human intellect has been at the origin of the ever faster evolution and changes which have occurred on this planet of ours in the past 25-odd centuries.

In the so-called *Axial Period* from about 600 to 300 BCE, the main religions of the world were founded. Ethical monotheism in the Middle East was first developed by ZARATHUSTRA, also called Zoroaster, in Eastern Persia, probably about 600 BCE but possibly earlier; Zoroastrianism (also called Mazdeism) spread in the Persian Empire starting in the 6th century BCE. Ethical monotheism also arose among the HEBREW PROPHETS in Palestine, starting in the 8th century BCE.

HINDU traditions of belief and social organization developed in the emerging Aryan society of India by 700–500 BCE, with the early sacred hymns or Vedas and the Brahman priesthood providing the foundations. The composition in the 8th to the 4th centuries BCE of the Upanishads provided systematic interpretation of the Vedas and are the foundation for much of later Indian philosophical and religious thought.

JAINISM was founded by Mahavira, who lived in the 6th century BCE (599-527), and died in Pavapuri, Bihar, India

BUDDHISM developed in India in these same centuries, beginning with the teaching career of SIDDHARTHA GAUTAMA, the BUDDHA (c.542–483), as a rejection of Brahman dominance and the caste system. The development of Hinduism and Buddhism created the distinctive world-views of Indian civilization by the end of the Axial era.

CONFUCIUS (551-479) lived during the 6th century BCE in China. His teachings provided a philosophical base for social loyalty and obedience.

TAOISM (or Daoism), which is usually traced to the legendary teacher Laozi (or Lao Tse), 580-500, followed by the egalitarian teachings of Mo-Zi (c.471–391), and the authoritarian legalism, most fully articulated by the later philosopher Han Fei (c.280-233).

GREEK PHILOSOPHY represents the intellectual culmination of the transformations in the eastern Mediterranean societies of the Mycenaeans and Dorians. Socrates (469–), Plato (427–327), and Aristotle (384–322), together they provided the basis for the main traditions of Greek philosophy emerging from the Axial age.

My life has been a rather varied one. At the time of our graduation from a Catholic senior high school in Belgium, we were with 36 students, of whom a remarkably high number of 16 entered a religious life to become a diocesan priest, a contemplative monk or an active missionary. Back in 1943, these vocations to the priesthood were considered by the Catholic parents of that time as the highest possible compensation and remuneration for their life of hard work, like it was still the common way of life for most people before the outbreak of World War II.

I chose for an active missionary life in the Belgian missionary congrega-tion of the Scheut (CICM) fathers. This became then, what I later called *my first life* of 21 years. One year of novitiate, two years of philosophical, and 4 years of theological studies, among which, English and in my case also Chinese, were the required studies to enter the priesthood and to be sent abroad to China to which country I was first destined to be sent. In 1950 five colleagues and myself left for Japan from Genoa on a Dutch cargo ship with sixteen passengers. Due to the communist regime, entry of China had become impossible, and because of the similarity in language, our destina-tion became Japan, where I spent 14 years in the service of the Church, with the mission of converting the Japanese to the Catholic faith. And try we did in the sincerest way, sustained by the innocent ideals of our youth, although with very little results. After the first year, which was spent on the study of the very difficult language, we were sent out as assistants to parishes in the Hyōgo prefecture, south of Kōbe. A great part of my time was taken up by kindergarten management, another part by teaching catechism to the parents of the children and to other people, another part by teaching English or French to the young and to businessmen as financial revenue and by other normal church activities.

End 1964, I took the painstaking decision to make an end to this first life of mine, for a lot of reasons. The main one was frustration with the slowness of the church authorities to permit an inculturation of the church ceremonies and practices into the culture of Japan. Another reason was my growing awareness of and integration in a society, enjoying a standard of morality, based on Buddhist and Confucian life and family concepts, much higher than in most Western countries. This was still before the resolutions of the Second Vatican Council (1962-1965) became effective, and gave a kind of green light to the long awaited changes by a/o the permission to switch from the Latin language, which had been used for the past centuries in all Catholic ceremonies the world over, to the local languages, and a world-first declaration of the obligation of respect for other religions and cultures.

And so began *my second life* as a businessman, starting with my entering in the service of a big Japanese trading house, my marriage with a Japanese, and our returning to Belgium in 1965, where I learned and became involved in international trade for 3 years at the Belgian office of the same trading house in Brussels. After this period, I started in 1968 on my own and with my own company, active for 21 years in trade and commercial consulting between Europe and Japan, until it was taken over in 1997 by our youngest son. Our main trump for success was our knowledge of the languages and customs on both sides.

On occasion of my more than 60 business trips to Japan and other countries in Asia and the US, I made it a point of conduct to always pay a visit to the slum quarters of all the big cities of New York, Los Angeles, San Francisco, Jakarta, Bombay, etc. The frightening images of poverty and misery I have witnessed there have been with me ever since, and have had their influence on my desire to do something about it in my third life.

The launching of the idea of creating a United Religions Organisation as a partner to the United Nations Organisation by Bishop William Swing of the Episcopal California Diocese in 1993, was the start of *my third life,* a kind of merger of my first and second life, dedicated to the promotion of the interfaith dialogue, with as main aim the collaboration between the world religions, traditions, spiritual movements and other convictions, now more commonly denominated as Faith Communities. This we considered to be the means by excellence towards the creation of a new world order of a world with more peace and justice for all.

My permanent solicitude in relation with our world problems of wars, conflicts, poverty, refugees, etc. and my searching how these destructive forces could be reined in and fashion a new universal civilization has led me to the conviction that only a global world organization like a kind of United Religions Organization, next to the United Nations, could become a one-voice moral forum of the world of the Faith Communities. Only such global forum could summon the necessary power to make the politicians of all involved governments mindful of their duty to take more efficient measures on a local and global scale to stop the proliferation of these world problems. The activities of all the NGO's of the world, while very plausible, remain limited to local remedies, without however really changing the overall dramatic situation, and the socio-economic and political systems, which are at its roots.

In Japan I became acquainted with and a part of the Japanese way of life, which is regretfully all too unknown outside Japan. The Japanese are rather introvert people and in particular so in their contacts with non-Japanese. They seldom talk about themselves and will do so only when they feel there is a real wish to learn and to understand, which then becomes a basis for conversation. The Japanese way of life is a way of life in harmony, where the common good stands above private interests, where the Confucian five basic relationships of husband and wife, father and son, older brother and younger brother, ruler and ruled, heaven and earth, are still practiced in everyday life. This has created a nation where harmony and perfection are standard aims in all domains and for all citizens. Comparing different kinds of capitalism, I read somewhere that the capitalism of Japan can be called a human capitalism, the capitalism of the EU a social capitalism and that of the US a capitalism of winners and losers.

Many of the texts which have been on my website since some years and of which some are published in this book have been influenced by what I have learned in Japan during a long relationship of 47 years (1950-1997). My own texts in this book are therefore the result of my becoming Japanese with the Japanese and of my 14 years involvement in the interreligious dialogue movement from 1993 till this day of 2007. Because I have wished to make the different paragraphs of this book into rather independent units, I apologize for some repetitions, which therefore have been unavoidable. Texts of other authors, which I consider to have been constructive elements in the promotion of the interreligious dialogue movement, are added under separate paragraphs. Dr. Hans Kûng, Catholic Theologian, professor emeritus of the Thûbingen University in Germany has expressed the need of dialogue as follows:

No human life without a world ethic for the nations.
No peace among the nations without peace among the religions.
No peace among the religions without dialogue among the religions.

The day after a most interesting and inspiring dialogue meeting with Buddhist monks in the city of Osaka, Japan, in November 1994, I was inspired to write down my main basic text "INTERFAITH DIALOGUE GUIDELINES", which has not substantially changed since that date and which has remained as the guiding principles for all my subsequent interfaith dialogue activities.

A text worked out by the Universal Solidarity Movement of Value Education for Peace, Indore, India, as qualities to be aimed at by their movement, expresses also a characteristic for each of the world religions, which characteristics should be studied as subjects of mutual enrichment:

Civilization of love on earth is built on the spiritual foundation
of the world religions.
'We visualize a nation with
the universal family spirit of Hinduism and Baha'i faith;
the discipline and fellowship of Islam;
the courage of Sikhism;
the compassion of Buddhism;
the non-violence of Jainism;
the creativity of Parsi religion;
the indomitability of Judaism;
the cosmic solidarity of Tribal religion;
the self-sacrifice and forgiveness of Christianity.'

* * *

Buddhism, Baha'i, Indigenous Traditions, Christianity, Hinduism, Islam, Jainism, Judaism, Shintō, Zoroastrianism, Taoism, Sikhism.

Lucien F. Cosijns Pr. Poppestraat 44, 2640 Mortsel, Belgium
T. +32 3 455.6880 F. +32 2 706 5883 lucien.cosijns@telenet.be
www.interfaithdialoguebasics.be

* * *

Before going to the core of this booklet, let's first have a look at some preliminary paragraphs.

Part 1 Preliminary Chapters

1. Our World Problems

Naom Chomsky(USA),*Year 501*, Verso, 1993, Hans-Peter Martin & Harald Schuman (D), *Die Globalisierungsfalle*, Rowolt, 1996, Bas de Gaay Fortman and Berma Klein Goldewijk (NL), *God and the Goods*, WCC, 1989, and others, in many books and articles, have claimed that the worldwide indoctrination of the common population and the ongoing world domination in the economic and financial sectors of 80% of the population of the industrialized world by 'the richmen's club' of 20% of that population, are at the basis of the proliferation of most of our world problems. Globalization is a mixture of an unavoidable world evolution of the human race accompanied by some less good side-effects which need a counteraction.

Poverty, material and intellectual:
- Wealth sharing of the 20% poorest: in 1960: 23%; in 1997 : 1%
- Wealth sharing of the 20% richest: in 1960: 30 times that of the 20% poor, in 1997: 78 times that of the 20% poorest.
- The 44 poorest countries control in 1998 only 0.3% of the world trade, compared with 0.6% in 1977. (UNCTAD data)
- World income increased almost 4 times, from US$ 6000 billion in 1960 to 23,000 billion in 1993. During the same period of 33 years however, the number of poor people increased by 18%.
- 3 Billion people survive with less than US$ 2.00 a day.
- 1 Billion people have no drinkable water.
- 800 Million people are illiterate. 125 million children never go to school, and each year 150 million of pupils drop out of school before having a usable capability of reading and writing.
- 1/3 of the African population has a life expectancy of 40 year.
- In 2004 at least 3 billion people lived in acute poverty, and at least 1 billion people lived in slums.
- International Aid Assistance: the rich countries give an average of 0.27% of their wealth to the so-called underdeveloped countries, while, since many years, the target has been set at 0.7%.

- **Britain:** in the past 20 years, and especially since the Margaret Thatcher government, the situation of the poor has unbelievably escalated, with now more than 27 million or 1/4th of the British population living below a humanly acceptable minimum, where the rich get richer and the poor poorer. According to the best available estimate of 1995, about 100.000 refugee children are living on the streets of the British cities, and 1.7 million people do not have their own bed to sleep in.
- **Mexico:** the poor increased in the last decade from 17 to 26 million, for a total population of 91 million. The number of extreme poor is now increasing each year by 1 million. in 1998 the UN Development Program spent some US$ 5 million on the extreme poverty in Mexico, as part of a total of US$ 80 million for this country.
- **India:** among a population of 1.027 billion, 400 million are considered as living below a minimum standard of life. The Dalit caste of the rural and tribal villages is as rigorous as ever, in spite of a democratic government of 50 years (1948-98). 340 Million illiterate Indians are the backbone of Indian economy. No government resources for primary education are available, although the Indian Constitution recognizes education as a basic right. The situation is now however since some years gradually improving with a rapidly growing middle-class population.
- **Brazil:** according to an International Labor organization study, 7 million children are working as slaves and prostitutes, while there are probably 7 to 8 million street children in the big cities like Rio de Janeiro.
- **Belgium :** even in a wealthy and prosperous country like Belgium, 13% of the 10 million population, meaning 100.000 citizens, live below the poverty line.

Despite all official and private aid assistance, the population of slums the world over continues to increase.

Debts of the poorer nations

The global world debt of 41 of the poorer nations, with a population of about 1 billion, has run up from US$ 567 billion in 1980 to 1.416 billion in 1992. Thirty three of these nations are on the Sub-Sahara African continent. The global international debt of these Sub-Sahara nations has since 1980 quadrupled to US$ 223 billion in 1997. There seems to be no other human way to get over this devastating world problem than an international study and cooperation by the creditor nations on how to work out ways and means on an annulment of these debts.

Conflicts and Wars

- W.W.II: 45 million victims of whom 2/3 civilians !!!
- 37 conflicts were active in the world in 1997. Since the end of the cold war period around 1991, bloody conflicts have resulted in 9.3 million

victims of which 90% are civilians.

Death Tolls of Selected Wars, 1500-1945
(State of the World 1999, p.154)

Table 1. 1

Wars and Conflicts	Time Period	Number killed	Civilian Victims %
Peasants'War (Germany)	1524-1525	175.000	57
Dutch Independence War (vs. Spain)	1585-1604	4 177.000	32
30-Year War (Europe)	1618-1648	4.000.000	50
Spanish Succession War (Europe)	1701-1714	1.251.000	n.a
7-Year War (Europe, North America, India)	1755-1763	1.358.000	27
French Revolutionary/Napoleon Wars	1792-1815	4.899.000	41
Crimean War (Russia, France, Britain)	1854-1856	772.000	66
US Civil War	1861-1865	820.000	24
Paraguay vs. Brazil and Argentina	1864-1870	1.100.000	73
French-Prussian War	1870-1871	1250.000	25
US-Spanish War	1898	200.000	95
World War I	1914-1918	26.000.000	50
World War II	1939-1945	53.547.000	60
Total	**1524-1945**	**99.549.000**	

Armament

- **Armament an Development Aid**

The yearly expenses worldwide run up to 900 billion dollar for armament and to 350 billion dollar for agricultural subsidies, but only a paltry 68 billion dollars can be made available for foreign development aid.

The 30 dollar per year needed to send a child to school are not being found, but as much as 150 dollar per year and per person is expended on so-called defense budgets. The agreed upon 0.7% of the GDP as foreign development aid would procure 200 billion instead of the current 0.3%, or 86 billion dollar.

- **Military forces in 1998 in the Far East** (Source: Defense Agency Japan):

Table 1. 2

Country	Troops	Aircraft	Vessels	Million Tons
North Korea	190.000	900	440	15
Russian Far East	000	610	730	10
South Korea	575.000	490	190	11
China	100.000	4.260	820	00
Japan	149.000	510	150	36
US-Force in Japan	21.000	140	n/a	n/a
US-Forces in S.Korea	27.000	90	n/a	n/a
US-Navy 7th Fleet	n/a	130	60	63
Taiwan	270.000	440	370	0.22
Total	2.332.0000	7.570	2.710	3.57

- **Main exporters of conventional weapons**: USA, France, UK, Russia and China. They sell 86% of all conventional weapons, of which 2/3 go to 10 developing countries.
- **Enlightening data**
- 200 million guns are in private hands in the USA. 800.000 security guards protect houses   and offices at a yearly cost of US$ 22 billion. Near to no guns in private hands in Japan with only 230 shootings per year recorded.
- Modern war costs: defense experts have estimated that the first 24 hours of the air attacks against Yugoslavia has cost more than Euro 85 million, and that every additional day costs from US$ 10 to 30 million (Euro 8.5 to 25.5) extra.
- American fighter/bomber planes & missiles cost in million Euro: F117A Nighthawk: € 104, F16 fighter plane: € 17, F15 Eagle: € 37, B52: € 26, B2: € 1.100, E3 Sentry: € 230, EA6B Prowler: € 44.3, BGM109 Tomahawk cruise missile: € 0.85, AGM86C cruise missile: € 0.99.

A study would be worthwhile on the background reasons for the remarkable differences in the data on Russia/US/Japan and some other countries in 2006 as hereunder.

Table 1. 3

Country	Criminality Rate/1000	Prisoners /100.000	Prisoners	Lawyers	Population
Russia	204.0	595	846.000		142.069.000
USA	92.0	696	2,078,000	1.850.000	298.444.000
UK	85.8	85	52.000		60.609.000
Germany	81.5	95	79.000		82.422.000
Belgium	76.1	67	9.000	7.500	10.379.000
France	61.4	92	56.000		60.876.000
Japan	21.5	54	69.000	50.000	127.463.000

Population movements
- Immigration in Europe: 17 million North-Africans, followed now by-many from other countries.
- Multireligious Europe: Islam has become the second religion after Christianity, with a Muslim population of 300.000 in Belgium, 600.000 inThe Netherlands, 4 million in France, 4.5 million in Germany.
- Refugees: external displaced persons (EDP) decreased to 9,2 million,while internal displaced persons (IDP) in the world increased from 12 million to 25 million in 2005. The total number of people who can be called refugees runs to 46 million, or 1 for 200 of the world population. This was 1 for 100 on the African continent. Between 1948 and 1992, the UNO has spent US$ 8.3 billion for assistance operations in military conflicts and in the problem of the fugitives.

World Globalization and Domination

The neo-liberalism of the last 30 to 40 years with its main overall purpose of money profits with the free market economy as the means thereto, has had an enormous impact also on scientific research. The main investment sectors have been the new materials, the information technology and the biotechnology, with, it has to be admitted, amazing results in all three sectors. The problem however, also here, is that these developments have been achieved, not for the benefit of humankind, but to cash in tremendously high profit margins by the transnational groups. This results in many cases in an increase in poverty and a still higher dependence of the poor in the developing countries on the world domination of the transnational corporations, without being subject to law regulations to protect the population, for example, from the dangers implicated in cloning, in transgening of animals and plants. The have-nots of this planet will be also here the victims of the patents, obtained by these transnational enterprises, and their monopolizing of the products.

The globalization is for 70 to 80% at the origin of the decline in employment in the developing countries to the advantage of the rich countries is the conclusion of a 1998 study by Marcio Pochmann of the Brazilian University of Campinas.

According to this study:
- the unemployed in the world increased between 1979 & 1998 from 44.6 million tot 130.6 million,
- tripled to 39 million in India,
- quadrupled to 6.65 million in Brazil,
- increased tenfold in the last 10 years to 10.6 million in Indonesia.

The 'terminator' project of the Monsanto Corporation is.only one example of this encroachment on the economic and social life. It means the marketing of good seeds but with sterility effect on the plants, with as consequence that the planters will depend for 100% on the supply of seeds by the corporation, like Professor Filip Polk of the Free University of Brussels described in an article in the Belgian-Flemish journal 'De Morgen' of December 14, 1998.

Economic and financial world domination 80/20 of the many by a few (World Bank and other reports):
- Transnational Corporations (TNCs) conduct 70% of global trade. D.Korten in his book "Then Corporations rule the World", concludes that the second industrial revolution, based on the exploitation of information and communication technology, is also based on processes of colonization, now defined more by class than by geography, and forcing ever more of the world's population in the ranks of the colonized.
- The share of total exports of manufactures of foreign US affiliates of US based firms increased from less than 18% in 1957 to 41% in 1984.
- Intra-firm trade within the largest 350 TNCs ran up to 40% of total

trade. More than a third of US trade is between foreign affiliates and their US-based parents. Over half of Malaysia's exports to the US are from US affiliates, and Taiwan's five leading electronics exporters are US firms, 47% of Singapore's exports in 1992 were by US-based firms.

- Protectionist measures of the industrial countries reduce national income of the South by about twice the amount provided by official aid, which is largely export-promotion most of it to the richer sectors of the less needy but better consumers in the developing countries.
- Non-tariff barriers of the industrial countries reduce Third World exports by almost 20% in affected categories, which include textiles, steel, seafood, animal feed and other agricultural products, with billion of dollars a year in losses.

Information: four news agencies control 96 % of the entire flow of news in the world, and 95% of all computers are in the developed countries. In 1992, 50 countries, inhabited by over half the world's population, had only one telephone line per 100 inhabitants. 71% of the telephone lines in the world are in high-income countries, while low-income ones own 4%.

In spite of all official and private laudable efforts, the world problem situation is deteriorating, instead of improving. Only a concerted global action by a union in collaboration among the world religions, traditions, spiritual movements and other convictions, and this in cooperation with the political and industrial world can arrive at efficient solutions and build the basis for a real new world order.

Réginald MOREELS, Belgian Minister of State in charge of international aid assistance in 1999, in his book "Hoop voor de naakte mens" (Hope for the naked human), Lannoo, 1997, states some concepts which all could be taken from the Japanese way of life: p.102: *A stable society is only possible when prosperity goes together with welfare for all, when freedom goes together with social justice, when justice goes together with truth.* p.125: International Aid : Moreels proposes 5 main sectors: *education, welfare, agriculture, small infrastructures, peace-initiatives or small-scale economic initiatives.* p.143: *Enterprises must serve their share-holders but also their stake-holders: workers, employees, consumers, local authorities, sub-contractors and suppliers, environment: harmony between shareholders and stakeholders.*

*   *   *

Here I wish to quote an article originally published in The Tablet on 05/01/2002 and reproduced here with permission from the editor and the author with as title The Path from Hate to Love by William Johnston, s.j.

2. The Path from Hate to Love

by William Johnston, s.j., based at Sophia University in Tokyo.

It gives a Japanese/Buddhist response to the theology of Juliana of Norwich (1342-1416) and shows a way out of the problems of our world.
Quote:
'No peace between the nations without peace between the religions', the theologian Hans Küng has said. And how can that be achieved? Pondering the terrorist attacks on the United States, a Jesuit skilled in East-West dialogue sees only one answer.

When I returned to Japan from Europe last November, I had an opportunity to speak to a group of Japanese friends about the crisis in today's world. All agreed that the attack on the World Trade Centre was a turning point in the history of humanity. The world will never again be the same. Many Japanese who watched that seemingly innocent plane head relentlessly towards its target in the blue sky of New York were reminded of another turning-point in human history. On 6 August 1945 at 8.15 in the morning a tiny silver plane appeared high in the cloudless blue sky of Hiroshima. People looked up in wonder. And then it parachuted down, the bomb that killed 100,000 people and left 100,000 wounded, blinded, paralyzed, their naked bodies scorched from head to toe. That day of terror ushered in the nuclear age.

In my many decades in Japan I have encountered little bitterness, little talk of revenge. The Japanese seldom speak about the bomb. Nevertheless now, more than 50 years after that unspeakable tragedy, it is legitimate to ask if there is any connection between the ruthless destruction of the Twin Towers in New York and the cruel bomb that wiped out Hiroshima.

The thesis of Samuel Huntington about the clash of civilizations is well known in Japan, where it has been widely discussed both in learned journals and in popular magazines. As my friends and I sat around a table drinking green tea, we began to speak about the clash of civilizations in this country. We reflected on the bloody clash that took place when Christianity came to Japan in the sixteenth century. The new religion, brought by St Francis Xavier, was at first warmly welcomed. In Nagasaki thousands joyfully received baptism, and the missionaries were filled with confidence. But the rulers of Japan began to see Christianity as a threatening colonial power, and after unleashing one of the fiercest persecutions in human history, they expelled all foreigners. For centuries Japan was cut off from the world, with only a few Dutch residents remaining in "the closed country". And what about today?

We agreed that the clash of civilizations continues in the hearts of the people, particularly in the hearts of Japanese Christians. It is described dramatically by the distinguished Japanese novelist Shusaku Endo. A committed Catholic with a personal love for Jesus Christ, Endo brought many Japanese to baptism, yet he felt uncomfortable with the exterior trappings of Western Christianity. He, a Japanese, was wearing Western clothing. His vocation in life was to change that Western suit into a Japanese kimono.

Asked concretely what the problem was, Endo replied that Christianity was too much a Western religion. It was dogmatic, uncompromising, patriarchal. It saw reality in terms of black-and-white. Its history was full of "I am right and you are wrong", bringing inquisitions, intolerance, punishment of dissidents and downright lack of compassion. Asian thought, on the other hand, was "grey", flexible, tolerant. It stressed "both-and" rather than "either-or". Above all, Asian thought was feminine, grounded in a predominantly yin culture. Endo often said that his faith came through his mother. I recall showing him a book about Julian of Norwich and "the motherly love of Jesus". He smiled enthusiastically. "Father, give me that book!" he said.

The clash of civilizations in Asia has indeed been fierce. Colonialism and religion are at its core. As we move into the third millennium, however, one great event gives ground for optimism: the clash between Buddhism and Christianity is becoming a powerful dialogue in which both religions are mutually enriched. Christians listen attentively to the wise words of the Dalai Lama and Sogyal Rinpoche; they learn meditation from Thich Nat Han and Zen teachers. Likewise, Buddhist teachers quote the gospels, and Buddhist scholars in Kyoto have made profound studies of the Christian mystics, particularly Meister Eckhart. And all this is complemented by cooperation in helping the poor and in working for world peace. Here there is real friendship.

And this raises the million-dollar question: can the Buddhist-Christian dialogue become a model for dialogue between the religions of the world? Can we all work together so that the clash of civilizations becomes a union of civilizations? Let me mention two aspects of Buddhism that are valuable yet controversial. The first is that while it has a wealth of teaching, Buddhism has no dogma. Buddhist teaching is upaya, a Sanskrit word usually translated into English as "skilful means", leading to an enlightenment like that of the Buddha. In itself it is not absolute truth but pragmatic truth. So the

Buddhist teacher will willingly use the New Testament or the scriptures of any religion provided they lead to enlightenment, which makes Buddhism very tolerant; but it can lead to a clash with Jewish, Christian or Islamic civilizations.

I believe that upaya (translated into Japanese as hōben) penetrates Asian society. Shusaku Endo, it seems to me, had something of hōben, and this was part of his struggle. He was deeply committed to Jesus Christ; but for him (and I hope I do him justice) the Church was a skilful means.

My second point is that Buddhism is a mystical religion which leads beyond words and thinking and reasoning to the silence of "transcendental wisdom". Buddhists teach meditation, whether through the repetition of the name or the contemplation of a mandala or the regulation of the breath. Their mystics, like many Christian mystics, enter into the emptiness, the darkness, the nothingness, the cloud of unknowing.

What can we – Christians, Jews, Muslims – learn from these two aspects of Buddhism? Assuredly we cannot abandon all dogma; but we can be less dogmatic. We can abandon fundamentalism, and recognize that much of our teaching is "pragmatic truth". Already we Catholics (if I may say it modestly) have become more tolerant, open to dialogue, open to compromise, open to recognizing the goodness and truth in others. We can now learn from others and recognize our mistakes. But we have a long way to go.

For this uncompromising attitude which is basically religious – common to traditional Judaism, Christianity and Islam – extends to the whole of Western thinking; and it played its part in the annihilation of Hiroshima. Think of the Second World War. The stance of the Allied powers could be summed up as: "We want unconditional surrender. We are good and our enemies are evil. We will have no truck with evil. We will have no negotiation, no dialogue, no talking, no mercy." The result was the carpet bombing of the German cities and the terrible destruction of Japan. Men, women, children and animals died in Hiroshima and Nagasaki. Even the mosquitoes were wiped out. In the fire bombing of Tokyo 100,000 people, almost all civilians, died.

No one in any official position apologized for Hiroshima and Nagasaki; and it would be idle to deny the existence of the same uncompromising mentality today. "No negotiation with terrorists" is the slogan. "We are good: terrorists are evil. Anyone who harbors a terrorist or shows any understanding will pay the price. Shoot to kill! Show no mercy!" And (horror of horrors!) this attitude often has the blessing of religious authorities. Now the frightening thing is that the Islamic fundamentalists who destroyed the Twin Towers have the same way of thinking. They, too, believe they are pitted against evil. They want to destroy the corrupt Western civilization. They want no negotiation and they will consider no dialogue. They will show no mercy. They will die rather than compromise. It is no secret that they are working might and main to get weapons of mass destruction. For them the attacks in New York and Washington were only the first step. And so we are faced with a very terrible confrontation. Is there any answer? I find it difficult to see an answer for the immediate future; but for the distant future there is surely an answer. The answer, the only answer, is dialogue and friendship between the religions, a dialogue in which the religions will challenge one another, lead one another to conversion of heart and help one another get away from fanatical fundamentalism. Through these means we will all find our authentic roots in love and compassion. Bernard Lonergan rightly says that all true religion is based on love; and he maintains that religious conversion is conversion to love.

Interreligious dialogue is the way of the future. There is now a Parliament of Religions which meets every year, working for a global ethic that will outlaw war and terrorism and killing. The indefatigable Pope John Paul has traveled the world, seeking union between the Catholic Church and other religions. Who can doubt that the Holy Spirit is working in human hearts? And there is a further movement, from dialogue to prayer. This was already clear in 1986 when representatives of the religions prayed for peace at Assisi; and John Paul made the extraordinary statement that the exigencies of peace transcend religion. The same Pope longs for the day when Jews, Muslims and Christians will unite in common prayer to our father Abraham. And the day will surely come – indeed it has already come – when children of East and West will unite in silent, mystical prayer at the core of our being. We used to say that dialogue between the religions is necessary for world peace. Now we can say that dialogue between the religions is necessary for world survival. Only prayerful dialogue between Judaism, Christianity, Islam, Hinduism and Buddhism can save our planet from destruction. What a responsibility we have!

We concluded our meeting last November by speaking about a Japanese Christian prophet and mystic who lost his all in the holocaust of Nagasaki. Dr Takashi Nagai worked tirelessly for the sick and wounded until he collapsed and could work no more. As he lay dying of leukaemia he cried out that war in the nuclear age would be suicide for humanity: "From this atomic waste the people of Nagasaki confront the world and cry out: No more war! Let us follow the commandment of love and work together. The people of Nagasaki prostrate themselves before God and pray: grant that Nagasaki may be the last atomic wilderness in the history of the world." Japanese Christians are rightly proud of their prophetic Takashi Nagai.. *unquote.*

It is however a sad reality that all too many 'words' are being spent on dialogue which are not sufficiently being followed by concrete actions. Instead of words there is urgent need for creative collaboration on a local as well as on a global scale. The way to world peace should be a way of collaboration!

3. The Way to World Peace

A way of collaboration

The last decennia of the 20th century have seen a remarkable growth in local, regional national and international activities, which all try to promote world peace, by information, demonstrations, gatherings, prayer-meetings, etc. The 0.2% of the national GNP, although still far from the engaged 0.7%, which many industrialized countries dedicate now on average to governmental and non-governmental activities in international aid cooperation projects in the underdeveloped countries also means an important contribution to more peace and better shared welfare.

These activities, how praiseworthy they are in themselves, contribute very little and surely not enough to the necessary structural changes in the economic and financial situations which, for a great part, lay at the basis of social humanly-degrading conditions of poverty, unjust sharing of the wealth-resources of our earth, arms circulation, conflicts, world-domination by the transnational enterprises and the consequential growing globalization with as side-effect that the rich become richer and the poor poorer. Peace achieving can only and will be proportional to the application of efficient solutions to change the socio-economic structures at the origin of most of these world problems.

As long as the political leaders of nations as India, Brazil, Mexico and other countries in South-America and India, are not put under international pressure to let the poor have a greater share in the national wealth, there is only a very meager or even no chance their governments will carry out the necessary structural changes. Only a pressure from international global authorities, sustained by international global organizations, can originate a move to find and to apply efficient solutions to the ever-escalating world problems.

By an unfair veto-system and other unilateral agreements between the big industrial nations, and by a lack of the necessary funds, the United Nations Organization and all its agencies do not arrive at fulfilling a sufficiently leading and authoritative role, which results in keeping their role limited in many cases to resolutions without real follow-up. The improvement of these obstructing situations should be a priority challenge to all concerned and involved nations and organizations.

In the past years, we have been able to observe a trend which means a revolution in world history, namely the growing recognition of spiritual values besides material values, a growing questioning of our consumption-based way of life, the growing recognition of the values of environment, of nature, of other cultures, and of other religions. Even the separation of Church and State, as it has been introduced in the Western world and in modern democracies is being questioned and looked at from different new angles. We have been able to observe also, as a rather new phenomenon, efforts to come to a collaboration between political and religious/ humanistic leaders - between politics and religion - to work together in finding solutions to our world problems. It is now being accepted more and more that there is an absolute need of global dialogue and global collaboration on a worldwide scale.

Thanks to the exceptional growth in the past twenty years of encounters and of literature in relation with the dialogue among religions, traditions and other convictions, and also thanks to the growing recognition that the multi-cultural and multi-religious society on all continents will be the society of tomorrow in a more homogeneous world, the necessary breeding ground is now at last present to enable the achieving of a new world order.

More and more, people arrive at the awareness and the conviction that only by a growth in mutual recognition, a closer collaboration between peace organizations, a closer collaboration between world Faith Communities on one side, and the political, economical and financial world on the other side can lead to more peace and justice. The transnational corporations (TNCs), thanks to the growth in communication means and to their aim of profit-above-all, have already achieved an advanced global union in collaboration, with its many good and bad side effects.

Also these interfaith dialogue and peace movements need the power to influence the political, industrial and financial world of ours on a global scale. Many may wonder whether 'power' can be used by 'religious' people. While it has been used by church-institutes in various wrong ways, the time has come now to use it in the right way, in real collaboration based on mutual respect. Christ himself used his human and divine-inspired power to enforce his good tidings of love, sincerity, goodwill, compassion, and so many other human virtuous values in the troubled world which surrounded Him.

Is it not high time that such a union in collaboration becomes a reality between the peace promoting organizations and between the world Faith Communities? Recent texts of the papal guidance of the Catholic Church, many texts and interreligious meetings as edited and organized on a high level by the Pontifical Council for Interreligious Dialogue of the same

Church are, without doubt, showing the right direction. There is need of a bigger awareness inside the Christian ecumenical movement of the importance and the necessity to get other non-Christian religions and traditions involved in this drive for union and in particular for collaboration. Thus only can a real union in collaboration be realized, by which could also be realized a support of global ideas such as for example the project of the United Religions Initiative, launched in 1995 by the Episcopalian Bishop of San Francisco, William Swing, with its aim of creating a United Religions Organization as a world-partner of the United Nations Organization.

Is it also not the time for the multitude of existing peace promoting organizations and also for the national and international interfaith dialogue organizations to follow the example of the economic world to live up to and to apply their basic doctrine of "care, love and compassion" to achieve this union in collaboration, even by mergers or at least by a much closer collaboration? Only from such unions in collaboration can there emerge a sufficiently strong voice-forum for more peace-achieving measures, and in the religious world for the creation of something like a United Religions Organization, as an acceptable and worthy discussion partner for the political authorities represented in the United Nations, and as always with the aim of working out together efficient proposals and solutions to our world problems, for more lasting peace on our mother earth.

*   *   *

From a permanent awareness of the problems of our world, from a path of hate and confrontation we have come to think about collaborative and constructive ways of coming to a more peaceful world. The remarkable process of historical changes towards a new world order which has occurred especially since the end of WWII, has created the necessary subsoil for interfaith and other dialogue movements. It can be said that the Catholic Church has been a forerunner in this process.

4. Global Changes in the Faith Communities

1) Evolution in the Catholic Church in the period of 1945-1965
In this period of 20 years, the Catholic Church has really acted as forerunner in the remarkable evolution and the consequent changes which have occurred inside the Church and which have created for the attentive believers a new image of God and new ways of looking at the Church as teaching and guiding institution. It is a manifest fact that the attitude of the faithful to the leading authorities of their Church has undergone radical changes in the past 60 years.

a) New Bible interpretation and worldwide switch from the Latin language to the vernacular languages.
The fertile ground for the development of the interfaith dialogue movement was created by the new more scientifically founded interpretation of the Bible, Old as well as New Testament, which application was put into practice in the theological studies at the diocese seminaries and monasteries from the time of the war years 1940-45. This revolution in the biblical exegesis first in Catholic theology and then followed by other Christian Churches, from the literal interpretation to a describing and relating interpretation, appropriate to the culture in which it originated, and the switching from Latin to the local languages has been the most valuable evolution and development of the last 50 years towards interfaith dialogue, real inculturation and a multicultural/ multireligious society.

The second Vatican Council (1962-1965) was a second important step in the recognition of the values of other Faith Communities and of the individual believer, with as one of the first concrete results the worldwide switch from Latin to the local languages and some other liturgical changes in the Eucharist celebration. Next to the ecumenical meetings towards unity between the Christian Faith Communities, the above changes have created the necessary basis for the globalization of interfaith dialogue encounters worldwide. One of its main results has been the now rather global acceptance of and respect for the values in other cultures and religions which is a completely new aspect in the cultural/religious history of humankind.
My Interfaith Dialogue Guidelines state in point 4:
"The tenets of world religions and other faith traditions have their roots

in their native culture, have developed on the basis of their culture's phi-
losophical and moral concepts, and have approached and proclaimed the
Ultimate Spiritual Reality in transient expressions and in culturally appro-
priate ceremonies. As pilgrims always on their way to new discoveries and
subject to change, no faith community should claim exclusive representation
of the Truth."

This new interpretation of the Bible, Old as well as New Testament,
which became gradually a commonly accepted practice from the years after
WWII, has been the first step towards real interfaith dialogue. The dialogue
with other Faith Communities has been further promoted by the new way of
looking at and better appreciating of the other religions and cultures as
promulgated by the Second Vatican Council of the Catholic Church (1962-
1965). Also in many other Christian Churches, it is now being considered as
self-evident that the formulation of a divine revelation is influenced for a
great part by the culture and the historical milieu in which it originated, and
that this form of presentation is not revelation itself. These presentations
have furthermore to undergo a continuously new interpretation, appropriate
to the ever-changing knowledge and ever-higher conscience- level of the
faithful, without therefore changing the essentials. As long as the texts of the
Qu'ran remain static unchangeable words of God and as long as this more
scientifically based interpretation of revelation is not accepted by the Islamic
Faith Communities, real dialogue and maybe even real world peace remain
most difficult assignments.

b) Disobeying of former precepts or prohibitions

In the past 60 years, we have seen still more changes in particular inside the
Catholic Church in the widely spread 'disobeying' or maybe better 'ignor-
ing' of former precepts or prohibitions by a majority of the faithful at least in
Europe and the United States, such as e.g. Sunday worship, renouncing meat
on Fridays, regular or yearly confessing of sins, prohibition of the use of
mechanical contraceptives, changing of the 40 days of fasting into a more
immaterial renunciation of personal attachments, and so many others. From
nowadays' pulpits in the churches, there is no talk anymore of sins in their
different forms and of the former terrifying punishments of hell and purga-
tory. Fear has at last disappeared from most of the Christian churches.

For memory's sake, I give you hereunder 'The Five Commandments of
the Catholic Church' as formulated in English speaking countries, and
slightly different with the formulation in non-English countries of Europe
where the 5th commandment is not mentioned, and which are all not being
considered anymore as obligatory duties by postmodern Catholics:

1. *You shall attend Mass on Sundays and on holy days of obligation and
   rest from servile labor.*
2. *You shall confess your sins at least once a year,*
3. *You shall receive the sacrament of the Eucharist at least during the*

Easter season,
4. *You shall observe the days of fasting and abstinence established by the Church*
5. *You shall help to provide for the needs of the Church.*

c) Less Belief in dogmas

Among the faithful and even among priests/clergymen and theologians, there is less, if still maybe uncomfortable, belief in many of the human-made dogmas of the Christian tenets of belief, such as: the infallibility of the Pope; the exclusive belief in Christ as the Son of God, the 'only' savior of human-kind; the immaculate conception of Mary; Mary's and Christ's bodily Ascension; Original Sin; the celibacy as obligatory condition for the priest-hood; the non-participation of women in the hierarchical structure of the Church institute; and so many others

These extraordinary changes which are now finding their way at least all over the western world have their origin in the new postmodern vision of catholic and protestant theologians as Edward Schillebeeckx, Dominican; Jacques Dupuis, Jesuït; Hans Küng, Catholic Theologian; Roger Leenaers, Jesuït, (see his book in bibliography); the Anglican theologian John Hick, and many others, and last but not least the writings of the theologians of the liberation theology in particular in South-America. All the changes in the Catholic Church and the new postwar movements such as the re-evaluation of nature, the new evaluation and acceptance of the values of other cultures and religions, the rise of the "Greens", the efforts towards a healthier environment, the ecological vision on our planet as the property of us all, a new positive approach between religion and science, a growing collaboration between the political world and the leaders of the Faith Communities, are all without doubt interrelated and interconnected. Each of them is undergoing the influence of the others in this evolution on its way of no return.

Another not less important change is occurring in the image of God, of the Divine, as conceived by many of the faithful, by which the monotheistic vision in Christianity has attained now a pantheistic bias, and by which we see now a new belief in and consciousness of the omnipresence of the divine Spiritual Reality not only in sentient beings but also in all created matter as their origin and their final destiny. In the Catholic Faith Community, the human body and its sexuality are no more considered as sinful, like it has been the case for so many centuries.

One example only of the changing attitude to and belief in the Christian fundamental doctrine of the original sin may be enlightening:

Original Sin and its Consequences

As information on the Catholic doctrine on original sin, I quote from the Catholic Encyclopedia on the Internet:

I. MEANING

Original sin may be taken to mean: (1) the sin that Adam committed; (2) a consequence of this first sin, the hereditary stain with which we are born on account of our origin or descent from Adam.

From the earliest times the latter sense of the word was more common, as may be seen by St. Augustine's statement: "the deliberate sin of the first man is the cause of original sin" (De nupt. et concup., II, xxvi, 43). It is the hereditary stain that is dealt with here. As to the sin of Adam we have not to examine the circumstances in which it was committed nor make the exegesis of the third chapter of Genesis.

VI. NATURE OF ORIGINAL SIN

This is a difficult point and many systems have been invented to explain it: it will suffice to give the theological explanation now commonly received. Original sin is the privation of sanctifying grace in consequence of the sin of Adam. This solution, which is that of St. Thomas, goes back to St. Anselm and even to the traditions of the early Church, as we see by the declaration of the Second Council of Orange (A.D. 529,) one man has transmitted to the whole human race not only the death of the body, which is the punishment of sin, but even sin itself, which is the death of the soul [cf. Denzinger-Bannwart, n. 175 (145)]. As death is the privation of the principle of life, the death of the soul is the privation of sanctifying grace which according to all theologians is the principle of supernatural life. Therefore, if original sin is "the death of the soul ", it is the privation of sanctifying grace.

(A/N: Orange is a town in the present department of Vaucluse in southern France)

Human beings are part of the evolution of the universe from the first exis-tence of seemingly pure material matter to the present higher and higher spiritualization of human beings, as it has been projected by Teilhard de Chardin. All existing matter is inherently linked to a condition of permanent changing from less to more, from less good to better, from less perfect to more perfect. Suffering in all its forms can be explained as a consequence of the imperfectness of sentient beings in their struggle for a better life. Evil, or sin in theological and moral terms, can be explained as everything that runs against this evolution of higher and higher spiritualization and is possible because of a free choice by intelligent beings. Good and evil are inherently linked to intelligence, to the knowing of what is good and what is bad. Hu-mans have by their free will the exclusive human faculty of being able to choose between good and evil. More and more people are in their search for a moral basis of this possibility of choosing turning to the Golden Rule of Conduct, which is accepted by all faith communities. In human society good should be remunerated and evil/sin be punished as a guidance by society authorities towards a better social community life.

In the definition of original sin by the Trent Council it is stated that sin is transmitted to all by generation (*propagatione*), not by imitation [Denz., n. 790 (672)]. According to Catholic doctrine all human beings are from their coming into this world hereditaryly stained on account of their origin from our first parents Adam and Eve. I am wondering more and more about what reason there could exist for this being stained by an original sin by two human beings of 4 million years ago, who are supposed to have still been then in a mental condition of very low intelligence, and very near to ape-like creatures.

This can be called a problem of utmost importance to Christian believers because Christian doctrine on sin as a state of privation of sanctifying grace and the whole development of the doctrine of salvation, by animal offers in the Old Testament and by the death on the cross of Jesus Christ, called the Son of God, the only Savior of humankind, is based on this idea of the need to purify and to save human beings from this original state of sin. Should the whole life and the preaching of Jesus Christ therefore not be reduced to the life and teaching by a Person filled to an exceptional degree by the Divine, with as main theme, active love to God and active love to all human brothers and sisters of the same human family?   For centuries one of the main subjects in sermons in Christian churches has been about sin, its origin and its consequences. A tremendous change has occurred since WWII by the fact that preaching about sin has almost totally disappeared in Christian churches. Might this have something to do with the lessening and even disappearance of the belief in original sin by post-modern church attendants? Belief in the original goodness of human beings has lead the Buddha to limit his instructions to moral guidance, without trying to and even refusing to explain the Divine by theological explanations and still less by the declaring of infallible dogmas.

What can be the meaning of this sanctifying grace, provided by the baptism ceremony? Is sanctifying grace not simply the condition of the human mind and the human heart, as a result of human conduct in union with the Divine? Is the belief that God, the infinite, unspeakable spiritual Reality is present as a loving Father in all matters and surely in a very special human-like way of mutual love in human beings, going as far as Jesus' command of loving one' s enemies, is this not the basic teaching of Jesus Christ and therefore of Christianity? Is being conscious at all times of this dwelling in oneself of the Divine, of the need to replace the personal self by the Divine Self as it is the goal of life in Buddhism, not the highest human way of living and does this not lead to a permanent consciousness of being a member of the global human family in union also with one's ancestors in the past, and with one's offspring in the future? Assisting in the deepening of this kind of consciousness in as many people as possible, should this not be the reason of existence of all faith communities?

2) Evolution in the Faith Communities in general

The main undercurrent that has influenced the radical changes, which have occurred and which continue to progress on their way of no return, is that the common people in most industrialized Western nations have reached an intellectual level by which they wish to be free, as individuals and sometimes as group, in deciding on the basis of their conscience and overall knowledge what they consider to be morally right or morally wrong.

The remarkable changes inside the Catholic faith community can be expected to take place without doubt also in other Christian Churches and other Faith Communities. A similar evolution inside the different schools of Islam would be a most welcome and most important contribution to real interreligious dialogue in a better and estimating understanding of the values and identity of the others, and surely also an important step towards global world peace.

a) Instability and uneasiness

The former stability of belief which has reigned inside and around Christianity for so many centuries has turned since WWII into an overall feeling of instability and uneasiness, under which reign the masses of the faithful are now looking around for new ways of believing. The belief in a God with all too many humanlike attributes is being questioned, while the conviction is gaining ground that there exists somehow and somewhere an Ultimate Spiritual Reality in which all material beings must find their origin and their final destiny in a onetime unification with it or through a maybe endless cycle of rebirths or reincarnations. Against the unease with and loss of trust in the church institutions, which has become a rather common phenomenon in the past decades in particular in Western countries, I dare to remark here as a matter of course that the Churches should be upheld as institutions, irreplaceable by whatever other organizations. Their role remains a matter of necessity in the holding up of the essence of the teachings of Christ and also from now on of a *globally acceptable ethic for the whole of humankind,* as pronounced already since many years by the German Catholic theologian Hans Küng. The declaration of this global ethic was acclaimed, on occasion of the second Parliament of World's Religions in 1993 in Chicago, by a majority of the 7.000 participants, as a valuable means for coming to a union in collaboration among the Faith Communities and as a most recommendable global basis for human conduct. The accepting and practicing of this golden rule should be the moral basis of a new world order.

b) Conciliation between the world of science and of religion

In both the world of science as well as in the religious and philosophical world there is a growing tendency towards a new recognition of each other's values and in the need of collaboration instead of confrontation in the common search for Truth. A close following of the media clearly shows that the efforts towards this kind of collaboration between science and religion is a manifest trend in the US, the EU and probably also in other parts of the world.

d) Christian inspired activities by enterprises

Another most interesting evolution is happening in the industrial world. In the past ten years, hundreds of enterprises in Holland, Belgium and maybe other European countries have joined hands in regular meetings to do something about the north-south gap by arranging for financial bank loans and by the dispatching of technical people, no strings attached, to give aid assistance to local smaller enterprises in the poorer countries mainly in Africa and South America. From a Christian inspired look at the world and its problems, they are now carrying out what for centuries has been a task reserved to monasteries and other church institutions of Christian Faith Communities.

e) Faith Communities without prescriptions and prohibitions

From Buddhism, we learn that a faith community without prescriptions and prohibitions is a real way of life for Buddhist believers the world over. Buddhism has a wealth of teaching but has no dogma, nor strict commandments. It is a mystical religion, which leads beyond words and thinking and reasoning to the silence of "transcendental wisdom". The Dalai Lama, who is admired and even venerated by so many all over the world, never speaks from a pulpit or teaching attitude, he never commands or prohibits. In stead, his advices and counsels are being admired and accepted as emanations of universal profound mystical wisdom. Most of the spiritual movements, like e.g. the Brahma Kumaris, most of the indigenous Faith Communities and the humanist faith community have already this non-commanding but guiding approach as a basic attitude of their followers and sympathizers.

Might it be possible that the interfaith encounter and dialogue among Christian and Buddhist Faith Communities could lead, admittedly in a rather far away future, to religions without commandments and prohibitions, without do's and don'ts? Could this be in the future the true way of all the Faith Communities of our world? Could the Catholic Church and the other Christian Churches without this "Go and Teach" attitude uphold their authority in the moral and spiritual guidance of their faithful and as such in the guidance of humanity as a whole? In this context, the image of the Catholic and other Christian Churches as institutions is undergoing a radical change in many aspects of what until now has been considered and believed in as unchangeable tenets of belief. One sees a pronounced change from an attitude of "Go and Teach" to an attitude of "Go and Learn", of guidance instead of commanding and of testifying instead of proselytizing.

f) Another image of what we call God

Dionysius the Areopagite (First Century CE) is being called the founder of the so-called negative theology and was of great significance tot the mystics. He stressed that God is always infinitely greater than all what we can say or think about Him.

Another evolution which is going on in the background of this above discussed commendable evolution from commanding and prohibiting towards guidance, is the growing acceptance of the incapacity of the human intellect in its actual dimension to grasp, and still less to understand the *Ultimate Spiritual Reality*. It is also more and more accepted that all human words to explain this Reality remain very limited and subject to necessary periodic adaptations in accordance with deeper scientific and even mystic insights in the characteristics of the material and the spiritual world. It should therefore be beyond doubt that each of the Faith Communities does not share the whole final truth but only part of it. This involves also that the 'revelations' by the founders of the world Faith Communities should not be proclaimed anymore as infallible dogmas, because each of them, reveal in limited human words, influenced and formed by the cultural environment of their time, only part of the Ultimate Spiritual Reality. It is now becoming more and more commonly accepted that the 'revelations' as proclaimed by the founders of the world Faith Communities and all their holy scriptures concern the same unique divine spiritual reality. The dividing of the religions in monotheistic and pantheistic or whatever else is losing its meaning into a combination of monotheistic as well as pantheistic characteristics of the same Divine Reality. The acceptance of this new way of thinking should bring the Faith Communities and also all organizations committed to interfaith dialogue nearer to each other not in a unity yet but in a union of collaboration.

Diversity: It has been said that "Diversity is God's gift to humanity". In my humble opinion, I don't know whether, as such, this can be called a gift from God. Diversity in all existing things is essentially linked to the temporariness or transience of all existing matter, non sentient as well as sentient. In the case of human beings this is also linked to the human faculty of disposing of a free will. The human diversity in everything and in particular the diversity in the different Faith Communities of our world seems to me to be a result, in the case of human beings, of their free faculty of free will. This free will, essentially connected to the faculty of intelligence is without any doubt a gift from God.

Diversity, just like the whole of humanity, through centuries of evolution of the human mind and of the quest of humanity to learn more about the meaning of life and death, is moving on a way not of 'clash' but of convergence towards a gradual better understanding of their final destination, viz. unification with the ultimate spiritual reality. The road of diversity is a road of centuries of totally separated diversities from the beginning of the human existence. The period after WWII can be considered as the start of a new age of dialogue in getting acquainted with, in study and understanding and respectful acceptation of the others. This will automatically be followed by an evolution over surely many more years towards a still deeper global knowledge of the one spiritual entity which we Christians and many others call God and of further unification of the religious diversities into a unified humanity. The diverse contacts with other Faith Communities should always be a mutually enriching encounter.

Double Belonging: to belong to more than one religion is also a rather new concept of practicing one's belief. Catholics who practice Zen Buddhism meditation is now a widely practiced way of meditation also in the Christian religious world of the European Union and the USA. Some Catholics call themselves Buddhist-Catholics. Catholics are now allowed to go and pray at Protestant churches or Buddhist temples, a Catholic priest gives a sermon at a Protestant service while a Protestant clergyman/woman presents a religious talk in a Catholic church. A most advisable booklet on the subject is 'Many Mansions? Multiple Religious Belonging and Christian Identity' authored by Catherine Corneille, Orbis Books, Maryknoll, NY, 2002, in which there are articles by the author herself, and by Jan Van Bragt cicm, John B. Cobb Jr., Joseph S. O'Leary, Francis Clooney s.j., Jacques Dupuis s.j.., Elisabeth J. Harris, Claude Gefré op., Werner G. Jeanrond and Ramon Panikkar.

3) The Future: collaboration between the political and the religious world

Another remarkable and most commendable evolution is the apparent signs of interest in an up-to-now unique quest for collaboration between the political and the religious world. The United Kingdom can be considered as an example in this quest for collaboration, for which testify the multiple and regular contacts and meetings on local, regional and national levels between political and religious leaders in that country. The same quest is going on since more than ten years now in the European Union and more specifically through the activities of the Forward Studies Unit inside the EU Commission, still an initiative of Jacques Delors, and which since 2001 is working under the name of Group of Policy Advisors. One of their four fields of concentration is 'Dialogue with Religions and Humanisms'. More and more political and also industrial leaders are sharing the conviction that only a joining of hands with the leaders of the Faith Communities can lead to a world in more peace and justice for all. The former anti-religious attitude of the political world in Europe is now changing into a recognizing of the reality that peace and justice can be realized only by a collaboration between the Faith Communities and the political world. A change in the socio-economic structures which are for a great part at the origin of poverty and illiteracy of hundreds of millions of people in India, in South America and in so many countries on the African continent can only be achieved by political pressure from inside and from outside. This kind of needed pressure on the political world for more peace and social justice can only be produced by a global union in collaboration of the Faith Communities of the world.

An economic, financial and political union of the world is in progress by the creation and activities of the United Nations Organization with its now 192 member-states, and by the creation in the past 60 years of thirteen and maybe more international organizations and four important universal declarations as hereunder:

- **World Bank** in 1944 with 184 member countries, 7.000 employees in Washington headoffices and over 3.000 in offices in other countries.
- **United Nations Organisation** created on 24.10.1945 with now 192 member states. Preceded by the first international organization in our world, called the **League of Nations**, signed in Paris in 1919, at the Peace Conference after WWI., joined by sixty one nations but without the United States
- **International Monetary Fund** (IMF), established in 1945 as an international organisation with now 184 member countries.
- **North-Atlantic Treaty Organisation** in 1949 consisting of 19 country members.
- **International Court of Justice** established as a judicial organ of the United Nations which began work in 1946 in the Peace Palace in The Hague in the Netherlands, when it replaced the Permanent Court of International Justice which had functioned there since 1922.
- **World Trade Organisation** (WTO) which came into being in 1995 as successor to the General Agreement on Tariffs and Trade (GATT) established in the wake of the Second World War.
- **European Union,** becoming a reality by the Treaty of Maastricht in 1992, followed by the implementing of the Euro as common currency on January 1, 2002, uniting now 25 countries since 2004 with a population of 455 million.
- Very recently, the preparation towards a '**Asian Union**' and a **"African Union"**, similar to the EU, are in progress on both continents. The same evolution is taking place in the Latin American countries towards the creation of a **South American Community of Nations** (SACN) of 12 countries, with head office in Lima (Peru) and a South American Bank in Brasilia.
- **Millennium World Peace Summit of Religious and Spiritual Leaders** in 2000 attended by more than thousand religious leaders from all world faith communities, a global gathering of religious leaders that was held, in part, in the UN General Assembly Hall, and that involved UN officials, but was regretfully, not officially endorsed by the UN.
- **The Millennium Summit of the United Nations,** 6-8 September 2000. was followed by the creation of:
  1) The World Council of Religious Leaders (WCRL), 2001.
  2) Board of World Religious Leaders, Israel, 2003.

3) Leaders of World and Traditional Religions, Republic of Kazakhstan, 2003.
4) European Council of Religious Leaders (ECRL) 2002.
See details in the paragraph "Councils of Religious Leaders"

- **World Social Forum** which took place in 2003 in Porto Alegre, Brazil, which was attended by more than 100.000 people from all over the world.
- Towards a **Single Euro Payments Area (SEPA).** The SEPA implies that customers will be enabled to make payments throughout the whole euro area as efficiently and safely as in the national context today. In the White Paper of May 2002, 42 European Banks and the European credit sector associations declared that a full migration to the SEPA would be achieved by the end of 2010. This can be considered as one of the steps leading in the future to a global worldwide payment system.
- **Universal Declarations** of Human Rights in 1948, of Non-Violence in 1990, of a Global Ethic in 1993, and of Human Responsibilities in 1995.

A global union in collaboration between the Faith Communities of our world should result in the creation of a global one-voice forum, a kind of United Religions Organization, as a worthy discussion partner to the United Nations Organization, which idea has first been launched by the Episcopal bishop of California, the Right Rev. William Swing, in 1995, and which idea should be sustained and supported by all interfaith organizations worldwide.

One of the main handicaps on this road of "uniting" towards the creation of a global one-voice forum is the problem of coming forward with leaders who can be accepted by their communities as real representatives. The need for a representative authoritative body is now acutely being felt in the Islamic communities, in Buddhism and Hinduism, and also in the Orthodox and non-catholic Christian communities. Only the Catholic Church disposes of the Vatican as a guiding and representative authority, represented on each continent by the Conference of Catholic Bishops. The efforts by the EU-Commission in the past ten years to come to a dialogue with the Faith Communities clearly show this problem of not finding yet real representative organizations or institutes of the Faith Communities, which are acceptable as discussion partners to the leaders of the political world.

It should be clear that the aim of creating a union of the Faith Communities is not the creating of one religion but of a union in collaboration and in joining hands and forces, by the different world Faith Communities (religions, indigenous traditions, and other convictions of humanists, freemasons, etc.), each keeping to its own identity and values. Interfaith dialogue should also result in a mutual enrichment of the own religious and cultural identity. The words which the Dalai Lama keeps repeating to his Christian admirers is the way to follow: "By the study of Buddhism, Christians should become better Christians, and Buddhists should become better Buddhists by the study of Christianity."

In order to really influence the political, industrial and financial world, the world of the Faith Communities needs the unified power of their billions of believers. At the actual stage of growing rapprochement, this can only be realized by a joining of hands towards the creation of umbrella interfaith dialogue organizations on the national and continental levels. The joining of forces then of these national and continental umbrella organizations will act as so many stepping stones towards the creation of a powerful one-voice forum of the world Faith Communities as a supranational body and as a worthy partner to the UN. This will be an important further step in the
evolution of the growing unifying economic, financial, religious and political globalization of our world.

After many years of activity in the interfaith dialogue movement worldwide, it has become my conviction that, as a most important step towards the realising of this aim of creating a global organization as a worthy partner to the United Nations Organization, is that a still closer collaboration between some of the interfaith organizations would be a most appropriate and opportune step towards its realisation. The two western organizations which might be most advanced towards such a merging are without doubt the Council for a Parliament of the World Religions (CPWR, Chicago) and the United Religions Initiative (URI, San Francisco), which both might be joined in this uniting by the World Congress of Faiths (WCF) of Oxford, UK. The three of them together might then also work out a much needed global interfaith magazine which could become a reinforcement of the existing interfaith magazine 'World Faiths Encounter', edited by the WCF, and since 2003 edited under the new name of Interreligious INSIGHT, eventually in collaboration and a cross-exchange of articles with the Thai magazine "Seeds of Peace", edited by the International Network of Engaged Buddhists (INEB), Thailand, and other similar magazines.

While the industrial and financial world is undergoing a process of joining hands - of uniting - by the ever increasing merging of enterprises and financial institutes, it is apparent that this kind of uniting is still not being accepted and still less being aspired at in the world of Faith Communities and interfaith dialogue organizations. Each one of the hundreds of interfaith organizations in the west and in the east (see the two lists in annex) remains bound to its own local, regional or national interests. The words of uniting in the preambles and intentions of their charters are not sufficiently being followed up by deeds of real collaboration and even still less of merging, which by itself would mean a giving of priority to the common good above the interests of the community, group or organization.

4) Final Target: a World Forum of the Faith Communities

From a lot of initiatives and global activities it is now becoming apparent that we can observe a growing interest for everything that can contribute to dialogue and union in collaboration, which can also be said to be a matter of primary importance towards more peace on earth. This remains a subject for further discussion in the political as well religious world. It must be recognized that most of the worldwide initiatives have originated from Christian communities. Some will without doubt object that this might be an all too western dream originated in the Christian world. The other non-Christian Faith Communities should join this movement by a more active participation of ideas and activities from their own religious and cultural values and background.

Many organizations a/o those involved in interreligious dialogue and NGO's (Non-Government Organization) have thought it useful if not necessary to have an affiliation with the UNO. In 2004, there were some 130 organizations affiliated with the UN. The organizations were located as follows: 36 of Europe, 50 of the US, 20 of Asia & the Middle East, 18 of Africa, 3 of Latin America and the Caribbean, and 4 of Oceania. In 2006 about 1,500 NGOs were associated with the Department of Public Information (DPI) of the UN.

One may wonder if it is the right way for religions and religious organizations to link themselves so closely to the political world, and whether such an affiliation does not run the risk of becoming too closely bound to the political world. The history of the past centuries has shown that religions had better avoid whatever close inside links with the political world, which has lead ultimately to our present separation of church and state in most democratic nations. This is another reason why a separate organization outside the UN but as an acceptable discussion party to the UN, and with the support of their billions of adherents should be the way to exert influence on the activities of the political world towards more effective ways to improve the problems of our world.

Is their still need to repeat that the aim of creating a United Faith Communities Organization, as a one-voice global interfaith forum, is not the creating of one religion but of a union in collaboration and in joining hands and forces, by the different world Faith Communities (religions, indigenous traditions, and other convictions like humanists, freemasons, etc.), each keeping to its own identity and values.

5) A new important concept:
The Universal Declaration of Human Responsibilities
The most advanced definition of an ethical code can be seen in *The Universal Declaration of Human Responsibilities* drafted by the InterAction Council (IAC, www.interactioncouncil.org). Founded in 1983 by Takeo Fukuda, former Prime Minister of Japan and Helmut Schmidt, former Chancellor of the Federal Republic of Germany. The IAC is a group of former heads of government or state, who use their experience to help solve world problems.

The IAC sent its proposed declaration to the UN on 1 September 1997, and they are still waiting for it to be discussed at the international diplomatic level.

This declaration can be considered as an emanation of the Japanese and eastern way of life, reflecting the cultural values of eastern civilizations, giving priority to responsibilities and duties above rights, in other words a giving of priority to the common good. The Japanese way of life, based on this priority of the common good, should be an example to the other countries of the world. (See in Addition Paragraphs 'For a more genuine Image of Japan'). The proposed *Universal Declaration of Human Responsibilities* is not a replacement of the *Universal Declaration of Human Rights* but is designed to supplement it. This declaration could also be considered as another moral basis for the economic globalization process.

Yehudi Menuhin, one of the greatest violinists of our time, has said: "The Declaration of Human Responsibilities is the first assertion of human dignity. We need to agree on at least one self-evident truth that human rights can never exist without human responsibilities. They form one coin, two sides of one and the same coin".

*   *   *   *

It remains a manifest reality that the claim by whatever religion of being unique, of being in possession of the whole truth, of being exclusive and above other religions is one of the main obstacles to interfaith dialogue. At this point of our meditative study, let us listen to the declaration of 35 theologians and religious scholars from Asia, Europe and the United States at an international meeting on September 6-9, 2003 at the University of Birmingham, UK.

5. 'No One Religion is better than the Others'

'The Pluralist Model: A Multireligious Exploration".

Accepting this statement can be considered as a must to arrive at real dialogue among the world Faith Communities. The gathered theologians and scholars called on all religions of the world to recognize their mutual validity and to desist from claiming that any one religion is the 'one and only' or the 'best'. This conference was organized by Prof. John Hick (University of Birmingham, Prof. Paul Knitter (Xavier University, Cincinnati), Prof. Leonard Swidler (Temple University), and Prof. Perry Schmidt-Leukel (University of Glasgow).

In his book *God and the Universe of Faiths* (1973) John Hick called for a paradigm shift in thinking about religion. He suggested that each of the world's religions should be viewed as "different human responses to one divine Reality. . ."

Participants recognized the link between absolute truth claims and the exploitation of religion to promote violence. They explored resources within their religious traditions (Hinduism, Buddhism, Sikhism, Judaism, Christianity, Islam) to show that no religion can claim to have the 'absolute truth' or to be better than all the others.

The participants agreed on the following 'Key Principles of Religious Pluralism':

1. Interreligious Dialogue and engagement should be the way for religions to relate to one another. A paramount need is for religions to heal antagonisms among themselves.
2. The dialogue should engage the pressing problems of the world today, including war, violence, poverty, environmental devastation, gender injustice and violation of human rights
3. Absolute truth claims can easily be exploited to incite religious hatred and violence.
4. The religions of the world affirm ultimate reality/truth, which is conceptualized in different ways.
5. While ultimate reality/truth is beyond the scope of complete human understanding, it has found expression in diverse ways in the world's

religions.

6. The great world religions with their diverse teachings and practices constitute authentic paths to the supreme good.

7. The world's religions share many essential values, such as love, compassion, equality, honesty, and the ideal of treating others as one wishes to be treated oneself.

8. All persons have freedom of conscience and the right to choose their own faith.

9. While mutual witnessing promotes mutual respect, proselytizing devalues the faith of the other.

*   *   *

A consensus is being formed in the past years that the clerical culture supporting the Catholic priesthood needs to be reformed. But... how? A Jesuit priest Fr William Johnston s.j., based at the Sophia University in Tokyo, sets out some guidelines. What is essential is to meet modern society's desire for spirituality. I add here his article "We need a revolution", which was published in the Catholic newspaper of the UK, the Tablet, on 01/06/2002.

6. We need a Revolution

by William Johnston, S.J.

The scandals in the Catholic priesthood have been reported in press and television throughout the world; and church authorities realize that extensive reform in the priesthood is vitally necessary. It is not just that the Catholic Church has been humiliated and has lost credibility. That could even be salutary. More important is the fact that the priest presides at the Eucharist, which, Catholics believe, is the core and centre of Christian worship. Already, since the middle of the twentieth century, we have heard of millions deprived of "the bread of life" because there are too few priests. And now the Spirit is surely calling for a reform that will remedy this sad situation, ensuring that the command of Jesus, "Do this in memory of me", may reach fulfillment throughout the world.

Under these circumstances we have to go beyond the sort of reform initiated by the Council of Trent. It is not enough that the assembled bishops decide to expel errant priests, compensate the victims, screen future candidates for the priesthood, encourage priests to pray, and return to a Church dominated by celibate priests, bishops and supreme pontiffs. Such a Church, modeled on the Roman Empire, will not be valid in the third millennium.

For the signs of the times indicate that Christianity in the third millennium will be neither western nor eastern but global. Catholicism will learn not only from other Christian denominations but from the cultures of Asia and Africa, while remaining faithful to the New Testament and the Christian tradition.

Reform will come probably not through a decision from above but through the prayer and aspirations of the people of God throughout the world. This accords with the teaching of the Second Vatican Council which speaks of growth that comes through the people: "For there is a growth in the understanding of the realities and the words that have been handed down. This happens through the contemplation and study made by believers, who treasure these things in their hearts (cf. Lk 2:19,1), through the intimate understanding of spiritual things they experience" (Dei Verbum 8). In ways we do not yet know, the Spirit will teach the whole Church, perhaps through an ecumenical council (held not in the Vatican but in Manila or Rio de Janeiro or some Third World capital) in which lay men and women will play their legitimate role. And, as Jesus predicted, the Gospel will be preached in the whole world. What a reform will come when the Eucharist is celebrated everywhere from the rising of the sun even to the going down thereof!

And a renewed priesthood will need a renewed theology, less dogmatic and more oriented to prayer and holiness of life. Again, this new theology will not come from above but from the prayer of the people.

The split between theology and spirituality is one of the main causes of the crisis in the priesthood. Seminarians and students of theology assert almost unanimously that their theological studies did little for their life of prayer.

In dogmatic theology the principal textbook was the little manual of Heinrich Denzinger, which set out in clear propositions what one must believe and the penalties incurred if one did not believe. What mattered was fidelity to the official teaching of the Church and unquestioning obedience to ecclesiastical superiors.

The same kind of theology was popularized in the catechism. Children were trained to give "the right answer". The Church seemed less interested in religious experience. Stress on orthodoxy - faithful adherence to the exact words of dogmas - goes back to the time when Christianity moved out of its Jewish environment into the Graeco-Roman world. Councils defined dogmas, telling Christians to believe or face excommunication.

Then there was the Inquisition, the spirit of which remains, even though the Pope has apologized for its excesses. A Roman congregation continues to guard orthodoxy with the utmost care, scrupulously insisting that certain propositions, expressed in Western terminology, be firmly believed. At a time when sexual harassment by priests was passed over in silence, this congregation punished theologians who looked for new ways. Small wonder that some cynics asked if in the Catholic Church dissent from official teaching was a greater sin than pedophilia.

And now the reaction has come. We hear it said that spirituality is necessary, but religion is not. How did religion get so far from the Gospel?

Side by side with scholasticism and dogmatic theology, however, there has always existed in the Catholic Church a powerful tradition of prayer, and a vision of Christianity quite simply as the following of Jesus. Then there is a mystical theology, which, unfortunately, played only a minor part in the education of priests and seldom reached the laity.

But since the middle of the twentieth century this spiritual tradition has swept into the secular world in a remarkable way. In universities we find scholarly studies of the desert fathers, of Eckhart and the Rhineland mystics, of The Cloud of Unknowing, of the Carmelite mystics, studies that are pursued avidly by students looking not just for theoretical knowledge but for religious experience. There is also widening interest in the Eastern Church with its tradition of "the Jesus Prayer" and the icon. People are searching less for theory and more for what in Asia is called "practice".

Religious thinkers such as Teilhard de Chardin, Carl Jung, Ken Wilber and Bede Griffiths speak of an evolution in human consciousness. They claim that humankind is transcending the rational consciousness of reasoning and dualistic thinking to enter into a mystical consciousness wherein one sees the unity of all beings. Karl Rahner, in a much-quoted sentence, said that the Christian of the future will be a mystic or nothing. His contention is not so startling. Dominican theologians in the early twentieth century spoke of "the universal vocation to mysticism".

Then there is Asia. At the Asian synod held in Rome in 1998 several bishops spoke of Asia's difficulty with Western, particularly scholastic, theology; whereas the West uses a plethora of words, Asia prefers silence. One bishop spoke of the Western penchant for separating and dividing and distinguishing. Asia, on the other hand, is contemplative, seeing God in all things and accepting quite naturally what the Western mystics call "the coincidence of opposites". Asian ways of meditation are making a greater and greater impact on Christianity.

The signs of the times would indicate that in the third millennium the people of God will ask for priests - whether men or women, celibate or married - who will preside at the Eucharist and preach the word of God. While dogma will have its role, actively living the Gospel will come first. Perhaps the Roman congregation that carefully preserves orthodox doctrine might even be replaced by a congregation that promotes prayer and the great commandment of love, as Teilhard and others have predicted. Human consciousness is evolving towards mysticism, and there will be a need for celibate monks and nuns who devote their lives to prayer while studying the Christian mystical tradition and that of Asia. In this study, mystical theology could be the queen while other forms of theology act as handmaidens.

The reform of the priesthood, when it comes, will bring a revolution in the Catholic Church. It could bring an end to clericalism, making us more and more faithful to the Gospel of Jesus Christ. Christianity presented as a spiritual path of love, rather than as a series of propositions in the catechism, will attract millions of searchers in today's world.

*   *   *

The following text 'Beliefs of Catholics in Asia' are considerations by Edmund Chia, fsc. (De la Salle Brother) on the questionnaire empirical survey which was sent out to persons from all across Asia, in which he hints in all openness at the occurring and still much more needed change in the religious conception of Asian Catholics. Br. Chia from Malaysia worked at this time in Thailand as executive secretary of the Office of Ecumenical and Interreligious Affairs of the Federation of Asian Bishops' Conferences.

7. Beliefs of Catholics in Asia

by Edmund Chia, fsc,

1. *DOMINUS IESUS* AND THE *SENSUS FIDELIUM*

The Vatican *Declaration Dominus Iesus,* released by the Congregation for the Doctrine of the Faith (CDF) in September 2000, became the most "talked about" Vatican document in recent Church history. A significant criticism of the document is that it does not resonate well with the ground realities of the Church's relations with persons of other religions. In an article written for an issue of an Indian theological journal specifically dedicated to *Dominus Iesus,* American theologian Paul Knitter even suggests that, on the basis of these many and varied criticisms, "the 'sense of the faithful' (*sensus fidelium*) in regard to other religious believers has been clarified, thanks to the CDF's declaration.". Knitter then went on to specifically point out that among the issues raised and clarified is the issue of "the uniqueness of Jesus Christ as the one redeemer and mediator of salvation for humankind." He was actually quoting from an article by his fellow American Richard McBrien who in his article also advanced the thesis that among the Asian theologians there is the possibility that some may have erred: "In two or three cases, theologians may have gone too far in collapsing any meaningful distinction between Jesus of Nazareth as the Christ of faith and other so-called 'Christ figures'."

Knitter agreed with McBrien that the issue of the uniqueness of Jesus was a point of controversy but disagreed with the latter's suggestion that this had arisen as a result of the work of "two or three" theologians. Knitter, who himself has been very much engaged in interreligious dialogue and is also a keen observer of Asian theology, asserts: "I find that there are many Catholics who are painfully struggling with the traditional teachings that Jesus is the one and only savior of all other people. In view of their encounter with the depth of religious experience in their non-Christian friends, many Catholics, both Asian and American, find it difficult to continue insisting, to these other religious friends and to themselves, that a saving experience of God must come only through Jesus and find its fulfillment only in him and his church."

Even if McBrien's "two or three" is not taken literally but understood to mean that an insignificant number of Asians have "denied the uniqueness of Jesus Christ," [1] one wonders how he arrived at such a conclusion. Has he met enough Asians to come to that conclusion? Has he read enough Asian books – not only those available in the West, but also those by Asian publishers -- to surmise that only very few Asians have problems with Jesus' uniqueness? On the other hand, one can also ask how Knitter arrived at his own conclusion that McBrien is probably wrong? Does he have any data to substantiate his claims that "many" Catholics in Asia find it difficult to profess Jesus as the one and only savior? Does he know anything about what the ordinary lay Catholic on the pews of Asian churches -- not just Asian theologians -- believe?

These questions, asked of McBrien and Knitter, could also be posed to everyone else writing on Asian theology. Few, if not none, of the Asian theologians actually have any data to substantiate their hypotheses, be it in support of McBrien's position or Knitter's, or the CDF's, for that matter. At best, theologians project their personal theological orientations onto their Catholic brothers and sisters and suggest it to be the *sensus fidelium* of the People of God in Asia. This "false consensus bias" influences much of the theological writings of Asia, especially when one attempts to speak on behalf of the Church in Asia. Moreover, many Asian theologians do not have too much contact with the Church and Christians living in other Asian countries other than their own. In fact, it is not surprising to find more Asian theologians who have visited and/or lived in European and American cities as compared to those who have done the same in another Asian city. Consequently, when the Indian theologian speaks of "Asian theology" s/he is in fact speaking from her/his own experience of India rather than of Asia as a whole. Likewise, when a Taiwanese theologian claims something to be "not in harmony with Asian beliefs," chances are that s/he has never ever been to Manila, Delhi, or Jakarta but has often visited Paris, New York, or Rome. In a way, theirs is really a comparison between the West and their experience of their own particular country rather than the West and Asia as a whole. To confound the problem, there is little valid data on what Catholics in Asia believe, just as there is little literature written from a truly pan-Asian experience.

2. AN EMPIRICAL SURVEY

It is in view of this absence of data that an empirical survey was conducted to get a feel of the *sensus fidelium* of the Asian Church on the issues raised by *Dominus Iesus*. Thus, a questionnaire survey was sent out by means of email to persons from all across Asia. For a period of 8 weeks between January and March 2002, a total of 394 responses were received from nearly twenty countries, from as far West as Pakistan, India and Sri Lanka to as far

East as Indonesia and the Philippines to as far North as Japan, Korea and even Mongolia and China.

2.1 Analysis: In light of *Dominus Iesus*

A descriptive analysis of the data of the survey, in light of the themes raised by *Dominus Iesus* (*DI*), is as follows:

First, *Dominus Iesus* insists on the fullness and definitiveness of the revelation of Jesus Christ (*DI*, 5-6). The survey showed that out of a total of 394 respondents, 97% believe that Jesus is God's revelation, while only 72% believe that he is indeed the "fullness" of God's revelation. However, 44 % of these respondents believe on the one hand that Jesus is the fullness of God's revelation and believe, on the other hand, that revelation is also given elsewhere, for example, in the other religions. Only 17% of the respondents who believe in the fullness of Jesus' revelation assert its definitiveness in that they believe this revelation is given "only" in Jesus and not anywhere else. Whereas, 62% of the respondents believe not so much in the "fullness" or "definitiveness" of Jesus' revelation but that revelation is given in Jesus as well as in the other religions.

Second, *Dominus Iesus* postulates the unicity and universality of the salvific mystery of Jesus Christ (*DI*, 13-15). The results of the survey showed that out of a total of 394 respondents, 91% believe in Jesus as savior of Christians as well as savior of humankind. However, only 50% claim the unicity of this belief, asserting that Jesus is indeed the "only" savior for all of humankind, while 25% of the respondents believe in Jesus' universality as well as the possibility of other saviors for humankind.

Third, *Dominus Iesus* insists on the necessity of the Church for salvation (*DI*, 20-21). This does not mean, however, that everyone has to be baptized, as the document also states that those who do not belong to the Church can still be saved through the Church, even if it is not known how that happens (*DI*, 20). Not taking into account the apparent ambiguity these statements raise, the survey, nevertheless, showed that 84% of the respondents believe the Church to be a means of salvation. However, only 36% of the respondents believe in the "necessity" of the Church for salvation. Of these, only 12% would rule out absolutely the possibility of salvation through other religions. On the other hand, 20%, while believing in the necessity of the Church for salvation, also admit that other religions could be means of salvation. More significant is that 58% of the respondents hold that the Church is indeed a means of salvation -- albeit not a "necessary" means -- and at the same time hold that other religions could also be means of salvation.

Fourth, *Dominus Iesus* asserts that those who are in the Church have the fullness of the means of salvation (*DI*, 22). 62% of the respondents believe in this assertion, while 24% oppose it. The document then goes on to contrast this with the followers of other religions who are regarded as being in a gravely deficient situation. Of those who believe the first assertion that those who belong to the Church have the fullness of the means of salvation, 35% also believe in this second assertion that the followers of other religions are indeed in a deficient situation, while another 35% disagree with this second assertion.

Fifth, *Dominus Iesus* posits that the Church reserves the designation of inspired texts only to the Bible (*DI*, 8). Of the 394 total respondents, 92% believe the Bible is indeed the inspired Word of God. However, only 22% would go as far as *Dominus Iesus* to insist that the Bible is the "only" inspired text or sacred Word of God. Whereas, 47% accept the Bible as God's Word and at the same time accept the possibility of other sacred scriptures as God's Word.

Sixth, *Dominus Iesus* asserts that the true religion exists in the Catholic Church (*DI*, 23) and distinguishes this as "theological faith" as compared to other religions which are regarded only as mere "beliefs" (*DI*, 7). he results of the survey showed that 91% of the respondents believe Christianity to be indeed a true religion. However, of these, only 30% would assert that there can be no other true religions while 45% subscribe to the view that there can be other true religions just as Christianity is a true religion.

Seventh, *Dominus Iesus* warns against the spirit of indifferentism characterized by a belief that "one religion is as good as another" (*DI*, 22). The results showed that 36% of the respondents are indifferent and subscribe to the idea that belonging to one religion is as good as belonging to another, while 48% of those who responded disagreed with the idea.

Eight, *Dominus Iesus* warns against relativistic theories which seek to justify that it is indeed within God's plan that different religions exist *de jure* [in principle] (*DI*, 4). The results of the survey revealed that 49% subscribe to the notion that religious pluralism exists *de jure* while 20% disagreed with the notion.

Ninth, in keeping with the advances made by the Second Vatican Council, *Dominus Iesus* insists that interreligious dialogue "retains its full force and necessity" (*DI*, 22). Of the 394 respondents, 95% agreed that Catholics in Asia should be engaged in interreligious dialogue with their neighbors of other religions, while only 1% disagreed with the idea.

A summarized version of these results are presented in the table as follows:

Table 7, 1

THEOLOGICAL ISSUES RAISED BY *DOMINUS IESUS*	TOTAL RESPONDENTS (394 responses)	
1. Yes, Jesus is God's revelation	(382)	97 %
2. Jesus is <u>fullness</u> of God's revelation	(284)	72 %
3. Jesus is <u>fullness</u> of God's revelation, but God's	(172)	44 %

	revelation also given elsewhere		
4.	God's revelation given only in Jesus and not in other religions or elsewhere	(66)	17 %
5.	Jesus is God's revelation (not fullness) and God's revelation also given elsewhere	(245)	62 %
6.	Jesus is savior for Christians	(359)	91 %
7.	Jesus is savior for all	(357)	91 %
8.	Jesus is the only savior for all	(196)	50 %
9.	Jesus is savior for all, but there are also other saviors for all	(99)	25 %
10.	The Church is a means of salvation	(329)	84 %
11.	The Church is necessary for salvation	(140)	36 %
12.	Other religions are not means of salvation	(49)	12 %
13.	The Church is necessary for salvation, but other religions are also means of salvation	(79)	20 %
14.	The Church is a means of salvation (but not necessary), and other religions are also means of salvation	(229)	58 %
15.	Christians have the fullness of the means of salvation	(246)	62 %
16.	Christians do not have the fullness of the means of salvation	(96)	24 %
17.	Other religions are deficient, as compared to the Church	(139)	35 %
18.	Other religions are not deficient, as compared to the Church	(139)	35 %
19.	The Bible is the Word of God	(362)	92 %
20.	The Bible is the only Word of God	(88)	22 %
21.	The Bible is the Word of God, but other scriptures are also Word of God	(184)	47 %
22.	Christianity is a true religion	(357)	91 %
23.	Christianity is the only true religion	(120)	30 %
24.	Christianity is a true religion, but there are also other true religions	(178)	45 %
25.	One religion is as good as another	(142)	36 %
26.	One religion is not as good as another	(191)	48 %
27.	It is God's plan that there be different religions (pluralism de jure)	(195)	49 %
28.	It is not God's plan that there be different religions	(79)	20 %
29.	Yes, to Interreligious dialogue	(374)	95 %
30.	No, to Interreligious dialogue	(5)	1 %

3.   DISCUSSION ON THE RESULTS

3.1 The Statistics Speak

From the results of the survey, a few observations can be made. Firstly, it is clear that the following items yielded very high percentages, viz. more than

90%: No.1, No.6, No.7, No.19, and No.22. In other words, more than 90% of the 394 respondent sample affirm the theological assertions of the numbered items concerned. Specifically, they affirm that Jesus is God's revelation (97%), that Jesus is savior for Christians (91%), that Jesus is savior for all humankind (91%), that the Bible is God's Word (92%), and that Christianity is a true religion (91%). Since these are the most funda-mental and basic faith affirmations which distinguish Christians from those who are not Christians, it is safe to say that more than 90% of the respondent sample are believing Christians. The remaining who did not affirm these fundamental Christian beliefs are probably nominal Christians, skeptics, and/or people who project themselves as agnostics for the purpose of the present survey. In any case, since these latter didn't seem to identify with Christianity's basic beliefs, their responses in the survey were discounted. For, it would make no sense to include a response from them which claimed that other religions are not true if, in the first place, they also do not believe in Jesus or the Church either.

That only five of the numbered items received such unanimous affirma-tions speaks volumes of the *sensus fidelium* of the People of God in Asia. In particular, it reveals that amongst Asian Catholics, only these five doctrinal assertions are widely adhered to. In a way, if *Dominus Iesus* was re-written for Asian Catholics, this is probably how it would begin its first article: "The fundamental contents of the profession of the Christian faith for Catholics in Asia are expressed thus (cf. *DI*, 1): I believe in one God, the Father, Al-mighty. I believe in the Lord, Jesus Christ, who is God's revelation and who is savior for Christians as well as for all of humankind. I believe that the Bible, the canonical books of the Old and New Testaments, is the sacred Word of God. I believe that the true religion exists in Christianity in general and the Catholic Church in particular." That's it. There will probably be no affirmation of Jesus as the only savior or of the Church as necessary for salvation. On the other hand, of course this does not suggest that Asian Catholics do not affirm other doctrines of faith. It only implies that as far as the theological themes raised by *Dominus Iesus* are concerned, these are the only ones which they overwhelmingly subscribe to.

A second observation is that even if more than 90% of the respondent sample are decidedly Christian, a significant proportion amongst this same 90% are also decidedly open to and receptive of other religions. For example, 62 % believe God's revelation is also given in other religions (No.5), 25% allow the possibility of other saviors (No.9), 58% acknowledge that other religions could be means of salvation (No.14), 35% do not believe persons of other religions are deficient as compared to Christians (No.18), 47% allow for other scriptures as God's Word (No.21), 45% believe that there could be other true religions besides Christianity (No.24), and 49% accept religious pluralism as within the plan of God (No.27). Averaging these seven percentages would give a figure of between 40 and 50%. Hence, in very general terms, one can say that about 40-50% of Asian Catholics have a sense of openness to other religions. Indeed, contrary to the presuppositions and demands of *Dominus Iesus*, this significant proportion of Asian Catholics do not believe that either Jesus, the Church or Christianity is the sole, unique or normative repository of truth. It is important to be reminded that these same respondents also affirm the basic beliefs which *Dominus Iesus* postulates, except that they reject some of the more extreme and exclusive assertions, especially those which seem to question the integrity and authenticity of the other religions.

Thus, if *Dominus Iesus* were to be re-written for Asia, it would probably not begin -- as does *DI*, 1 -- with the mission mandate: "Go into the whole world and proclaim the Gospel to every creature. He who believes and is baptized will be saved; he who does not believe will be condemned" (Mk 16: 15-16). Instead, it would probably begin with: "Stop judging, that you will not be judged" (Mt 7: 1) or "Do to others whatever you would have them do to you" (Mt 7: 12). Such is the respect Asian Catholics have for their neigh- bors of other faiths and such is the respect they expect others to have for them in their believe of Jesus, the Church and Christianity.

A third observation is that a very small percentage of the respondent sample affirmed the more exclusivistic assertions of *Dominus Iesus*. Specifically, only 17% of the 394 respondents affirm that God's revelation is given only in Jesus and not in the other religions (No.4), 50% affirm that Jesus is the only savior and that there can be no other savior figures (No.8), 12% affirm that the other religions are not means of salvation (No.12), 35% affirm that the other religions are deficient as compared to those in the Church who have the fullness of the means of salvation (No.17), 22% affirm that the Bible is the only Word of God and that other scriptures are not God's Word (No.20), 30% affirm that Christianity is the only true religion (No.23) and 20% affirm that it is not within God's plan to have many religions (No.28). Leaving aside No. 8, where a significant 50% of the respondents affirm Jesus as the only savior, the percentages of the other six items average about 20-25% of the respondent sample. In other words, in very general terms, only about 20-25% of Asian Catholics would subscribe to the very exclusivistic aspects advanced by *Dominus Iesus* which do not acknowledge that truth can also be found in other religions.

It cannot be glossed over that a significant 50% of the respondent sample affirm the assertion that Jesus is indeed the one and only savior for all of humankind. To be exact, it was 49.7% as 196 out of the total of 394 respondents affirm this theological doctrine. On the other hand, 198 (50.3%) did not affirm the doctrine. This, however, does not mean they reject the doctrine. Out of this 50.3%, about half or 25% affirm the possibility of other savior figures while the other half are undecided on the issue. The finding is significant as it is primarily this issue of the possibility of other saviors which has been most sensitive and controversial. That 25% of the respondents were unable to declare their position on the issue is also significant. To be sure, the theory of the plurality of saviors remains ambiguous and is not as definitive as *Dominus Iesus* has made it out to be. The *sensus fidelium* of the People of God of Asia certainly reveals that. Moreover, even *Dominus Iesus* is not as definitive as it seems. In fact, article 14 of the document invites the Church "to explore if and in what way the historical figures and positive elements of [the other] religions may fall within the divine plan of salvation" (*DI*, 14). The findings of the research, therefore, call to question the very strong reprimands -- such as "it must be firmly believed" or "it is contrary to the faith" -- which *Dominus Iesus* employs. To be sure, the issues are far from firm and final. Moreover, if the *sensus fidelium* does not correspond to these doctrinal positions, no matter how insistent the Vatican is about them, such beliefs cannot be forced upon the People of God, especially in Asia, where Christians experience other religions everyday of their lives.

In summary, therefore, one can say that amongst Asian Catholics, more than 90% believe in the basic tenets of the Christian faith. Amongst these, about 40-50% also display a theological openness to other religions while only half that number, or 20-25%, harbor theological positions which exclude the viability of the other religions.   ....

4. DISCUSSION ON THE SURVEY

A final area which needs to be discussed is the feedback received on the survey itself. To be sure, many of the respondents expressed surprise at a survey of the present nature. This is in part because academic surveys are not as common a feature in Asian cultures as they are in the West. Moreover, surveys which deal with religious questions are even more atypical.

Thus, it did not come as a surprise that many of the respondents sent additional email messages expressing their fascination at the nature of the survey. One message read: "I'm interested in these sort of surveys. Do forward me more if any. Just wondering if there are any these type of on-line questions and answers in regards to the Catholic faith." Aside from those who found the survey interesting others were so interested that they asked that the results be shared with them. One respondent even asked: "Do you have 'model' answers? If you have I like to have them." A few of the respondents asked why the study was being done and how the questions came into being. Some shared that even if this was the first time ever that they had come across questions such as those asked in the survey, they found them thought provoking. Some wanted to know if they were the only ones responding the way they did as, for example, a message which read: "I hope I do not scare you with my 'radical' way of thinking. I would be interested to be kept informed of the consolidated results of your survey to see if my thinking is 'average'." A few wrote back to request for more time to work on the survey, saying something to the effect that "I want to reflect carefully on the questions because I think they will help me to work through my beliefs." One person said she was making photocopies of the survey and would request her parish priest to distribute it to all the parish-council members, for "it will be good for them to do." On the basis of some of these feedback, it looked as if the survey had become more than a statistical instrument to measure Asian Catholics' beliefs as it had also taken on the function of a formation tool.

These observations beg three points. Firstly, if many of these respondents expressed surprise at the nature of the questions it is because they had not come across the document *Dominus Iesus*. If they had, they would have recognized that the issues raised in the survey were really those of the document. Of course, a few respondents did recognize the document when they wrote to say, "Looks like you are working on *Dominus Iesus*!" The majority, however, had no idea where the issues came from or why they were being discussed because they had equally no idea of the existence of *Dominus Iesus*. Given that the survey was conducted more than a year after the document was officially issued, it only suggests that the Vatican document had not trickled down to the masses. Perhaps the bishops of Asia found the document too complex and technical and so decided that it should remain on the shelves of libraries rather than being disseminated. Perhaps the bishops found the issues raised by *Dominus Iesus* simply unimportant or irrelevant to the peoples of Asia and so decided against passing it on to their parishes. Whatever it is, these facts speak volumes of the reception of the document, which is supposed to have the status of "universal Magisterium."

Secondly, if the Asian bishops had decided that the document *Dominus Iesus* was irrelevant it is more because the "answers" were so, but by no means the questions. One respondent, a parish priest from Japan, who left many of the questions unanswered, commented: "I found that most of the questions if answered with A, B, or C, are too black and white and do not give a true reading of what a lot of us are thinking along these lines." Another respondent, also a priest but from India, who refused to accomplish the entire questionnaire, expressed similar sentiments: "I found the questions rather tricky especially since I strongly feel that we are caught in our own language game." Thus, if *Dominus Iesus* was deemed irrelevant it could be because it attempted to provide too many "black and white" answers which had to be "firmly adhered to," without taking note of the "language games" which we trap ourselves into.

A third point which the observations raise is that even if many of the respondents were unfamiliar with the nature of the questions asked, they found the questions truly interesting. To be sure, the questions were not only interesting, but also thought provoking and for some even bothersome or at least bordering on the sensitive. A Religious Sister from the Mekong Valley had this to say: "May I not answer the questionnaire. It's very catching. My superior in the house told me in a joking manner she is afraid she might lose her faith while reflecting on the questions asked!" A few more messages which expressed similar sentiments were equally friendly. Other friendly messages also advocated caution as, for example, one message which read: "This could be controversial so brace yourself for some negative feedback by some well meaning Catholics." Two messages, however, were particularly pointed. The first, which had responded to the questions half-way, had this to say: "I don't like to answer your questions anymore. If you like to know more, it is better you ask the bishops, especially those who have doctorate degrees. Please excuse me if I am too rude." The second, with a similarly angry tone, was even more direct in his challenge to me: "To Edmund. I come straight to the point. Why are you doing this survey? Why is it necessary for you to do this survey? Why are you targeting Catholics? Who authorized you with those questions in your so-called survey? Are you trying to doubt the Catholics' faith, or create confusion? What's your objective?"

As can be seen from the preceding comments, the questionnaire was not only thought provoking but viewed with a certain degree of suspicion as well, in view of the questions which seemed to have hit at the core of the Christian's being. In fact, the questions seemed to have caused much tension as they questioned the respondent's faith, especially in relation to her/his lived reality of religious pluralism. Of course, one way to deal with such tension is to block out the lived reality and act as if persons of other religions did not exist. Another way is to simply relegate them to the "unsaved" and be contend that Christianity is the superior and only true religion. The sincere seeker, however, will find such strategies of dealing with the tension untenable and could end up being even more confused and vulnerable. An emotive comment from one respondent captures this sense of vulnerability well: "I believe that only Christianity is for me, and it is different from the rest in a special way. However, I feel uncomfortable in saying my religion is the best, simply because that would imply that the other religions are not good and doing something wrong. That is difficult to say because a lot of religions preach goodness, and it is difficult to say goodness is wrong, just because it is of a different religion. Yet, I also am torn by the fact I've learnt all the time in Sunday-School that Christianity is the true religion. It is true, but does it necessarily mean that others are not? What is religion anyway? Common beliefs? Ultimate truths? Argghh... this is confusing." Another response, which expressed a similar dialectical tension, had this to say: "This is what I believe, although deep in my heart wish this is not 100% right, so more people can be saved from hell."

Edmund Chia is a De La Salle Brother from Malaysia but works in Thailand as Executive Secretary of the Office of Ecumenical and Interreligious Affairs of the Federation of Asian Bishops' Conferences. (edchia@pc.jaring.my)

[1] Knitter argues that Asian theologians do not actually "deny" Jesus' uniqueness. To be sure, they have no difficulty accepting Jesus as savior. They only ask if Jesus is indeed the "only" savior. "Truly but perhaps not only," is Knitter's mantra.

*   *   *

Herewith we come to the core text of this book 'Interfaith Dialogue Guidelines' which was worked out in 1994, one year after my becoming involved in the interfaith dialogue movement.

8. INTERFAITH DIALOGUE GUIDELINES

1.   WE BELIEVE that dialogue is only possible, not in mere tolerance, but in acceptance in mutual respect of the others in their typical individuality. Knowledge of others in their cultural setting is an essential condition towards such acceptance. By recognizing and accepting diversity on the social, cultural and religious levels, an exchange of mutual values and a union in collaboration will ultimately lead to the final unity of humankind.

2.   WE BELIEVE that we, as human beings together with all of nature and with all living creatures, are actively involved in a continuous growth process towards a better world in an ever higher intellectual and spiritual environment (Teilhard de Chardin 1881-1955). In this optimistic life-view and in our new world of global trans-border communication, the awareness that all human beings belong to the same brotherhood through their common Origin and their common Destination, should lead to a higher universal responsibility by all to put this into real practice in the everyday life.

3.   WE BELIEVE that, towards the creation of a better world order in peace and in justice, the inspiring role of the leaders of world religions, traditions, and other convictions, in whatever form they may be organized, is of prime importance. Their churches, organizations and institutions are, in their cultural and philosophical traditions, the organizations par excellence capable of proclaiming and sustaining universally accepted moral principles.

4.   WE BELIEVE that the tenets of all world religions and other faith traditions have their roots in the culture where they originated, that they have developed on the basis of the philosophical and moral concepts of that culture, and that they have approached and proclaimed the faith in transient expressions and in ceremonies proper to the culture to which they belong. As pilgrims on their way to always new discoveries and subject to change, no adherents to whatever religion or other faith tradition should claim exclusive representation of the Truth nor superiority over others.

5.   WE BELIEVE that, as an apparent consequence, there is need to convert the missionary activities and goals of the world religions from an "approach of converting" to an "approach of testifying". The essential valuable elements of the own faith should be presented in a language understandable by the local faithful, so that the dialogue among the world religions and traditions should lead to a better mutual knowledge and understanding, and

to an exchange of the mutual values as an enrichment of the own faith and of the faith of the others.

6.   WE BELIEVE that in the passionate search for the truth and for a more comprehensive approach to spirituality, meditation should be re-evaluated and more universally practiced as the road by excellence to a deeper awareness of the Divine presence. Meditation is the crucial approach to the Divine that crosses the boundaries of religious culture and is also universally shared and accepted. Meditation in silence should be part of all interfaith encounters.

7.   WE BELIEVE that a permanent awareness of and solicitude with the escalating ecological, social, economical as well as financial problems of our world should always be present in the minds of all people involved in interfaith dialogue. Acceptance of these guidelines could become a major steppingstone to a union in collaboration between the world Faith Communities (world religions and other faith traditions), transcending the doctrinal differences. Such dialogue in collaboration with the political world would be the most effective contribution towards more efficient solutions to our world problems, and at the same time an important stepping stone to a new world order in more peace and justice for all.

ELUCIDATION

The seven points of these Interfaith Dialogue Guidelines propose a basis for mutual recognition of and collaboration between the world Faith Communities: Christianity, Islam, Buddhism, Hinduism, Baha'i, other religions, religious traditions, humanists and spiritual movements. The 7 propositions can be considered as essential conditions towards the aimed at way of life: peace on earth to all people of good will.

These guidelines, which were conceived in 1994 and have grown up to the present text, will no doubt be judged by many as a dream. Having dreams however, belongs to the essence of the progress of human civilization and human society. Dreams are the source of development and of progress. To realize these dreams, they must have a foundation in a system of values assuming, among others, that:

• all human beings are equivalent with equal rights and also equal duties,
• human happiness lies in love and in returning in that love to the Ultimate Reality,
• confrontation should be replaced by collaboration in mutual respect,
• real human freedom consists in having the interior capacity to do what is commonly considered as right and to refrain from what is commonly considered as wrong,
• intercultural and interfaith dialogue leads to a mutually enriching union and in the long run will lead to a more universal homogeneity and a fi-

nal global unity,
- support of education and science should be the fundamental aim of all development aid assistance,
- all wars and acts of violence are a loss to all,
- limitation of arms-production, traffic and possession is the shortest way to peace and to a peaceful society,
- a common universal language, besides one's own native language, should be promoted as a much needed carrier for smooth worldwide communication,
- the treasures of our planet (oil, gas, minerals, etc.) should be considered as he property of the whole of humankind and should not be the sole property of nations which happen to be geographically situated above or near to some of these treasures. A tax on those who profit from these treasures should be levied and used for the common welfare of humankind. (this paragraph has been added in 2001)

On the basis of these values, these guidelines aim to be a basis for mutual acceptance and cooperation between the world Faith Communities: Christianity, Islam, Buddhism, Hinduism, Baha'i, etc., spiritual movements, humanists, and other convictions. Its seven paragraphs are limited to what can be considered as the essential requirements for arriving at the intended objective 'peace and justice on earth to all people of goodwill'. Remarks and advice of many readers have resulted in various adaptations over a period of 12 years, while the original conceptions have been maintained.

1) WE BELIEVE that dialogue is only possible, not in mere tolerance, but in acceptance in mutual respect of the others in their typical individuality. Knowledge of others in their cultural setting is an essential condition towards such acceptance. By recognizing and accepting diversity on the social, cultural and religious levels, an exchange of mutual values and a union in collaboration will ultimately lead to the final unity of humankind.

Real dialogue is only possible when knowledge and acceptance of the cultural and religious values is present on both sides. Racism can be described as intolerance and non-acceptance of other cultures and of the people belonging to them, with ignorance as its main cause. All opponents of racism argue for tolerance. Tolerance is a word which, in recent years, has been used commonly in almost all intercultural and interfaith activities, in meetings, in the media and in the mouths of the common people as a to be recommended attitude in ecumenical and in intercultural and interfaith encounters. The word itself however, implicates discrimination because one tolerates something which one would prefer that it is not there. Tolerance can be no basis for a real dialogue and should be replaced by acceptance of the others in respect of the values inherent in their culture, in their religion and in their peculiar customs. Accepting others has to mean more than just tolerating them. It should mean acceptance of the others as members of the own community, without necessarily loss of one's own identity. This acceptance from both sides should result in an integration of the values of both sides into a culturally richer community. Where there is respect, there will be willingness and readiness even to take over some of those values to integrate them in the own way of life, as a means of enrichment of the own cultural and religious values. It is obvious that this attitude of respect of the others is not possible without a certain knowledge of the others, their history, their historical and cultural development, their ways of life. The increase of such knowledge, thanks to the expansion of communication means, the availability of books on other cultures and religions, a growing amount of articles devoted to cultural and religious subjects, in the last twenty years, all have been valuable stimuli in intercultural encounters all over the world.

This attitude of accepting the others in mutual respect is becoming the attitude of more and more religious leaders, and to show that even in my Catholic church, although the time is not ripe for their supporting publicly these 7 points, remarkable changes are occurring from the grassroots up to the highest level in the Vatican. I quote the words of Pope John Paul II which he pronounced on occasion of the Interfaith Prayer Vigil for Peace in Assisi on January 9, 1993: *"...only in mutual acceptance of the other and in the resulting mutual respect, made more profound by love, resides the secret of a humanity finally reconciled... we wish to oppose the wars and conflicts, with humility but also with vigor, with the demonstration of our harmony that respects the identity of each one".*

The abundance of books on the islamic-arabic world and on Buddhism, in recent years in Europe and the USA, is a very fortunate development in the fostering of this necessary knowledge of these other worlds, not yet sufficiently known to most people outside the Islam and the Buddhist world. The numerous Zen-meditation sessions now being held on a regular basis in many European monasteries and the more than 250 Buddhist societies in the UK alone, testify to the growing interests in the Buddhist faith and in its beliefs and prayer-practices. The growing knowledge and acceptance of the values in other cultures and religions and other faith traditions will ultimately lead to the final unity of humankind, as children of the same mother-earth.

2) WE BELIEVE that we, as human beings together with all of nature and with all living creatures, are actively involved in a continuous growth process towards a better world in an ever higher intellectual and spiritual environment (Teilhard de Chardin). In this optimistic life-view and in our new world of global trans-border communication, the awareness that all human beings belong to the same brotherhood

through their common Origin and their common Destination, should lead to a higher universal responsibility by all to put this into real practice in the everyday life.

To dream about the future demonstrates a sense of optimism, believing in a growth towards an always better world. The five volumes of the books of Pierre Teilhard de Chardin (1881-1955), Jesuit, geologist and palaeontologist, - Le Phénomène Humain, L'Avenir de l'Homme, La Vision du Passé, Le Milieu Divin, L' Avenir de l'Homme -, have given us a vision of hopeful expectation and confidence in the slow but sure spiritualization of humankind in its centuries long growth.

Alvin Toffler describes in his book Power Shift (1990) the development of communication connections from an intra-intelligent and an extra-intelligent system towards an electronic nerve-network as an ever-expanding web across our earth. Both scientists, each in his own way, see the future of the world in a growing value-shifting from the material to the spiritual, in which the human mind plays an always greater role. It is obvious that in this growth process a crucially important role is reserved not only for the Christian churches, which have been at the origin of this vision, but also for the other world Faith Communities. This growth process is being realized not only in and across human beings. All what lives and moves on earth is involved in this ascendance to a higher spiritualization, to a unitive approximation to the divine mystery, the Ultimate Reality, foundation of all beings.

The 1992 10-pages document "The Global Community and the Need for Universal Responsibility" of the Dalai Lama remains a most valid document, calling the attention of all towards more responsible attitudes and a more responsible way of life by all members of the one human family. A most important and recent development is that this is now also in the progress of being recognized by political personalities in Europe, inside the EU Commission, as well as in the US.

The belief in the continuous growth of mankind from a animal-inspired way of life in the first thousands of centuries of the human existence into an ever higher intellectual way of life is an important aspect of this optimistic vision on the development of humanity in its long period of evolution. It is already common knowledge that this growth will know a still faster development in the years to come. This growth in knowledge has resulted in totally different ways of life - from feudal societies through the Middle Ages to our modern democratic systems of government, free trade and free travel - with an ever higher intellectual heritage passing on from one generation to the other. In olden times just a few were the owners of the land, while the common people were the subjects who by the work of their hands had to sustain the wealth of the owners. The common wealth has now become shared, at least in most of the democratic countries of the West and in Japan, by almost all citizens on an improving and relatively equal basis. Nobody can deny that, generally speaking, the life of the people of our times is of a higher intellectual and therefore of a more human level than in the past centuries. The remarkable increase of cultural activities and of interest in these activities in most countries is surely a sign of this higher quality of the daily life. The whole of the relatively recent world developments also in transport and in other communication means has automatically resulted in a tremendous increase in traveling for business as well as for leisure, in immigration and emigration movements of millions of people, to which, regretfully, also the domestic revolutions and wars between countries have contributed their part.

Millions of people have in this way come in contact with cultures and with religions, other than their own. This also is a way of no return and is only the very beginning of the new multicultural and multireligious world of tomorrow, which will become a reality much sooner than is normally thought of. Already in Europe, and this in spite of the language differences, frontiers between the countries of the European Union have been removed. As a totally normal consequence, the importance of the countries as geographical and political entities will know a rapid decrease, while the language regions are becoming more and more preponderant as new important components of the Europe of tomorrow. This has been well understood by the government leaders of India when they decided the state borders to be on the basis of the language of the region, which is maybe in this scale unique in the world. A very important point in relation with the interfaith and intercultural dialogue is that in parallel with this global trend towards unification, there is a strong tendency to stress the identity of communities belonging to the same culture and language and the stress on keeping on to that identity. This development towards unification and homogeneity on one side and towards a protection of the own cultural identity on the other side is a development which is and will become more than ever an object of discussion by all political leaders, first of all in Europe and in the US and of course also by all who are active in the interfaith dialogue movements, the world over. Governments of countries having problems with separation movements should be aware of this world trend and try to find solutions not in separation but in collaboration towards federal state solutions.

Jacques Delors, former president of the EU-Commission in Brussels, has created inside the Commission a "Forward Studies Unit" with as purpose the study on the ethic dimensions of the European Union. This unit has organized already some interfaith symposia, one in Toledo in 1995, one in Florence in 1996, one in Brussels in 1999, to which also Bishop William Swing was invited to give a talk on the United Religions Initiative, and in 2000. This Forward Studies Unit has also produced some very interesting reports and documents on the relation between religion and politics and on ways of coming to collaboration. In this way, I believe that the European Union can be considered as a forerunner in this field, and let us hope that this example will be followed by many other governments. I quote EU Commission Director of the Unit, Dr. Wolfgang Pape in one of his 1997 thesis-papers: "*Values and religion are now expected in Europe to provide us with a new source to legitimize the necessary ethical limitations on science and rights/democracy ("process") for the common good without borders in space or time*" - "*Ethics will no longer be deducted from abstract eternal principles of thought, but from communication and world-wide dialogue on the values necessary for our individual and collective survival will take center-stage.*"

3) WE BELIEVE that, towards the creation of a better world order in peace and in justice, the inspiring role of the leaders of world Faith Communities, in whatever form they may be organized, is of prime importance. Their churches, organizations and institutes are, in their cultural and philosophical traditions, the organizations par excellence, capable of proclaiming and of sustaining universally accepted moral principles.

After world war II, there was hope and expectation that people would now at last draw the necessary lessons from the traumas of this war. The dream of a world in peace was there. Again our world politicians have not been able to realize this expectation. And yet, we continue to believe that this dream will come true somehow and sometime. In a long-term view, the world religions can fulfill their important task, on condition that they achieve dialogue and cooperation on a worldwide scale. It is the task of popes, patriarchs, bishops, priests and ministers, imams, gurus, geshés, rishis, ripotchés, lamas or whatever their names may be, in short of the leaders of the Faith Communities to stress the essentials of the faith of their founders, and to find therein the necessary basis towards unity in diversity and in collaboration. This collaboration should manifest itself in one authoritative voice from a global supranational organization like e.g. a "United Religions" as proposed in 1995 by the Episcopal bishop W. Swing, San Francisco. This can become a bridgehead for the world Faith Communities to create a United Faith Communities Organization, and in this way support a global ethic and contribute in an effective way to a new world order in which the human individual stands central in his social and spiritual dimension.

In the individualistic world of the west, there is a growing tendency by which the individual is placed in the foreground as the decision maker in moral matters, on the basis of his individual conscience. This comes to expression in the attractiveness of movements like New Age and the innumerable new religious sects which are fighting for new adepts also in the countries where poverty and misery are still rampant like in some South-American and African countries. Many of the deep-believing faithful of the Catholic Church and of other Christian churches have, till now mainly in the West, lost faith in their churches as institutes. This is, in my personal opinion, a dangerous trend, which is due for a great part to the slowness of the highest church authorities in following the needs and the trends of the time, of the progress in science, in scriptural studies, in the new comprehension of how biblical and other old religious scriptures have come into existence. It can be explained also as a normal evolution in the general trend towards more independent thinking and behavior based on the own individual intelligence and conscience. Because man/woman on this earth will always remain man/woman with their good and their bad sides, it is obvious that guidance from above remains an essential and irreplaceable element in the moral behavior of people in general. It is also clear that besides the world religions as institutes, there is nothing which could actually replace these organizations. On the contrary, the world religions, as institutes joining with the recent enunciations of freethinking humanists, should become united on a global scale in a union of collaboration to increase the effectiveness of their moral and ethical guidance not only in personal matters but also in world matters. This is still a dream, and at that a most difficult to realize dream, which however, could and should be the final aim of all interfaith dialogue movements. This kind of global dreams will, without doubt, receive the enthusiastic support of the young people all over the world who are searching for a new ethical basis for their lives. The ethical basis for such a union in collaboration is available in the global ethic declaration as worked out by the Catholic theologian Hans Küng and his colleague Karl-Josef Kuschel of Germany. This global ethic, after vigorous discussions, has been enthusiastically received, tentatively approved, and publicly declared on occasion of the Parliament of World's Religions meeting in Chicago in 1993, attended by 7.000 religious and spiritual personalities from all Faith Communities. Its main ideas are summarized in following three catch phrases:

'No human life without a world ethic for the nations;
No peace among the nations without peace among the religions;
No peace among the religions without dialogue among the religions'

A second important ethical document is the Universal Declaration of Human Responsibilities, announced to the public on September 1, 1997, by the InterAction Council, in Tokyo, supported by elderly statesmen of 28 different countries, headed by the late Prime Minister Takeo Fukuda and the former German Chancellor Helmut Schmidt. This declaration can be considered as an emanation of the Japanese and Eastern way of life, reflecting the cultural values of Eastern civilizations, giving priority to responsibilities and duties above rights. It means also a most opportune addition to the Universal Declaration of Human Rights. It is obvious that both documents are worth to become central pivots in the lay-out of the planned global forum of the Faith Communities.

After my reading of many books, magazines and news-editions on the subject of interfaith dialogue and after having participated in quite some interfaith symposia and meetings, it appeared from all this that there are many ways to come to interfaith dialogue, which ways have consisted mainly of academic seminars and of prayer-meetings. What has struck me, as layman and as businessman, is that the participants in those meetings were almost exclusively academic people and religious and spiritual leaders, while common lay-people, active at the grassroots, like myself, were a real rarity and an exception. Another matter about which I have been wondering is why there is no more effort to make these activities known to the general public. This is probably one of the reasons why lay people are so few in attending, while I suppose that many of the active grassroots people, women and men, who dedicate a precious part of their time to parish work and other social activities would be ready to dedicate themselves to this all-important dialogue task and to participate actively in the interfaith dialogue encounters. I am thinking here of the thousands of socially engaged people in most religions, of the volunteers in so many aid assistance projects in the poorer developing countries, of all the religious-minded persons who have in India and other south-east Asian countries put into practice the Jain motto "Ahimsa paramo dharma" - non-violence is the highest religious obligation - such as Mahatma Ghandi and his disciple Vinoba Bhave with their 'swadeshi' concept, Vivekananda and his Rama-Krishna Mission in India, Sheik Mujibur Rahman in Pakistan, Maha Ghosananda in Myanmar, Khan Abdul Ghaffar Khan in Bangladesh, the Dalai Lama and many Tibetan monks now spread out over the world, and many others.

4) WE BELIEVE that the tenets of all world Faith Communities have their roots in the culture where they originated, that they have developed on the basis of the philosophical and moral concepts of that culture, and that they have approached and proclaimed the faith in transient expressions and in ceremonies proper to the culture to which they belong. As pilgrims on their way to always new discoveries and subject to change, no adherents to whatever religion or other faith tradition should claim exclusive representation of the Truth nor superiority over others.

This position is more and more being accepted and postulated by Bible and Qu'ran exegetes and by many theologians in the Christian and Islamic faiths. It is now being considered as self-evident that the formulation of a divine revelation is influenced for a great part by the culture in which it originated, and that this form of presentation is not revelation itself. These presentations and interpretations have to undergo a continuous change, appropriate to the ever-changing knowledge and ever higher conscience-level of the faithful, without therefore changing the essentials. The revolution in the biblical exegesis from the literal interpretation to a describing and relating interpretation, appropriate to the culture, especially in Christian theology, is the most valuable evolution and development of the last 50 years towards interfaith dialogue and real inculturation. It is to be hoped for that the same evolution will occur in relation with the Holy Scriptures of other Faith Communities like Hinduism, Buddhism and Islam. In the Islamic Declaration of Human Rights the right to change one's religion is not mentioned, and as long as the texts of the Qu'ran remain static unchangeable words of God and as long as this more scientifically based interpretation of revelation is not accepted by the Islamic Faith Communities, real dialogue and maybe even real world peace remain most difficult assignments. Acceptance of the above position has as automatic result the acceptance of the others on a basis of equality, limiting to a reasonable degree whatever kind of superiority there might still be felt.

The liturgical changes in the Catholic eucharistic ceremonies, by which a/o the Latin language has been replaced by the local language, have also been an important step forward in this adaptation evolution. It is regrettable that this has resulted in the disappearance of the atmosphere of 'divine mystery presence' in the church buildings. Voices for renewal and adaptation are being heard also in the Buddhist churches of Japan, e.g. to replace the old semi-Chinese semi-Japanese language of the prayers into a language more understandable by the faithful, while hopefully, keeping the main statue(s), representing the divine mystery, the Ultimate Reality, in their symbolic semi-darkness.

Since many years, interfaith dialogue has been a subject and even an action program for many religions. Baha'u'llah, the 19th century prophetic founder of the Baha'i religious community has, much in advance of the times, maybe been the first to proclaim the need for a world government as unifying organization and as the only real solution to prevent wars and social injustice. The ecumenical movement between the Catholic church and other Christian churches has been a subject for many meetings in the last 50 years. The first interfaith world conference in 1893, was organized by the Parliament of World's Religions in Chicago, on which occasion Rev. Vivekananda of India was one of the most remarked speakers. After a long period of one hundred years of silence, a second similar meeting was organized in 1993 by the same organization and also in Chicago. It is only in the last 30 years that interfaith meetings have followed each other successively, starting with the New Delhi International Interfaith Symposium by the Ghandi Peace Foundation in 1968.

It has to be recognized that the interfaith dialogue movement up to now has been a meeting place mainly of religious academics and of religious leaders at prayer-meetings such as the Buddhist Tendai Church yearly Summer meetings in Japan, and many others in Europe and in the US, the monastic exchange-visits between Catholic monks of Europe and Zen Buddhist monks of Japan, the Muslim-Christian Consultations, which have been held with several partners in Europe on a yearly basis since 1984 through the collaboration of the Al Albeit Foundation in Amman, Jordan, and the numerous conferences organized by the main international interfaith organizations the world over. All this has certainly resulted in a growing understanding of other religions and cultures, and also recently to a growing mutual respect and acceptance of the values of each other. This has even resulted in an integration effort of cultural and religious values of the others in the own faith-life as a rethinking and an enrichment of the own faith. It is however only in the last decade(s) that, on one hand, the technological advances of the global communication network, and on the other hand, the growing migration of multitudes of people into countries of other cultures, followed by an unavoidable inculturation process, have created the necessary conditions of a fertile soil for the interfaith dialogue on a worldwide scale.

5) WE BELIEVE that, as an apparent consequence, there is need to convert the missionary activities and goals of the world religions from an "approach of converting" to an "approach of testifying". The essential valuable elements of the own faith should be presented in a language understandable by the local faithful, so that the dialogue among the world Faith Communities should lead to a better mutual knowledge and understanding, and to an exchange of the mutual values as an enrichment of the own faith and of the faith of the others.

Most of us accept the existence of a spiritual power, of a spiritual 'being', whether it is considered and believed in as a person with a sublimation of human characteristics, such as compassion and love, or as a difficult to define 'dharma' or 'buddhahood', to which spiritual existence all human beings and all existing matter belongs as its origin and as its final destination. It is now being admitted by most religious scholars, that each world religion has its origin in a particular culture and that the wordings of the eternal truth and the religious ceremonies of each religion are part of that culture. It is a fact of history that culture changes through the centuries, because of the continuously upgrading changes in general knowledge, in science, and in the ways of life. Life at the time of the founders of the Christian, Muslim, Buddhist and other religions, or at the time of the Veda's, Upanishad's and other holy Scriptures of India, was totally different with the life and conceptions of our times. The ways of expressing things 2000 years ago were very dependent on the life conceptions of those times, and therefore liable to erroneous interpretations in later times. Thanks to the development of philological, archeological and anthropological research, it has now become possible to better understand and to more rightly interpret the old writings on which the world religions have been founded and developed in their contemporary context and surroundings.

These venerable texts are therefore, because of their local and not global origins and characteristics, subject to change and can therefore not be claimed as exclusive, nor as total and final. The eternal Reality cannot be limited to one particular culture or religion, because it must be, by its essence, global and universal. Returning to the roots and to the essence of those teachings, not encumbered by the influences of olden times, next to the recognition that some concepts of belief may be subject to interpretations based on new scientific grounds, will help to overcome a lot of problems in practical dialogue consequences.

From all kinds of publications and public declarations of religious authorities, it appears that there still remains an underground aim of converting the others to the own faith. This apparently is still the case in the Roman vision of the Catholic church and in some Protestant churches where Jesus Christ is still being proclaimed by some as the only Redeemer of Humankind, and partly in the Islam. In the Christian churches, the infallibility claim in possession of the whole truth has become an unsustainable dogma in the light of modern research in the historical development of the doctrines of the Old and New Testaments, from the origins up to the present state of the Christian faith. The same is true for the study of the Qu'ran and for the historical development of the Islamic doctrine. Buddhism, with the exception of some of the post-war new religions in Japan, has not proclaimed this kind of exclusive dogmatic doctrine.

The Second Vatican Council (1962-5) has authorized a significant shift in attitude within the Catholic Church. 'Nostra Aetate', (Oct. 1965) one of the sixteen documents of the council, dealt specifically with the relationship of the Church to non-Christian religions. It declares : *'The Catholic Church rejects nothing which is true and holy in these religions. She looks with sincere respect upon those ways of conduct and life, those rules and teachings which, though differing in many particulars from what she holds and sets forth, nevertheless often reflect a ray of the Truth which enlightens all men.'*

That not all is well yet, becomes apparent when one listens to another document 'Ad Gentes' (Dec. 1965) of the same council, which declares: *'The Church is missionary by her very nature'*, and in which the purpose of mission is defined as *'evangelization and the planting of the Church among those peoples and groups where she has not yet taken roots'*. Since there is however only *'one Mediator between God and men, himself man, Christ Jesus'* and *'neither is there salvation in any other'*, the text concludes: *'therefore, all must be converted to Him as He is made known by the Church's preaching. All must be incorporated into Him by baptism, and into the Church which is His body'.*

These texts of 'Nostra Aetate' and 'Ad Gentes' and also the later declaration 'Dominus Jesus' (Sept. 2000, see 'Beliefs of Catholics in Asia') seem and are intrinsically contradictory, as one does not see how they can be combined in practical life. An encouraging evolution has however been going on in the Catholic Church, not at the highest top yet, but at the grassroots and even among the priests, bishops, and monastic monks, by which in the practical religious life the rather exclusive text of 'Ad Gentes' is being ignored and the text of 'Nostra Aetate' has become the common practice and attitude of the grand majority.° As long as there is no real and public renunciation of this centuries old dogma of the one-time complete and final revelation of the Divine in the Bible as well as in the Qu'ran, a real dialogue in mutual acceptance seems rather inconceivable. Although more and more people are acknowledging that the origin of most of what has gone wrong in Western history - inquisition, crusades, colonization with its repudiation and even destruction of other cultures and cultural assets, slavery, and last but not least the superiority mentality of the Western people - has to be found in this claim of exclusivity, the renunciation of this claim will, without doubt, still take some time in mental preparation. This renunciation would, without doubt, eliminate one of the main obstacles to real dialogue and be the bridge for a mutually enriching exchange of each other's values.

Many fear that the acceptance of other cultures within the own cultural borders means a loss of the own values. This fear comes mainly from those who have no or little knowledge of or contacts with other cultures. Anyone who knows another language, learns by experience that the knowledge of another language brings each time an important human enrichment. The same can be said of each globetrotter with an open mind to other cultures. Each acquaintance with people and values of other cultures brings an enrichment of one's own culture-values. A unification and further homogeneity of the world population in acceptance and acknowledgement of the cultural values of others can only result in enrichment of the own culture and of world-culture in general.

This can also be applied to religious perception. From the moment there is a renunciation of claiming the possession of the absolute truth, there is no sense any more in the attempt to convert believers of other religions to one's own faith or church. As each world religion has its own unique values, the passing on of these values, not for converting but for deepening the faith of others, means an important element in mutual drawing together. This can also mean, as a consequence, an end to the rivalry between the churches, allowing individual free conversion from one church to another as fully acceptable and understandable. Each of the world religions has through the ages developed a core of religious values, resulting in a proper identity of their own, with an inherent right to keep to that own identity, which however should be kept open for growth and amelioration.

The acceptance and even the taking over of values from other faiths should mean in any case an enrichment and deepening of one's own faith. Such acceptance and experiencing of these values and truths will also result in a growth in knowledge and perception of the Ultimate Reality, the final and eternal truth.

The evident aim of all interfaith dialogue is to come to a better mutual understanding and, which I personally believe to be most important, to common activities in an attitude of reconciliation to avoid the mistakes of the past centuries and with the aim of arriving at a better world in peace, in a more equal sharing by all in the wealth resources of our earth, and in a better providing for the underprivileged of our world. As it becomes more and more evident that a union in doctrine is as remote as ever and that it should even not be the real aim to strive at, the drive for union in doctrine or in one church or in one religion should be converted into a drive for union in collaboration to do something together, rising above discussions on similarities and differences in doctrines and ceremonies.. Such union in collaboration is only possible in diversity and in conserving as much as possible the own identity in a world growing unavoidably more and more homogeneous, which are not contradictory but rather converging developments. This is true for nations and countries where borders are becoming less important or even disappearing, and also for religions. It seems evident that such union can only be realized by collaborating with each other in a global common range of activities.

6) WE BELIEVE that in the passionate search for the truth and for a more comprehensive approach to spirituality, meditation should be re-evaluated and more universally practiced as the road by excellence to a deeper awareness of the Divine presence. Meditation is the crucial approach to the Divine that crosses the boundaries of religious culture and is also universally shared and accepted. Meditation in silence should be a part of all interfaith encounters.

The growing contacts in the past decades with Hindu and Buddhist spirituality and their religious practices of meditation have most probably for a great deal contributed to the recent interest in all kinds of spiritual practices, from yoga up to Zen meditation sessions and New Age meetings and even to many of the songs and musical texts of the popular jazz, hippy and other song-festivals. Where the West has been used to more active prayers and active intellectual meditation as religious practices, the East has surprised us by their other ways in their holy scriptures of approaching the inexpressible Ultimate Reality. In their dictionary, there is no comprehensive word like the word 'God' in the monotheistic religions. The Divine lives and is present in everything and especially in the self of each human being. Doing away with the 'self' to discover the real 'Self' by becoming free of thoughts, of desires, by becoming empty of the 'self' so the 'Self' can reign has been the way of Buddhist and Hindu meditation and contemplation. This is a way maybe still reserved for a few, but these few are on a remarkable increase, not only among the elder but also among the young. To dedicate each day some time to this kind of meditation, there is no direct need to sit in the lotus position which may be reserved still for a few. Meditation can be practiced by everyone. It is a matter of living the daily life in conscious awareness of the others as members of the same family and of all the things around us just being aware helps to concentrate on the essentials, to eliminate stress of all kinds, and especially to become aware of our brothers and sisters of the one earth-family under the same Heaven.

7) WE BELIEVE that a permanent awareness of and solicitude with the escalating ecological, social, economical as well as financial problems of our world should always be present in the minds of all people involved in interfaith dialogue. Acceptance of these guidelines could become a major stepping stone to a union in collaboration between the world Faith Communities, transcending the doctrinal differences. Such dialogue in collaboration with the political world would be the most effective contribution towards more efficient solutions to the world problems, and at the same time an important stepping stone to a new world order in more peace and justice for all.
In the present stage of the growth process of the doctrines of the diverse religions, it is obvious that they are not ripe yet to come to a unity of fusion. The unity which should be aimed at by all world Faith Communities in the actual conditions is only possible in collaboration. All the Faith Communities are, to a more or lesser degree, concerned about the welfare of all human beings as individuals and also as global community. Searching together for solutions to the acute and escalating problems of mankind, such as poverty, wars, manufacturing, traffic and possession of arms, unjust sharing in the earth resources, and so many others, should be a priority aim of the collaboration between the religions of this world. Only with this clear goal in mind, rising above the doctrinal and other differences, can a unity in collaboration be achieved.

From the media and the general interest of the public in the search for a new moral basis in a world of all too fast changes on the road to a multicultural and multireligious society, a growing interest in religious matters is apparent, even from the political world where there is coming about a looking for a closer collaboration with the religious world in the search for solutions to our world problems. This presents an extraordinary opportunity, unique in the history of the world, to all world Faith Communities to become a guiding beacon, proclaiming to the whole world universally accepted moral codes from a unanimous one-voice authority of a world-organization, like a United Religions or a United Traditions, as mentioned above.

If the organizations active in interfaith dialogue and in dialogue for peace really believe what they believe, then the most direct and most efficient way to realize a one-voice world forum of the world Faith Communities, like it is the object of the United Religions Initiative, would be that the main interfaith and peace organizations, such as the Parliament of World's Religions, the World Conference of Religions for Peace, the World Congress of Faiths, the International Association for Religion and Peace, and maybe others, transcending their self-interests join forces with the United Religions Initiative in a kind of federal combination under one flag, in order to create this kind of global world organization as a worthy collaborating partner to the United Nations Organization. This would be a creation, which would reverberate through the world, of a real human spirit of mutual love and compassion, and also of the Japanese and Eastern spirit of harmony in forgetting the self for the common welfare.

Many organizations involved in interreligious dialogue have thought it useful if not necessary to have an affiliation with the UNO. In 2004, there were some 130 organizations and NGO's (non-government organization) (36 of Europe, 50 of the US, 20 0f Asia & the Middle East, 18 of Africa, 3 of Latin America and the Caribbean, and 4 of Oceania) which had an affiliated relationship with the United Nations. One may wonder if it is the right way for religions and religious organizations to link themselves so closely to the political world, and whether such an affiliation does not run the risk of becoming too closely linked to the political world. The history of the past centuries has shown that religions   had better avoid whatever close links with the political world, which has lead to our present separation of church and state in most democratic nations. This is another reason why a separate organization outside the UN but as an acceptable discussion party to the UN should be the way to exert influence on the activities of the political world for a better world for all.

It is obvious that the Global Ethic as proposed in 1993 by the theologian Hans Küng (Germany), the Universal Declaration of Human Responsibilities (Japan) in 1997, the 'Turning Point for all Nations' a 1995 document of the Baha'i community and last but not least the 1992 document of the Dalai Lama 'The Global Community and the Need for Universal Responsibility' are so many appropriate complements to the Declaration of Human Rights, which could and should become the basis for the world Faith Communities, to effectively contribute toward a new world order in which man/woman stands central in their social and spiritual dimension.

(Original version: 1994   Latest revision: April 2006)

*　*　*

We enter now into the many aspects of the interfaith dialogue movement. The following text 'Interreligious Dialogue Review' gives a summarized situation in some countries of the interreligious dialogue movement, which text was brought about in 2003 after 10 years of intensive promotion activity.

Part 2 Interfaith Dialogue in its many Aspects

9. Interreligious Dialogue Review

In the USA

Since the first international interreligious dialogue meeting in Chicago in 1893, organized by the Parliament of World's Religions (PWR) and especially since the 1930s, we notice an acceleration in the interreligious dialogue encounters in the USA, crowned by their second international encounter in 1993, as well as in Europe. The participants in most of these encounters were for the most part academics, priests and religious ministers, with a small minority of common lay people. (See the list of organizations in annex.)

Against the background of the growing unification of the world, many at last have become conscious that there is great need for more collaboration and also coordination among the activities of these interreligious dialogue organizations and equally among the NGO organizations. Without collaboration, coordination and even mergers, as it is now a common practice in the industrial and financial world, there is no noticeable *power* which could exert efficient influence on the political world and which also could be accepted by the public-media as worthy of their attention.

A long-awaited rapprochement has started now in the US between the Council for a Parliament of World's Religions (CPWR) and the United Religions Initiative (URI), with respectively as contact person Mr. Dirk Ficca (dirk@cpwr.org) and Rev. Charles Gibbs (office@uri.org), by which a representative of both has now a seat on the board of directors of the World Congress of Faiths. They publish now since 2004 the quarterly Interreligious Insight with Rev. Alan Race as chief editor (arace@leicester.anglican.org). One of the aims was and is to expand the scope of its news coverage to the American world, and later on maybe to other parts of the world. (See "Western Interfaith Organizations" on my website)

In the English speaking world, next to the above mentioned magazine, there is one more good quarterly in the Eastern world namely "Seeds of Peace", edited in Bangkok, Thailand (Siam), by the International Network of

Engaged Buddhists, Bangkok. (see below on Thailand). A regular cross-exchange of articles between both magazines with the aim to increase the mutual knowledge in the field of interfaith/intercultural dialogue between the Western world and the countries of Southeast Asia would be a most recommendable issue.

Without doubt, as most important encounters can be considered the meeting in Chicago in 1993 with some 7.000 participants (a/o declaration of the World Ethic of the Catholic theologian Dr. Hans Küng), 100 years after a similar meeting in 1893, the meeting in Cape Town, South Africa, in 1999, with 8.000 attendants, both organized by the mentioned CPWR of Chicago, and the subsequent meeting in Barcelona, Spain in 2003, also with thousands of attendants. One of the stated issues in Cape Town was the need of not just toleration but of acceptance of the others in their own identity and of more collaboration among the organizations for dialogue and for peace.

Also inside the other organizations in the US like The Temple of Understanding and the World Conference of Religions for Peace, there is now a growing insight in the need towards more collaboration in order to create the possibility to establish, besides the United Nations Organization, a religious one-voice world forum, like it was the aim, at least in its be-gin-period in 1995 of the founder of the URI, Mgr. William Swing, Episco-pal Bishop of the diocese of California, to create a United Religions Organi-zation, not inside the UNO but outside of it as an independent entity. In the preamble of their charter they state *"We, people of diverse religions, spiritual expressions and indigenous traditions throughout the world, hereby establish the United Religions Initiative to promote enduring, daily interfaith coop-eration, to end religiously motivated violence and to create cultures of peace, justice and healing for the Earth and all living beings"*.

To realize however such a global organization, there is obviously need for more local collaboration at the roots and surely also on a national and continental level. IARF, WCRP and now also URI have a representation inside the UNO and the UNESCO. This however makes them, surely unintentionally, being involved in the world of politics, while history has learned us that this is not the appropriate base for Faith Communities. This is the main reason why priority should be given to this idea of a global organization outside the UNO, and preferably with office on the European continent, as probably more acceptable to non-Christian Faith Communities.

In the European Union

Each European country has now its regular interfaith dialogue meetings with participation of all main Faith Communities. Most of the encounters are between Christians, Jews and Muslims.

Also here the understanding and acceptance of the need for a union in collaboration on the regional, national, European and international level seems to be becoming gradually a subject of discussion.

It is a conspicuous reality that among all the interfaith organizations there is no or very little collaboration in trying to *do* something together about the problems of our world, while these problems, as a matter of course, should be an always present subject at all interreligious dialogue meetings. Isn't it strange that for example three important interfaith dialogue organizations in the UK, World Congress of Faiths (WCF), International Interfaith Centre (IIC) and International Association for Religious Freedom (IARF), have their office on the same floor of the same building in Oxford, each with its own news bulletin and its own interests and objectives.

A supranational organization cannot, in my personal opinion, be realized without the existence of national and/or continental umbrella organizations. An important step in this direction is the creation of a European umbrella organization. Since three years, I have tried by all means to propagate this idea to the leaders of the existing interfaith dialogue organizations in Europe. The EU Commission is looking for collaboration with the European Faith Communities and has been organizing since some years one-day meetings between religious and political leaders. The problem of the Commission is that to further work out these contacts into a closer collaboration there are, besides the Catholic Church, no organizations which can be considered as fully representative for the other Faith Communities and which could act as its discussion partners. The Commission is still working on solutions to this problem.

On 12 March 2002, Senior European religious leaders announced the launching of the European Council of Religious Leaders (ECRL) (see paragraph Councils of Religious Leaders). It should have as task also the editing of a European interfaith dialogue news magazine with English as basic language. Is the ECRL acceptable to the EU Commission as representative of the Faith Communities? The World Council of Churches in Geneva with its 342 members (in 2006) of Protestant and Orthodox Faith Communities could eventually play a role in this issue.

Also in the Islamic world, there seems to be a growing demand for a body which could represent the various Muslim schools, and be fully entitled to be a mouthpiece for the European as well as for the supranational political and media world. This might be a long way off but could mean an important step in the meeting possibilities with the other Faith Communities and also with the political bodies like the EU Commission and the UNO. To treat the Muslim imams and religious teachers in Belgium on an equal subsidizing footing with the other main Faith Communities, the Belgian government has in 2000 put as condition the creation by democratic election of an Islam Executive as a representative partner to the government. This resulted in 2001 in the establishment of such an Executive body with as consequence that also the Islam 'clergy' and the teachers of the Qu'ran will be salaried by the government, just like the clergy and religious teachers of other main

Faith Communities in Belgium.

In JAPAN

Japan is really a world apart in this field, with Buddhism and Christian churches as main partners. Like in Islam, also in Buddhism there is no hierarchical umbrella authority. All "Churches" or sects or schools and even all temples are independent, also financially, and most are being managed from father to son. Like in Islam, Buddhist universities can be consulted on theological matters and do have a kind of authority but not conclusive nor binding like it is the case of the Vatican in the Catholic Church. Since some years now, there seems to be a move ahead inside the various schools towards more regular dialogue for closer collaboration within each school and between the different schools. This could take still quite a long time, like it always does in Japan to obtain a final consensus, and the creation of a representative body which could speak out to the world, like the Dalai Lama is doing as representative for Tibetan Buddhist schools, will only be possible after the intra-school and between-schools dialogue towards collaboration has been worked out. The lack of a representative institutional body remains a handicap for Japanese Buddhism to come to a union of collaboration with the other Faith Communities in Japan and a still bigger handicap in communication with other Faith Communities outside Japan.

A special case is the two-yearly prayer meeting of the main Faith Communities of the world, organized by the Buddhist Tendai faith community on Mount Hiei in Kyoto, which is attended by many high personalities such as Mgr. Francis Arinze, when he was still chairman of the Pontifical Council for Interreligious Dialogue.

Some of the new post-war religions do have interest in the interreligious dialogue. Risshō Kōsei-kai (1938, Nichiren origin, 5 million adherents) has been at the origin of the creation and of the financial support of WCRP, and supports also financially IARF, Oxford.

Sōka Gakkai (1930, Nichiren origin, 17 million adherents) (Kōmeitō is its political party) has good relations with the Catholic Focolare movement. Also some Shintōist communities like Konkō Church of Izuō, The Omoto Foundation, Kurozumikyō, and Myochikai Religious Movement are active in interfaith dialogue worldwide and participate in many of the international meetings.

In INDIA

There is probably no country in the world where there are more interfaith dialogue meetings than India. According to my latest information on occasion of my third visit to that country, Jan. 27 to Feb. 21, 2002, there are probably more than 200 organizations active in interfaith dialogue. All these organizations have however no or very few contacts with each other, what is confirmed by the fact that there is no list available of addresses of these organizations. This was confirmed by Rev. Dr. A. Suresh, secretary at that time of the Committee for Ecumenism and Dialogue of the Commission of Bishops' Conferences of India (CBCI), whom I met in Delhi. There is little or no sign of any collaboration neither on a regional nor on a national level. From all the meetings I had on this occasion, it became apparent that, as a typical Indian phenomenon of attitude, there was no sign of any real interest in what is going on outside India in this and also in other fields, and what is still stranger no sign of any eagerness to learn from the others.

The India of the millions of the poor and of the caste system with its 150 million Dalits or untouchables is on the verge of unavoidable important societal changes. The middle class has an intensifying vitality with a growth in numbers of people who rise from the lower castes into a better way of life and of becoming more accepted and appreciated by their fellow citizens. Besides the poverty still of some 200 million of citizens, living admittedly not in hunger except in cases of natural calamities, there is a growth in employment and in familial income, resulting in the rise of many of the poor up into the middle class group of citizens, by which men as well as women enter into a way of life more and more independent of the caste system.

The caste system itself is becoming more accepted in a human way, while the values of each caste are becoming more appreciated as societal elements with their own identity, not to be ashamed of. Also this evolution is becoming a part of the interfaith dialogue by the spontaneous conversion of many of the lower castes to Christianity or Buddhism. However, there is still great need of a recognizing of the societal value of the Dalits and other lower castes, and surely of a consciousness by the group of the 200 million of rather rich citizens, who apparently only have interest in the poor as under-paid workers in the industrial as well as the agricultural sector. Theirs should be the care and the financial support of the social activities of the NGOs and other organizations, which is now being provided almost exclusively from abroad. As a footnote, it might be interesting to know that more than 90% of all Christians and of their clerical leaders originate from the Dalit caste, and that these pastors and professors are being accepted and respected in their different functions by the common people. The Catholic seminary in Bangalore, where I stayed for three days has 2 years of philosophy and 4 years of theology taught to a thousand students with 10% of females, in an atmosphere of religious enthusiasm like we knew it in Europe in the years just before WWII. Most Indians consider Europe now as being lost to Christianity and to religion in general, and drowning more and more into a morass of immorality and materialism.

All these are reasons the more to hope that the Indian interreligious dialogue organizations become more united in a union of collaboration and to hope also that mutual knowledge between India and the West may increase by more news and dialogue exchanges between the East and the West. Especially in India, they need power to exert influence on the political leaders, who are the only ones who could change the socio-economic infrastructures which are at the basis of the problems of India.

See the names and coordinates of the main Indian interfaith dialogue organizations in Annex 1 Main Interfaith Dialogue Organizations in the World.

India and the silk-road

In 1980 and subsequent years, the Japanese National NHK TV has sent a research team of scientists and reporters to travel the old 10.000km silk road from X'ian, the old capital of China to Egypt, Rome and Byzantium, and made a most remarkable TV documentary, broadcasted in regular programs. The same year a series of books based on this TV program, started being published in the Japanese language.

The export of silk from China started around the third century BCE till the 8th century CE, with the Indians and Persian as main intermediaries. This silk-road, which has been in almost continuous usage from around 400 BCE till the beginning of the 15th century CE, has resulted in a permanent cross-exchange of languages, human races and of cultural and religious values between all the nations on this road. In the centuries before Christ, the famous city of Taxila in the Ghandara region (now northeastern Pakistan, of which now only some ruins remain) was an important turning point on the silk-road, enjoying also a most famous university to which Persians, Greeks and Chinese came to study. The passing of the armies of Alexander the Great from 332 to 325 BCE through Mesopotamia and the other countries up to northern Pakistan and India, meant an important acceleration of these cultural and religious exchanges.

Emperor Asoka of India who reigned between 272 and 231 BCE converted to Buddhism, and became one of the first governors in the world of a multireligious and multicultural society, in peace between the religions of that time, Buddhism, Hinduism, and Zoroastrianism. His social prescriptions were carved on styles and granite blocks, of which so many have remained as tourist attractions in the India of today.

He has sent out Buddhist priests as missionaries to China, Ceylon (Sri Lanka) and to the other end of the silk road, Memphis and Alexandria in Egypt. The Buddhist councils which he convoked on regular periods may be seen as the oldest forerunners of the interreligious dialogue movement. Dion Chrysostomos (40-112) confirms in one of his writings that people from India stayed in Alexandria at the beginning of his new millennium.

There is quite a literature on the possibility that Jesus might have been acquainted with the teachings of the Buddha, which could explain the similarity of parables used by Jesus and by Buddha, and even that he may have been in contact with adherents of Buddhist missionaries in Egypt who were probably active in Alexandria and Memphis around his time. Some even go as far as trying to prove that Jesus spent the hidden years of his life, from his 14 till his 27 years, in Persia/Iran and mostly in the Pamir region of India under the name of Issa, as it seems to be written in some of the old Buddhist scriptures.

Some book titles: The Original Jesus, The Buddhist Sources of Christianity, Elmar Gruber & Holger Kersten, Element Books, 1995 // The Lost Years of Jesus, Elisabeth Clare Prophet, Book Faith India, 1994 // Jesus lived in India, Holger Kersten, Penguin Books, 1994.

Mogul Emperor Akbar, reigned from 1556 to 1605 and is known as a very broadminded monarch who treated all religions of his time, Hinduism, Buddhism and Christianity, as having equal values. He had discussions with Jesuit priests (Frs. Monserate, Aquaviva, Pigneiro, Xavier a/o) who stayed at his court between 1570 and 1605. In 1575, he built a "House of Worship" as a multireligious meeting place where on Fridays (the Muslim Sabbath) he held discussion meetings between religious personalities of his time. In the beginning it was limited to the different schools of Islam, but later from 1578 on also Hindus, Christians and other religions participated.

In Bangladesh

My point that there is need in all religions of an updating modern scientific interpretation of the Holy Scriptures has been proclaimed also in Hinduism by some personalities in the politico/religious world of Bangladesh, a/o RAMMOHUN ROY (1772-1833), his study of different religions convinced him that since every religion had the same end, namely, the moral regeneration of mankind, each stood in need of reinterpretation and reassessment in changing circumstances of the time.

The infallibility of the Vedas began to be questioned by the radical section of the Brahma Samaj amongst whom the most prominent was AKSHAY KUMAR DATTA (1820-1886). Hitherto Vedic infallibility had been regarded as the essential part of the Brahma religious creed. Around 1847 the Brahma leaders after a thorough scrutiny were convinced that the doctrine of Vedic infallibility was no longer tenable.

Keshab Chunder Sen (1838-1884) advocated complete abolition of caste distinction and actively promoted the cause of social reform, particularly the movement for female education and emancipation. He inculcated the popular Hindu conception of Bhakti or devotional fervor in his religious practice and stressed the doctrine of 'God in conscience'. Finally, his religious ideas took some definite shape when in January 1880 he proclaimed his new religious creed called Navavidhan or the 'New Dispensation'. It advocated faith in a living God and the several religions of the world as interpretations, diverse and fragmentary, but mutually complimentary rather than exclusive.

In Thailand

Sulak Sivaraksa (www.sulak-sivaraksa.org), the well known Buddhist social activist, is fighting here and in other countries of Southeast Asia for the human rights of the tribe people living in mountainous forests and for the educational development of the still very undervalued Buddhist nuns in Thailand and Sri Lanka. He is also the founder and the soul of the "International Network of Engaged Buddhists" (INEB) with their valuable quarterly on dialogue "Seeds of Peace". This quarterly magazine should be approached as a worthy partner by the American/English quarterly "Interfaith Insight" for more news exchange between East and West. On the matter of interfaith dialogue. He has good contacts with the Christian Faith Communities in his country, which he adamantly calls with its old name of Siam, but there are not real interfaith dialogue encounters with them, although he himself participates in many international meetings in the West.

In Sri Lanka

Many organizations, Buddhist as well as Christian and Muslim, are active in the interreligious dialogue, with Catholic priests and Buddhist monks as the main driving forces. The main four organizations are: Inter-Cultural Research Centre (inculture@eureka.lk) Religious Peace Foundation (nad@sit.lk), Interfaith Fellowship for Peace and Development (IFPD) (ifpdgn@itmin.com), and Centre for Society and Religion (csrlibra@slt.lk).

My very good friend Dr. Anthony Fernando is the director of an Inter-Cultural Research Centre near Colombo, where he together with his wife Sumana teaches English and computer practice to more than five hundred students mainly of the lower less privileged classes. He has published two remarkable and very recommendable booklets "Buddhism made plain" and "Christian Path to Mental Maturity" (the latter one translated in Dutch and published by the Teilhard de Chardin Foundation in Holland (sttdc@worldonline.nl).

Christian-Buddhist Monastic Interreligious Dialogue:

Monastic Interreligious Dialogue (DIM/MID) is an organization of mainly Benedictine and Trappist monks and nuns committed to fostering interreligious and intermonastic dialogue at the level of spiritual practice and experience. Mutual spiritual exchanges of Catholic Monks and Sisters from the EU and the US with Buddhist Monks and Sisters from Japan and India have taken place on a regular yearly basis since 1979. The 10th exchange sojourn by Catholic Benedictine monks and nuns, together 10 persons, in Buddhist monasteries in Japan took place in 2004.

*   *   *

As a view into the future evolution and most advisable action-aim for the global interreligious dialogue movement, hereafter a historical perspective on a world body for the world religions by Rev. Marcus Braybrooke.

10. A World Body for the World Religions?

by Marcus Braybrooke

'There is one thing stronger than all the armies in the world; and that is an idea whose time has come' (1). The idea of a United Religions Organization or a World Council of Religions is not new. It may be sensible to look back and see why previous initiatives have failed to realize the hopes of those who had this dream so that, God willing, we may be more successful at this moment of both crisis and opportunity.

The World Congress of Faiths

The hope for a new world order is a recurrent theme in the wartime writings of Sir Francis Younghusband who founded the World Congress of Faiths (WCF). A religious basis, he insisted, was essential for the new world order. In one of his chairman's letters, he referred to the efforts of Rudolf Otto, best known for his book The Idea of the Holy, to create an Inter-Religious League as a parallel to the League of Nations. In a subsequent letter, he referred to a book by Professor Norman Bentwich, called The Religious Foundation of Internationalism in which Bentwich expounded in detail the idea of a League of Religions. At a subsequent meeting, Bentwich said the idea had a long history. Leibnitz had propounded it and so had Rousseau. Then, quite independently, on April 4th 1943, Dr George Bell, the Bishop of Chichester. Spoke in the House of Lords of 'the acceptance of an absolute law with a common ethos to be secured in the dealings of nations with each other' and 'of an association between the International Authority and representatives of the living religions of the world;. The Bishop was subsequently invited to submit his proposal to the Executive of WCF. In a letter dated April 17th 1943, recognizing that the League of Nations lacked a supporting religious body, he wrote 'my idea was whether there could be some group officially recognized of representatives of all religions'. The WCF Executive asked Dr Bell to set up a private committee to examine the proposal in detail and to report back. The Committee included, Lord Perth, late Secretary General of the League of Nations, Lord Samuel, Sir S. Runganadhan, Indian High Commissioner, Baron Palmstierna and M .Mo'een Al-Arab, Secretary of the Royal Egyptian Embassy in London.

After several meetings it was unanimously agreed to ask WCF to circulate the Three-Faith Declaration on World Peace. The American Three Faith Declaration had been issued in October 1943 over some 140 signatures of authoritative leaders of the Protestant, Catholic and Jewish communities.

The Declaration proclaimed:
1. That the moral law must govern the world order.
2. That the rights of the individual must be assured.
3. That the rights of the oppressed, weak or colored (sic) peoples, must be protected.
4. That the rights of minorities must be secured.
5. That international institutions to maintain peace with justice must be organized.
6. That international economic co-operation must be developed.
7. That a just social order within each state must be achieved.

In Britain, the statement gained the support of the Council of Christians and Jews. The Bishop of Chichester's committee invited WCF to make the Declaration and Statement known to religious leaders of the world and to enlist their support. This was done through embassies, legations and rectors of foreign churches in London. By mid 1946, one thousand and fifty copies had been dispatched. Several copies sent to European countries were returned by the censor. WCF kept Dr Lois Finkelstein of the Jewish Theological Seminary of the USA, who was one of the original signatories, informed of the response. Pamphlet 27 of 1946, shows an interesting range of supporters, including the Sheikh of the Mosque at Mecca, as well as Muslim leaders from Iraq and Syria. The Dewan of Travancore affirmed his sympathy as did the Raja of Aundh. The Sadharan Brahmo Samaj published the document in full in its newsletter. The Archbishop of Sweden, after consultation with the Swedish Ecumenical Committee, expressed his whole-hearted agreement. There was little backing for the initiative from most Christian leaders. The Communist block prevented the United Nations from any public endorsement of religious principles. A reception was arranged for members of UN delegations during the first meeting of the Assembly in London in 1946 to tell them about the Declaration, but only a few people turned up. WCF had done all it could, but religious leaders failed to build on this initiative.

In 1953, there is a report in the WCF archives of a meeting of a member of WCF, Heather McConnell, with Mr. R. C.. Roper, Executive Vice-President of the World Parliament of Religions. This had been founded in February 1952, at the Presbyterian Labor Temple, New York. The aim was to establish a permanent World Parliament of Religions to work with a permanent United Nations to stop war and the causes of war and to extend the more abundant life among all peoples on earth. A leaflet describes the distinguishing features of the organization:

This is a movement of individuals ...

1. This movement for peace through cooperation of governments and religions is unique in all history. Governments, acting alone, cannot stop war and the causes of war. Religious, divided and competing, cannot stop war or the causes of war. But – governments, acting together, through the United Nations and religions, acting together, through a permanent World Parliament, both cooperation, can stop war and the causes of war.

2. This movement seeks to affiliate the moral and spiritual forces of the religions of the world, upon the basis of their common unities. There are a few subsequent references in the WCF archives to this organization and rather more to the World Alliance of Religions, but neither initiative seems to have had a lasting impact (2).

The Temple of Understanding

The Temple of Understanding in its first years held a number of Spiritual Summit Conferences to parallel the Summit Conferences of world leaders. At the second such meeting, in Geneva in 1970, on the theme 'Practical Measures for World Peace', it was agreed to establish a 'Continuing Conference on World Religions', 'to promote understanding and enduring appreciation of the different faiths, and to bring to bear all the resources at our disposal toward the solution of human problems, both personal and social'. Nothing came of this resolution, although the Temple of Understanding, through a variety of activities and the many contacts of its energetic International Director, Father Luis Dolan, has continued itself to bring religious influence to bear upon the work of the United Nations (3). In 1995, the Temple of Understanding, with a Council of Religious and Interfaith Organizations, took the initiative in arranging services in New York to mark the fiftieth anniversary of the United Nations.

The World Conference of Religions for Peace

The World Conference of Religions for Peace convened for the first time in Kyoto, Japan, on 16-21 October 1970. It is interesting in this context to recall the original vision of the World Conference of Religions for Peace. Dr Homer Jack quotes the dreams of several of the founders. For example, Shri R. R. Diwaker said, 'What seems necessary today is ...concentrated effort for peace by a kind of united religious organization of the whole world'. Dr Jack, with characteristic honesty, then analyzed reasons why WCRP has failed to live up to the initial high vision. 'The vision of the founders of WCRP was not modest' he concludes, 'for they hoped to engage all world religions everywhere in peacemaking and peacekeeping activities...The first two decades has lowered the expectations... despite a few successes, WCRP remains a modest organization'. He suggests several reasons why WCRP may not have lived up to its founders' vision.

"First was the 'representativity' of board members of WCRP and especially some of its influential chapters When WCRP was established, its leaders acted as individuals and not as official representatives of their religious organizations. They were more free to act on controversial war/peace situations. Today there is more talk in WCRP of representativity – even though this has not shown itself in financial statements of the organizations. Yet even discussion of representativity seems to weaken the courage which is needed for the organization to take risks. A second brake on WCRP activity may be the fact that the present leaders have little detailed knowledge of the history of the organization... A third factor ... perhaps is a change in priorities. Ironically the adoption of a holistic definition of peace may have diluted the organization's focus and urgency. Peace is not just the absence of war; it is fulfilled only when its many causes are eradicated – from poverty to discrimination. And yet if WCRP devotes itself to each of these "root causes", its holistic nature makes it diffuse. Attention to everything from apartheid to Zionism can result in WCRP losing sight sometimes of its "war against war" and the necessity to oppose war from every angle. A fourth and final deterrent to prophecy may be the very professionalism all organizations seek for sheer efficiency... Among the other dangers for the future of WCRP are that it might emphasize religion to the exclusion of peace and that it might emphasize study rather than action" (4).

A World Council of Faiths

In each decade of the UN, a similar suggestion for a world religious body has emerged. In 1986, a meeting of representatives of international interfaith organizations was held at Ammerdown, near Bath. There was a call for the establishment of a 'World Council of Faiths'. The plan was to bring together the main international interfaith organizations, identified as the International Association for Religious Freedom, the World Congress of Faiths, the Temple of Understanding and the World Conference of Religions for Peace, into one world body – rather in the way that forty years before the World Council of Churches was formed by the merging of Faith and Order, Life and Work and the International Missionary Council. It was recognized that the organizations had different emphases and that these were complementary. Their offices were located in different parts of the world, so a world structure might be established. The creation of a united organization would avoid competitive requests for funding, it would reduce the many demands on religious leaders to attend international conferences. One world body would make it easier for other international organizations to consult the religious world and also make it easier for members of one religion to consult members of others and to engage in joint work. Despite some discussion following the first Ammerdown conference there was little enthusiasm for the suggestion. The idea of a World Council of Faiths re-emerged in the

early nineties. The Won Buddhists and then Dr John Taylor, formerly
Secretary General of WCRP, made suggestions, which were taken up by Sir
Sigmund Sternberg, Chair of the International Council of Christians and
Jews, in an address at the Chicago Parliament of the World's Religions in
1993. Similar suggestions were made in several places during the 1993 Year
of Inter-religious Understanding and Co-operation.

Since 1993

Since the 1993 Chicago Parliament several initiatives have been taken. In
Chicago, The Council for a Parliament of the World's Religions has been
established. Besides work in the metropolitan area of Chicago, the Council
has an international program, with Dr Jim Kenney as the Director (succeeded in 2000 by Dirk Ficca). The Council plans to hold periodic 'Parlia-
ments of Religion' in different parts of the world. (A similar suggestions was
made in 1893). The first such Parliament was held in Cape Town, South
Africa in 1999 and followed in 2004 by a similar meeting in Barcelona,
Spain, both times with about 7.000 participants. The Council for a Parliament of the World's Religions also continues to promote the Declaration
Toward a Global Ethic, which was issued at the 1993 Parliament.

In 1995, the *Peace Council* held its first meeting at Windsor Castle,
near London. Dr Daniel Gomez-Ibanez, who was Executive Director of the Chicago Parliament, took the initiative and is the Peace
Council' s first Director. At the heart of the Peace Council is a
simple idea: a forum where about 25 religious and spiritual
individuals who are internationally known and respected and who
want to work together to overcome centuries of misunderstanding,
division and violence meet and agree to support each other's work
for peace. Initially, in response to a call from Maha Ghosananda,
the Council is supporting calls for a ban on land mines. The next
meeting of the Council, at the invitation of Bishop Samuel Ruiz
Garcia, will be in Mexico in November 1996.

Recently, the fiftieth anniversary of the signing of United Nations'
Charter in San Francisco has occasioned the proposal from Bishop
Swing for a United Religions Organization. The intention is to
provide the world's religions with a permanent gathering place
where, through daily prayer, dialogue and action, they may use
their spiritual and moral resources for the good of all life on this
earth. Other initiatives, such as Interfaith International could be
mentioned as well as those, such as the Alliance of Religions for
Conservation, which focus on a particular issue could be mentioned. Other existing bodies, such as WCRP, which held its Sixth
Assembly in Italy in 1994, the World Fellowship of Inter-Religious
Councils, which is planning an international conference in India in
August of this year and the International Association for Religious

Freedom, which will hold its 29th Congress in Korea, also this August.

What hope of success?

Is a new initiative, such as the United Religions Organization, needed and likely to be successful. I am sympathetic to the ideal, but I cannot avoid asking why previous attempts have been unsuccessful. Maybe we can avoid the mistakes of our predecessors, maybe this is the 'window of opportunity'. There are several reasons to think this is an opportune moment:

1. The dangers of religious extremism are now seen as an important item on the political agenda – it is not just a concern for religious professionals.
2. The collapse of communism has made the UN open to religious influence in an unprecedented way. Many people working in UN agencies now recognize that there is a spiritual and moral dimension to the great problems facing our world.
3. The interfaith movement has a new outward-looking concern. The 1993 Chicago Parliament was shaped to address the critical issues of our day. Much earlier interfaith work had to be directed at removing ignorance and prejudice and at encouraging religions to rethink their attitude to each other.
4. A growing number of religious leaders recognize the importance of inter-religious understanding and cooperation, as well as the dangers of religious extremism and hostility.

I am not clear whether we need a new organization, whether we should seek to develop an existing organization, most obviously WCRP, or find a means for all engaged in interfaith work to, on occasion, be able to speak together. The difficulty of a new organization is to see how it will make the break-through that other bodies have failed to achieve. It would need the initiative and energy of the leaders of several religions – not just their names on the notepaper. It would need, to my mind, also the active backing and involvement of political and economic leaders. It could not just be a 'religious' body. The problem of building on an existing organization is that it requires of that organization great flexibility and a willingness to treat others as equal partners. The difficulty of a co-operative structure of interfaith organizations is whether it can have the authority to make an impact. The International Interfaith Centre can become a useful place of information about interfaith work, but it has no mandate to speak for the interfaith movement. In Britain, the relief agencies do come together as a 'Disaster Committee' to present a joint appeal to the public when there is a disaster. Different organizations can work together for particular purposes, as some did to promote Sarva Dharma Sammelana. The experience of preparing for that conference in Bangalore suggested that there are many approaches to interfaith work. Organizations have their own particular emphasis. They may

also have their own constituencies. I doubt whether those who take initiatives want to be subject to someone else's control. Often the founding figure
of a group is a charismatic leader who inspires a number of followers. There
are I think several concerns that plans for a United Religions Organization
needs to address.

Concerns to address

Such an organization may be bureaucratic and seem too 'Western'. It should
certainly be multi-centred, that is to say with major offices in each of the
continents, so that control did not appear to rest with the West. There are
also fears that some people might try to manipulate such a council for
political purposes. There remains too the suspicion in some quarters that a
World Council of Faiths might become an attempt to create one world
religion. There are serious questions about who would constitute the
leadership of a World Council of Faiths.

I was sent once a small 'dictionary' of religious leaders. In the introduction, it was said that no one who qualified would have thought of himself or
herself as a religious leader. Humility should be the quality of a truly
religious person. In some religions there are clearly designated leaders – the
most obvious example being the Pope and Cardinals of the Roman Catholic
Church. Other religions, especially Hinduism, are not structured in this way.
Is religious leadership determined by the office held or the spiritual authority
of a person? – sometimes the two coincide. In planning any major interfaith
conference, the question of whom to invite is a major concern. Usually it is
clear that participants speak for themselves, but will what they say be
recognized and owned by other members of their faith community? I cannot
think of any religion that one would describe as a ' united religion' . Indeed,
what communities do you recognize as religious? This was a problem at the
Chicago Parliament, where the presence of some new religious movements
caused the Orthodox Churches to leave the Parliament. There are splinter
groups which the main religious community refuse to recognize. For
example, Muslims do not accept the claims of members of the Ahmadiyya
movement to be Muslims. These are only some of the complexities. Yet if
the voice of the religions is to be heard the need for an effective mechanism
remains. There are those who picture quite a small body of spiritual leaders
who would be listened to because of their personal authority and the wisdom
of what they say. Others look for a big representative body which would
have authority because it spoke for a large number of religious people. Some
bodies, which I prefer to call multifaith rather than interfaith organizations,
focus on a particular issue, such as the environment or the victims of torture.
At times, there is the suspicion that religions are being enlisted to serve a
predetermined cause. Yet Homer Jack's cautionary note that a holistic body
may become diffuse needs to be remembered. The variety of initiatives now
being proposed is evidence of the growing awareness of the need for

religious people together to contribute to efforts to meet the great crises facing the world. Many at the United Nations now recognize that issues such as population-control, the environment and world poverty have a spiritual and moral dimension. They require a wider consciousness and determination if they are to be tackled. Their solution may involve important changes in life style. Religious leaders may not be able to propose detailed solutions but they can help create an international conscience that demands effective political action.

This leads to my final consideration: How effective are religions in promoting peace and justice? It has been a persistent hope in the interfaith movement that people of faith should be able to act for reconciliation in situations of conflict. This has in fact proved very difficult. Those engaged in hostilities are reluctant to listen to outside voices. Sometimes religious difference is one of the causes of conflict and those involved will expect their co-religionists to identify with them. This is why an interfaith appeal from outside or a visiting interfaith delegation may be helpful. In some situations, religious people of different traditions may already be working for reconciliation, but be rejected by others in their own community. In such cases the main service those outside can offer may be to assure those who work for reconciliation that they are not forgotten. People of faith can help to shape public opinion and so to influence political decisions. Politicians are reluctant to admit their debt to others, but sufficient public demand will result in action. This has been seen in increased overt concern by governments on environmental issues, although there is a suspicion that sometimes the purpose of international conferences seems to be how to evade action and, on returning home, how to avoid acting on resolutions that have been passed. This is why sustained pressure from the religious communities is required and why there needs to be an effective instrument for this. There is a danger that religions will be used by politicians for their purposes rather than that they will influence politicians. Religious influence is often weakened by religious disagreement. There is a need for people of different faiths to meet together and to discuss in detail the complex moral and ethical issues that face our world with those with expertise in the particular concerns. It is easier to agree on the need to end poverty than on the methods of birth control that may be necessary to achieve this. If people of faith are to speak together on vital issues, then there has to be more on-going and detailed work. There has to be an understanding of the religious, philosophical, historical and cultural backgrounds which shape the approaches of different Faith Communities as well as adequate expertise on the issue discussed.

It is said of the United Religions Organization that 'the prime purpose for uniting the world's religions into a global organization is to eliminate violence in the name of religion, race or ethnicity'. An organization that makes this its primary task will have plenty of work to do. I hope any new organization will have a distinct focus, whilst recognizing that its long term objectives will only be achieved if it works closely with many other related bodies. Until religions clearly renounce violence, their creative contribution to building a new world order will be ignored. To many people today, religion is a threat rather than a promise and the public perception of religion as a cause of division and hostility is a disincentive to faith. If a United Religions Organization can purge the religions of what distorts and corrupts their witness, it can unblock the channels through which the healing wisdom of the great spiritual traditions will flow into our world.

Marcus Braybrooke, 20.3.1996   A paper submitted to the International Interfaith Centre Conference at Oxford in April 1996.

Notes
(1) From an anonymous author in Nation, 15.4.1943, but a similar idea was voiced by Victor Hugo in Histoire d'un Crime, written 1851-2, but not published until 1877, part 5, section 10.
(2) A fuller account and references are to be found in my forthcoming A Wider Vision: A History of the World Congress of Faiths, Oneworld Publications 1996.
(3) See my Pilgrimage of Hope, SCM Press 1992, especially Part VII.
(4) Homer A Jack, WCRP: A History , 1993, pp. 396-403.

*   *   *

The participants in a meeting "The Contribution by Religions to the Culture of Peace", organized by UNESCO and the Centre UNESCO de Catalunya, which took place in Barcelona from 12 to 18 December, 1994, expressed themselves as follows :

11. Barcelona Declaration 1994

On the role of religion in the promotion of a culture of peace

Deeply concerned with the present situation of the world, such as increasing armed conflicts and violence, poverty, social injustice, and structures of oppression; recognizing that religion is important in human life; we declare:

Our World

1. We live in a world in which isolation is no longer possible. We live in a time of unprecedented mobility of peoples and intermingling of cultures. We are all interdependent and share an inescapable responsibility for the well-being of the entire world.

2. We face a crisis which could bring about the suicide of the human species or bring us a new awakening and a new hope. We believe that peace is possible. We know that religion is not the sole remedy for all the ills of humanity, but it has an indispensable role to play in this most critical time.

3. We are aware of the world's cultural and religious diversity. Each culture represents a universe in itself and yet it is not closed. Cultures give religions their language, and religions offer ultimate meaning to each culture. Unless we recognize pluralism and respect diversity, no peace is possible. We strive for the harmony which is at the very core of peace.

4. We understand that culture is a way of seeing the world and living in it. It also means the cultivation of those values and forms of life which reflect the world-views of each culture. Therefore neither the meaning of peace nor of religion can be reduced to a single and rigid concept, just as the range of human experience cannot be conveyed by a single language.

5. For some cultures, religion is a way of life, permeating every human activity. For others, it represents the highest aspirations of human existence. In still others, religions are institutions that claim to carry a mes-

sage of salvation.

6. Religions have contributed to the peace of the world, but they have also led to division, hatred, and war. Religious people have too often betrayed the high ideals they themselves have preached. We feel obligated to call for sincere acts of repentance and mutual forgiveness, both personally and collectively, to one another, to humanity in general, and to Earth and all living beings.

Peace

7. Peace implies that love, compassion, human dignity, and justice are fully preserved.

8. Peace entails that we understand that we are all interdependent and related to one another. We are all individually and collectively responsible for the common good, including the well-being of future generations.

9. Peace demands that we respect Earth and all forms of life, especially human life. Our ethical awareness requires setting limits to technology. We should direct our efforts towards eliminating consumerism and improving the quality of life.

10. Peace is a journey - a never ending process.

Commitment

11. We must be at peace with ourselves; we strive to achieve inner peace through personal reflection and spiritual growth, and to cultivate a spirituality which manifests itself in action.

12. We commit ourselves to support and strengthen the home and family as the nursery of peace, in homes and families, communities, nations, and the world:

13. We commit ourselves to resolve or transform conflicts without using violence, and to prevent them through education and the pursuit of justice.

14. We commit ourselves to work towards a reduction in the scandalous economic differences between human groups and other forms of violence and threats to peace, such as waste of resources, extreme poverty, racism, all types of terrorism, lack of caring, corruption, and crime.

15. We commit ourselves to overcome all forms of discrimination, colonialism, exploitation, and domination and to promote institutions based on shared responsibility and participation. Human rights, including religious freedom and the rights of minorities, must be respected.

16. We commit ourselves to assure a truly humane education for all. We emphasize education for peace, freedom, and human rights, and religious education to promote openness and tolerance.

17. We commit ourselves to a civil society which respects environmental and social justice. This process begins locally and continues to national and trans-national levels.

18. We commit ourselves to work towards a world without weapons and to dismantle the industry of war.

Religious Responsibility

19. Our communities of faith have a responsibility to encourage conduct imbued with wisdom, compassion, sharing, charity, solidarity, and love; inspiring one and all to choose the path of freedom and responsibility. Religions must be a source of helpful energy.

20. We will remain mindful that our religions must not identify themselves with political, economic, or social powers, so as to remain free to work for justice and peace. We will not forget that confessional political regimes may do serious harm to religious values as well as to society. We should distinguish fanaticism from religious zeal.

21. We will favor peace by countering the tendencies of individuals and communities to assume or even to teach that they are inherently superior to others. We recognize and praise the non-violent peacemakers. We disown killing in the name of religion.

22. We will promote dialogue and harmony between and within religions, recognizing and respecting the search for truth and wisdom that is outside our religion. We will establish dialogue with all, striving for a sincere fellowship on our earthly pilgrimage.

Appeal

23. Grounded in our faith, we will build a culture of peace based on non-violence, tolerance, dialogue, mutual understanding, and justice. We call upon the institutions of our civil society, the United Nations System, governments, governmental and non-governmental organizations, corporations, and the mass media, to strengthen their commitments to peace and to listen to the cries of the victims and the dispossessed. We call upon the different religious and cultural traditions to join hands together in this effort, and to cooperate with us in spreading the message of peace.

*   *   *

The importance of a global religious forum with as moral basis a global ethic, a golden rule, acceptable to all Faith Communities and to all human beings has also been publicly declared by:

12. The Glasgow Ethic Declaration 2001

In Support of a Global Ethic

A Global Ethic and Its Relevance for the United Kingdom.
A multireligious conference. Glasgow, 29-30 October 2001.
Conference Report, Glasgow 2002.
University of Glasgow, Dept. of Theology and Religious Studies,
www.religions.divinity.gla.ac.uk/Centre-Interfaith/GlasgowDeclaration.pdf

(1) We, women and men from various Faith Communities, inter-faith organizations and academic institutions, have met in Glasgow to discuss the process of developing a "Global Ethic", its necessity and its prospects, its existing achievements and its relevance for the people of the United Kingdom in all their diversity. We, the undersigned, make the following declaration and further offer the suggestions, questions and inspirations collected in the workshop reports for consideration.

(2) At a time when human beings everywhere discover the increasing interrelatedness of all life on earth, the need of affirming a global ethic is evident. Its need and its difficulties are highlighted by the events of 11th September and later events and military action. Subsequent to the "Universal Declaration of Human Rights" (1948), this process of developing a global ethic emphasizes the need to keep rights and responsibilities in balance by establishing "a minimal fundamental consensus concerning binding values, irrevocable standards, and fundamental moral attitudes" "Declaration Toward a Global Ethic", adopted by the Parliament of the World's Religions in Chicago, 4 September 1993).

(3) The basis for such a global ethic has not to be created for it already exists: There are core values and moral insights which are held in common across the different philosophical and religious traditions despite the variety and diversity of beliefs and practices. It was this common ethical ground which the "Declaration Toward a Global Ethic" sought to express. We believe that the Chicago Declaration provides a valuable starting point for further reflection and refinement of the content of a global ethic.

(4) We endorse the essence of this global ethic which can be stated as:

"Every human being must be treated humanely!" This demand is unfolded in the most basic moral insight, widely testified to by the religious and philosophical traditions of humankind, that you shall not do to others, what you do not wish done to yourself, or – in positive terms – that you shall do to others, what you wish done to yourself.

Further we endorse the following four core values as expressive of this:

1. Commitment to a culture of non-violence and respect for all life.
2. Commitment to a culture of solidarity and a just economic order.
3. Commitment to a culture of tolerance and a life of truthfulness.
4. Commitment to a culture of equal rights and partnership between men and women.

(5) We are aware that there are moral issues which are difficult to decide. We know from our own traditions that a clear and unanimous judgment cannot always and in every ethical question be attained. However, if ethical discussion and debate is to be fruitful, a consensus on the most basic ethical principles is desirable. To establish this consensus serves as an antidote to forms of relativism that undermine any consciousness of moral obligation.

(6) It is not our intention to reduce religion to ethics nor ethics to religion. But morality is an indispensable element of religion and a fundamental basis of social life. Therefore we are convinced that the affirmation of common ethical principles gives the various relationships between our different Faith Communities a firmer basis for dialogue and a framework for common action as an important contribution to the foundations of our societies.

(7) We commit ourselves to promoting reflection and discussion within our Faith Communities and organizations on the content of a global ethic. The Chicago Declaration of 1993 can be of great help towards that aim. The awareness of shared moral values should serve as a cornerstone of all future interactions between our communities.

Signed by 58 religious leaders: *(A/N graphic layout by the author)*

Table 12.1

Baha'i	
1) Allan J. Forsyth (Baha'i)	33) Bishop Idris Jones (Scottish Episcopal Church)
2) Barnabas Leith (Baha'i)	
3) Kathryn Hendry (Brahma Kumaris)	34) John Riches (Scottish Episcopal Church)
Buddhists	
4) Vanessa Albrecht (Order of Buddhist Contemplatives)	35) Perry Schmidt-Leukel (Scottish Episcopal Church)
5) B.A.R. Coplans (Buddhist)	36) Peter Sampson (Unitarian)
6) Dharmacarya Kenneth Holmes	37) R.J. Berry (Christian)

(Tibetan Buddhism, Kagyu School)
7) Rawdon Goodier (Buddhist)
8) Nagapriya (Western Buddhist Order)
Christians
9) Michael H. Taylor (Baptist)
10) John Ferguson (Church of Scotland)
11) Tom MacIntyre (Church of Scotland)
12) Norman Shanks (Church of Scotland)
13) Brian E. Gates (Church of England)
14) Alan Race (Church of England)
15) Elizabeth J. Harris (Methodist)
16) Andrew MacKenzie (Methodist)
17) Nigel Dower (Religious Society of Friends)
18) Peter Jarman (Religious Society of Friends)
19) Josef Boehle (Roman Catholic)
20) Sr. Mary P. Cannon (Roman Catholic)
21) Regina O'Callaghan (Roman Cath.)
22) Maureen P. Cusick (Roman Catholic)
23) Sr Patricia Cusick (Roman Catholic)
24) Tim Duffy (Roman Catholic)
25) Thomas Fitzpatrick (Roman Catholic)
26) Clare Jardine (Roman Catholic)
27) Jim Kenney (Roman Catholic)
28) Hans Küng (Roman Catholic)
29) Ann Noonan (Roman Catholic)
30) Sr. Northcote (Roman Catholic)
31) Sr. Isabel Smyth (Roman Catholic)
32) Dominic Ind (Scottish Episcopal Church)

38) Eileen Crawford (Protestant)
Hindus
39) R. Chohan (Hindu Council UK)
40) S.M. Jaiswal (Hindu, Advaita Vedânta)
41) Ms. Diksha Joshi (Hindu)
42) Manjula P. Sood (Hindu)
43) Suraksha Vohra (Hindu)
Jains
44) Nathubai Shah
Jews
45) Ephraim Borowski
46) Jacqueline Tabick
Muslims
47) Batool Al-Thoma (Muslim, Sunni)
48) Imam Dr. Abduljalil Sajid (Muslim)
49) Nadeem Malik (Muslim)
50) Sayyed Mohammed Musawi (Muslim, World Islamic League)
51) Mona Siddiqui
Sikhs
52) Jaswant Singh Heera (Sikh)
53) Kirpal Singh Rai (Sikh)
Other or without specification
54) Concetta M. Kenney
55) Kamran Mofid
56) Victor Spence
57) Neil Walker
58) Brahma Kumaris

*   *   *

Once a global ethic is being accepted as a global rule of conduct, the obvious consequence is to accept the GOLDEN RULE as a global rule of conduct for the whole of humanity.

13. Golden Rule and Global Ethic

by Paul McKenna
Scarboro Missions (Toronto, Canada) in 2005
www.scarboromissions.ca/Interfaith_dialogue/gold_rule_global_ethic.php

The Golden Rule is considered to be the most prevalent and universal moral principle in history. To reflect on the Golden Rule is to reflect from the perspective of a universal wisdom. In this section, we examine the many dimensions of the Golden Rule, also known as the "Ethic of Reciprocity".
The Global Ethic is an international effort to develop a set of universal principles that calls upon the wisdom of the world's many cultures, religions and secular philosophies. Because the Golden Rule is found in so many religions and cultures, it is a key moral ingredient in the development of a Global Ethic

As a result of broad-based immigration patterns in recent decades, humanity is moving toward a global society with interaction among peoples in every conceivable way - economic, political, social, ethnic, cultural, technological, religious. Our shrinking "global village" is evolving into a multi-racial, multi-cultural and multi-religious society. Indeed, we are witnessing the emergence of a global consciousness - an increasing number of people are coming to see themselves as members of one family in an interdependent universe.

Across the planet, thousands of people including educators, humanitarians, social justice activists and religious people are working to develop a Global Ethic. This international effort to develop a set of universal moral principles calls upon the wisdom of the world's many cultures, religions and secular philosophies. The purpose here is to develop a universal ethic that will address major problems including racism, militarism, sexism, widespread poverty, violence, ecological destruction as well as intercultural and interreligious strife

The Global Ethic is an expression of the emerging global consciousness. Accordingly, every human being in our global village is called to become a "global citizen" with both rights and responsibilities.
Dr. Hans Küng, (Prof. Emeritus of the Tübingen University, Germany) a

noted scholar of world religions, is a key moving force behind the movement for a Global Ethic. For Küng, the Global Ethic cannot be implemented unless there is genuine dialogue among the world's religions:

No human life without a world ethic for the nations.
No peace among the nations without peace among the religions.
No peace among the religions without dialogue among the religions.

At the 1993 Parliament of World Religions in Chicago, Küng and others drafted A Declaration Toward A Global Ethic. This declaration challenges all people to commit themselves to:
- a culture of non-violence and respect for life
- a culture of solidarity and a just economic order
- a culture of tolerance and truthfulness
- a culture of equal rights and partnership between men and women

"We are interdependent. Each of us depends on the well-being of the whole, and so we have respect for the community of living beings... We must treat others as we wish others to treat us. We make a commitment to respect life and dignity, individuality and diversity, so that every person is treated humanely, without exception."   from "Towards a Global Ethic - An Initial Declaration", signed by 300 representatives of the world's religions at the 1993 Parliament of the World's Religions in Chicago.

"Golden Rule - Ethic of Reciprocity

The Golden Rule, known also as the Ethic of Reciprocity, is considered to be a key reference point for the development of a Global Ethic. The Golden Rule is arguably the most consistent and most prevalent ethical teaching in history. Many regard it as the most concise and general principle of ethics.

It is found in numerous cultures, religions, ethical systems, secular philosophies, indigenous (Native) traditions, and even in the mathematical sciences (e.g. the golden mean). And because the Golden Rule crosses so many traditions and philosophies, it possesses tremendous moral authority and reveals a profound unity underlying the diversity of human experience. The Golden Rule also emphasizes values of mutuality, interdependence and reciprocity.

Given its omnipresence across history, the Golden Rule could be described as a universal ethical principle. To reflect on the Golden Rule is to reflect from the perspective of a universal wisdom.

Accordingly, the Golden Rule is not just a moral ideal for relationships between people but also for relationships among nations, cultures, races, sexes, economies and religions. Clearly, the Golden Rule has the capacity to be the ethical cornerstone in developing a Global Ethic as the human family works together to build a peaceful, just and sustainable global society

The Golden Rule, with roots in a wide range of the world's cultures, is well suited to be a global standard to which different cultures could appeal in resolving conflicts. As the world becomes more and more a single interacting global community, the need for such a common standard is becoming more urgent."

The golden rule is best seen as a consistency principle. It doesn't replace regular moral norms. It is not an infallible guide on which actions are right or wrong; it doesn't give all the answers. It only prescribes consistency - that we not have our actions (toward another) be out of harmony with our desires (toward a reversed situation action). It tests our moral coherence. If we violate the golden rule, then we're violating the spirit of fairness and concern that lie at the heart of morality.

"Every religion emphasizes human improvement, love, respect for others, sharing other people's suffering. On these lines every religion had more or less the same viewpoint and the same goal." said the Dalai Lama.
Hereunder some passages on the golden rule from the religious texts of various religions and secular beliefs, with permission from the website of Ontario Consultants on Religious Tolerance, which all express the same idea of a golden rule for humankind:

Baha'í Faith:
"Ascribe not to any soul that which thou wouldst not have ascribed to thee, and say not that which thou doest not." *"Blessed is he who preferreth his brother before himself."* Baha'u'llah
"And if thine eyes be turned towards justice, choose thou for thy neighbour that which thou choosest for thyself." Epistle to the Son of the Wolf'.

Brahmanism:
"This is the sum of duty: Do naught unto others which would cause you pain if done to you". Mahabharata, 5:1517

Buddhism:
"...a state that is not pleasing or delightful to me, how could I inflict that upon another?" Samyutta Nīkaya v. 353
"Hurt not others in ways that you yourself would find hurtful." Udana-Varga 5:18

Christianity:
"Therefore all things whatsoever ye would that men should do to you, do ye even so to them: for this is the law and the prophets." Matthew 7:12, King James Version.
"And as ye would that men should do to you, do ye also to them likewise." Luke 6:31, King James Version.
"...and don't do what you hate...", Gospel of Thomas 6. The Gospel of Thomas is one of about 40 gospels that were widely accepted among early Christians, but which never made it into the Christian Scriptures (New Testament).

Confucianism:

"Do not do to others what you do not want them to do to you" Analects 15:23

"Tse-kung asked, 'Is there one word that can serve as a principle of conduct for life?' Confucius replied, 'It is the word 'shu' -- reciprocity. Do not impose on others what you yourself do not desire.'" Doctrine of the Mean 13.3

"Try your best to treat others as you would wish to be treated yourself, and you will find that this is the shortest way to benevolence." Mencius VII.A.4

Ancient Egyptian:

"Do for one who may do for you, that you may cause him thus to do." The Tale of the Eloquent Peasant, 109 - 110 Translated by R.B. Parkinson. The original dates to 1970 BCE and may be the earliest version ever written

Hinduism:

"One should not behave towards others in a way which is disagreeable to oneself." Mencius Vii.A.4

"This is the sum of the Dharma [duty]: do naught unto others which would cause you pain if done to you." Mahabharata 5:1517

Humanism:

"Humanists acknowledge human interdependence, the need for mutual respect and the kinship of all humanity."

"Humanists affirm that individual and social problems can only be resolved by means of human reason, intelligent effort, critical thinking joined with compassion and a spirit of empathy for all living beings."

"Don't do things you wouldn't want to have done to you, British Humanist Society.

Islam:

"None of you [truly] believes until he wishes for his brother what he wishes for himself." Number 13 of Imam "Al-Nawawi's Forty Hadiths."

Jainism:

"Therefore, neither does he [a sage] cause violence to others nor does he make others do so." Acarangasutra 5.101-2.

"In happiness and suffering, in joy and grief, we should regard all creatures as we regard our own self." Lord Mahavira, 24th Tirthankara

"A man should wander about treating all creatures as he himself would be treated.". Sutrakritanga 1.11.33

Judaism:

"...thou shalt love thy neighbor as thyself.", Leviticus 19:18

"What is hateful to you, do not to your fellow man. This is the law: all the rest is commentary." Talmud, Shabbat 31a.

"And what you hate, do not do to any one." Tobit 4:15

Native American Spirituality:

"Respect for all life is the foundation." The Great Law of Peace.

"All things are our relatives; what we do to everything, we do to ourselves.

All is really One." Black Elk.

Roman Pagan Religion:

"The law imprinted on the hearts of all men is to love the members of society as themselves."

Shintō:

"The heart of the person before you is a mirror. See there your own form"

Sikhism:

Compassion-mercy and religion are the support of the entire world". Japji Sahib

"Don't create enmity with anyone as God is within everyone." Guru Arjan Devji 259

"No one is my enemy, none a stranger and everyone is my friend." Guru Arjan Dev : AG 1299

Sufism:

"The basis of Sufism is consideration of the hearts and feelings of others. If you haven't the will to gladden someone's heart, then at least beware lest you hurt someone's heart, for on our path, no sin exists but this." Dr. Javad Nurbakhsh, Master of the Nimatullahi Sufi Order.

Taoism:

"Regard your neighbor's gain as your own gain, and your neighbor's loss as your own loss." T'ai Shang Kan Ying P'ien.

"The sage has no interest of his own, but takes the interests of the people as his own. He is kind to the kind; he is also kind to the unkind: for Virtue is kind. He is faithful to the faithful; he is also faithful to the unfaithful: for Virtue is faithful." Tao Teh Ching, Chapter 49

Unitarian:

"We affirm and promote respect for the interdependent of all existence of which we are a part." Unitarian principles.

Wicca:

"An it harm no one, do what thou wilt" (i.e. do what ever you will, as long as it harms nobody, including yourself). One's will is to be carefully thought out in advance of action. This is called the Wiccan Rede.

Yoruba: (Nigeria):

"One going to take a pointed stick to pinch a baby bird should first try it on himself to feel how it hurts."

Zoroastrianism:

"That nature alone is good which refrains from doing unto another whatso-ever is not good for itself". Dadistan-i-dinik 94:5

"Whatever is disagreeable to yourself do not do unto others. Shayast na Shayast. 13:29

Some philosophers' statements on this subject:

Epictetus: "What you would avoid suffering yourself, seek not to impose on others." (circa 100 CE)

Plato: "May I do to others as I would that they should do unto me." (Greece; 4th century BCE)

Socrates: "Do not do to others that which would anger you if others did it to you." (Greece; 5th century BCE).

Seneca: "Treat your inferiors as you would be treated by your superiors," Epistle 47:11 (Rome; 1st century CE).

*   *   *

Here follows now a declaration by a religious personality who is in our present world very highly respected and even venerated by so many, His Holiness the 14th Dalai Lama, Tenzin Gyatso, who is the spiritual leader of the Tibetan people. He was born on 6 July 1935, in a small village called Takster, in the Amdo province of northeastern Tibet. Born to a peasant family, His Holiness was recognized at the age of two, in accordance with Tibetan tradition, as the reincarnation of his predecessor the 13th Dalai Lama. The Dalai Lamas are the manifestations of the Bodhisattva of Compassion, who chose to reincarnate to serve the people. Dalai Lama means Ocean of Wisdom.

14. The Dalai Lama 1992 Statement

The Global Community and the Need for Universal Responsibility

The global community

As the twentieth century draws to a close, we find that the world has grown smaller and the world's people have become almost one community. Political and military alliances have created large multinational groups, industry and international trade have produced a global economy, and worldwide communications are eliminating ancient barriers of distance, language and race. We are also being drawn together by the grave problems we face: overpopulation, dwindling natural resources, and an environmental crisis that threatens our air, water, and trees, along with the vast number of beautiful life forms that are the very foundation of existence on this small planet we share.

I believe that to meet the challenge of our times, human beings will have to develop a greater sense of universal responsibility. Each of us must learn to work not just for his or her own self, family or nation, but for the benefit of all mankind. Universal responsibility is the real key to human survival. It is the best foundation for world peace, the equitable use of natural resources, and through concern for future generations, the proper care of the environment.

For some time, I have been thinking about how to increase our sense of mutual responsibility and the altruistic motive from which it derives. Briefly, I would like to offer my thoughts.

One human family

Whether we like it or not, we have all been born on this earth as part of one great human family. Rich or poor, educated or uneducated, belonging to one nation or another, to one religion or another, adhering to this ideology or that, ultimately each of us is just a human being like everyone else: we all desire happiness and do not want suffering. Furthermore, each of us has an equal right to pursue these goals. Today's world requires that we accept the oneness of humanity. In the past, isolated communities could afford to think of one another as fundamentally separate and even existed in total isolation. Nowadays, however, events in one part of the world eventually affect the entire planet. Therefore we have to treat each major local problem as a global concern from the moment it begins. We can no longer invoke the national, racial or ideological barriers that separate us without destructive repercussions. In the context of our new interdependence, considering the interests of others is clearly the best form of self-interest.

I view this fact as a source of hope The necessity for cooperation can only strengthen mankind, because it helps us recognize that the most secure foundation for the new world order is not simply broader political and economic alliances, but rather each individual's genuine practice of love and compassion. For a better, happier, more stable and civilized future, each of us must develop a sincere, warm-hearted feeling of brother- and sisterhood.

The medicine of altruism

In Tibet we say that many illnesses can be cured by the one medicine of love and compassion. These qualities are the ultimate source of human happiness, and our need for them lies at the very core of our being. Unfortunately, love and compassion have been omitted from too many spheres of social interaction for too long. Usually confined to family and home, their practice in public life is considered impractical, even naive. This is tragic. In my view, the practice of compassion is not just a symptom of unrealistic idealism but the most effective way to pursue the best interests of others as well our own. The more we -- as a nation, a group or as individuals -- depend upon others, the more it is in our own best interests to ensure their well-being.

Practicing altruism is the real source of compromise and cooperation; merely recognizing our need for harmony is not enough. A mind committed to compassion is like an overflowing reservoir -- a constant source of energy, determination and kindness. This mind is like a seed; when cultivated, it gives rise to many other good qualities, such as forgiveness, tolerance, inner strength and the confidence to overcome fear and insecurity. The compassionate mind is like an elixir; it is capable of transforming bad situations into beneficial ones. Therefore we should not limit our expressions of love and compassion to our family and friends. Nor is compassion only the responsibility of clergy, health care and social workers. It is the necessary business of every part of the human community.

Whether a conflict lies in the field of politics, business or religion, an altruistic approach is frequently the sole means of resolving it. Sometimes the very concepts we use to mediate a dispute are themselves the cause of the problem. At such times, when a resolution seems impossible, both sides should recall the basic human nature that unites them. This will help break the impasse and, in the long run, make it easier for everyone to attain their goal. Although neither side may be fully satisfied, if both make concessions, at the very least, the danger of further conflict will be averted. We all know that this form of compromise is the most effective way of solving problems -- why, then, do we not use it more often?

When I consider the lack of cooperation in human society, I can only conclude that it stems from ignorance of our interdependent nature. I am often moved by the example of small insects, such as bees. The laws of nature dictate that bees work together in order to survive. As a result, they possess an instinctive sense of social responsibility. They have no constitution, laws, police, religion or moral training, but because of their nature they labor faithfully together. Occasionally they may fight, but in general the whole colony survives on the basis of cooperation. Human beings, on the other hand, have constitutions, vast legal systems and police forces; we have religion, remarkable intelligence and a heart with a great capacity to love. But despite our many extraordinary qualities, in actual practice we lag behind those small insects; in some ways, I feel we are poorer than the bees.

For instance, millions of people live together in large cities all over the world, but despite this proximity, many are lonely. Some do not have even one human being with whom to share their deepest feelings, and live in a state of perpetual agitation. This is very sad. We are not solitary animals that associate only in order to mate. If we were, why would we build large cities and towns? But even though we are social animals compelled to live together, unfortunately, we lack a sense of responsibility towards our fellow humans. Does the fault lie in our social architecture - the basic structures of family and community that support our society? Is it in our external facilities -- our machines, science and technology? I do not think so.

I believe that despite the rapid advances made by civilization in this century, the most immediate cause of our present dilemma is our undue emphasis on material development alone. We have become so engrossed in its pursuit that, without even knowing it, we have neglected to foster the most basic human needs of love, kindness, cooperation and caring. If we do not know someone or find another reason for not feeling connected with a particular individual or group, we simply ignore them. But the development of human society is based entirely on people helping each other. Once we have lost the essential humanity that is our foundation, what is the point of pursuing only material improvement?

To me, it is clear: a genuine sense of responsibility can result only if we develop compassion. Only a spontaneous feeling of empathy for others can really motivate us to act on their behalf. I have explained how to cultivate compassion elsewhere. For the remainder of this short piece, I would like to discuss how our present global situation can be improved by greater reliance on universal responsibility.

Universal responsibility

First, I should mention that I do not believe in creating movements or espousing ideologies. Nor do I like the practice of establishing an organization to promote a particular idea, which implies that one group of people alone is responsible for the attainment of that goal, while everybody else is exempt. In our present circumstances, none of us can afford to assume that somebody else will solve our problems; each of us must take his or her own share of universal responsibility. In this way, as the number of concerned, responsible individuals grows, tens, hundreds, thousands or even hundreds of thousands of such people will greatly improve the general atmosphere. Positive change does not come quickly and demands ongoing effort. If we become discouraged we may not attain even the simplest goals. With constant, determined application, we can accomplish even the most difficult objectives.

Adopting an attitude of universal responsibility is essentially a personal matter. The real test of compassion is not what we say in abstract discussions but how we conduct ourselves in daily life. Still, certain fundamental views are basic to the practice of altruism.

Though no system of government is perfect, democracy is that which is closest to humanity's essential nature. Hence those of us who enjoy it must continue to fight for all people's right to do so. Furthermore, democracy is the only stable foundation upon which a global political structure can be built. To work as one, we must respect the right of all peoples and nations to maintain their own distinctive character and values.

In particular, a tremendous effort will be required to bring compassion into the realm of international business. Economic inequality, especially that between developed and developing nations, remains the greatest source of suffering on this planet. Even though they will lose money in the short term, large multinational corporations must curtail their exploitation of poor nations. Tapping the few precious resources such countries possess simply to fuel consumerism in the developed world is disastrous; if it continues unchecked, eventually we shall all suffer. Strengthening weak, un-diversified economies is a far wiser policy for promoting both political and economic stability. As idealistic as it may sound, altruism, not just competition and the desire for wealth, should be a driving force in business.

We also need to renew our commitment to human values in the field of modern science. Though the main purpose of science is to learn more about reality, another of its goals is to improve the quality of life. Without altruistic motivation, scientists cannot distinguish between beneficial technologies and the merely expedient. The environmental damage surrounding us is the most obvious example of the result of this confusion, but proper motivation may be even more relevant in governing how we handle the extraordinary new array of biological techniques with which we can now manipulate the subtle structures of life itself. If we do not base our every action on an ethical foundation, we run the risk of inflicting terrible harm on the delicate matrix of life.

Nor are the religions of the world exempt from this responsibility The

purpose of religion is not to build beautiful churches or temples, but to cultivate positive human qualities such as tolerance generosity and love. Every
world religion, no matter what its philosophical view, is founded first and
foremost on the precept that we must reduce our selfishness and serve others.
Unfortunately, sometimes religion itself causes more quarrels than it solves.
Practitioners of different faiths should realize that each religious tradition
has immense intrinsic value and the means for providing mental and spiritual
health. One religion, like a single type of food, cannot satisfy everybody.
According to their varying mental dispositions, some people benefit from
one kind of teaching, others from another. Each faith has the ability to pro-
duce fine, warmhearted people and despite their espousal of often contradictory philosophies, all religions have succeeded in doing so. Thus there is no
reason to engage in divisive religious bigotry and intolerance, and every reason to cherish and respect all forms of spiritual practice.

Certainly, the most important field in which to sow the seeds of greater
altruism is international relations. In the past few years the world has
changed dramatically. I think we would all agree that the end of the Cold
War and the collapse of communism in Eastern Europe and the former Soviet Union have ushered in a new historical era. As we move through the
1990s it would seem that human experience in the twentieth century has
come full circle.

This has been the most painful period in human history, a time when,
because of the vast increase in the destructive power of weapons, more people have suffered from and died by violence than ever before. Furthermore,
we have also witnessed an almost terminal competition between the fundamental ideologies that have always torn the human community: force and
raw power on the one hand, and freedom, pluralism, individual rights and
democracy on the other. I believe that the results of this great competition
are now clear. Though the good human spirit of peace, freedom and democracy still faces many forms of tyranny and evil, it is nevertheless an unmis-
takable fact that the vast majority of people everywhere want it to triumph.
Thus the tragedies of our time have not been entirely without benefit, and
have in many cases been the very means by which the human mind has been
opened. The collapse of communism demonstrates this.

Although communism espoused many noble ideals, including altruism,
the attempt by its governing elites to dictate their views has proved disastrous. These governments went to tremendous lengths to control the entire
flow of information through their societies and to structure their education
systems so that their citizens would work for the common good. Although
rigid organization may have been necessary in the beginning to destroy previously oppressive regimes, once that goal was fulfilled, the organization
had very little to contribute towards building a useful human community.
Communism failed utterly because it relied on force to promote its beliefs.

Ultimately, human nature was unable to sustain the suffering it produced.

Brute force, no matter how strongly applied, can never subdue the basic human desire for freedom. The hundreds of thousands of people who marched in the cities of Eastern Europe proved this. They simply expressed the human need for freedom and democracy. It was very moving. Their demands had nothing whatsoever to do with some new ideology; these people simply spoke from their hearts, sharing their desire for freedom, demonstrating that it stems from the core of human nature. Freedom, in fact, is the very source of creativity for both individuals and society. It is not enough, as communist systems have assumed, merely to provide people with food, shelter and clothing. If we have all these things but lack the precious air of liberty to sustain our deeper nature, we are only half human; we are like animals who are content just to satisfy their physical needs.

I feel that the peaceful revolutions in the former Soviet Union and Eastern Europe have taught us many great lessons. One is the value of truth. People do not like to be bullied, cheated or lied to by either an individual or a system. Such acts are contrary to the essential human spirit. Therefore, even though those who practice deception and use force may achieve considerable short-term success, eventually they will be overthrown.

On the other hand, everyone appreciates truth, and respect for it is really in our blood. Truth is the best guarantor and the real foundation of freedom and democracy. It does not matter whether you are weak or strong or whether your cause has many or few adherents, truth will still prevail. The fact that the successful freedom movements of 1989 and after have been based on the true expression of people's most basic feelings is a valuable reminder that truth itself is still seriously lacking in much of our political life. Especially in the conduct of international relations we pay very little respect to truth. Inevitably, weaker nations are manipulated and oppressed by stronger ones just as the weaker sections of most societies suffer at the hands of the more affluent and powerful. Though in the past, the simple expression of truth has usually been dismissed as unrealistic, these last few years have proved that it is an immense force in the human mind and, as a result, in the shaping of history.

A second great lesson from Eastern Europe has been that of peaceful change. In the past, enslaved peoples often resorted to violence in their struggle to be free. Now, following in the footsteps of Mahatma Gandhi and Martin Luther King, Jr., these peaceful revolutions offer future generations a wonderful example of successful, nonviolent change. When in the future major changes in society again become necessary, our descendants will be able to look back on the present time as a paradigm of peaceful struggle, a real success story of unprecedented scale, involving more than a dozen nations and hundreds of millions of people. Moreover, recent events have shown that the desire for both peace and freedom lies at the most fundamental level of human nature and that violence is its complete antithesis.

Before considering what kind of global order would serve us best in the post-Cold War period, I think it is vital to address the question of violence, whose elimination at every level is the necessary foundation for world peace and the ultimate goal of any international order.

Nonviolence and international order

Every day the media reports incidents of terrorism, crime and aggression. I have never been to a country where tragic stories of death and bloodshed did not fill the newspapers and airwaves. Such reporting has become almost an addiction for journalists and their audiences alike. But the overwhelming majority of the human race does not behave destructively; very few of the five billion people on this planet actually commit acts of violence. Most of us prefer to be as peaceful as possible.

Basically, we all cherish tranquility, even those of us given to violence. For instance, when spring comes, the days grow longer, there is more sunshine, the grass and trees come alive and everything is very fresh. People feel happy. In autumn, one leaf falls, then another, then all the beautiful flowers die until we are surrounded by bare, naked plants. We do not feel so joyful. Why is this? Because deep down, we desire constructive, fruitful growth and dislike things collapsing, dying or being destroyed. Every destructive action goes against our basic nature; building, being constructive is the human way. I am sure everybody agrees that we need to overcome violence, but if we are to eliminate it completely, we should first analyze whether or not it has any value.

If we address this question from a strictly practical perspective, we find that on certain occasions violence indeed appears useful. One can solve a problem quickly with force. At the same time, however, such success is often at the expense of the rights and welfare of others. As a result, even though one problem has been solved, the seed of another has been planted.

On the other hand, if one's cause is supported by sound reasoning, there is no point in using violence. It is those who have no motive other than selfish desire and who cannot achieve their goal through logical reasoning who rely on force. Even when family and friends disagree, those with valid reasons can cite them one after the other and argue their case point by point, whereas those with little rational support soon fall prey to anger: Thus anger is not a sign of strength but one of weakness.

Ultimately, it is important to examine one's own motivation and that of one's opponent. There are many kinds of violence and nonviolence, but one cannot distinguish them from external factors alone. If one's motivation is negative, the action it produces is, in the deepest sense, violent, even though it may appear to be smooth and gentle. Conversely, if one's motivation is sincere and positive but the circumstances require harsh behavior, essentially one is practicing nonviolence. No matter what the case may be, I feel that a compassionate concern for the benefit of others -- not simply for oneself -- is the sole justification for the use of force.

The genuine practice of nonviolence is still somewhat experimental on our planet, but its pursuit, based on love and understanding, is sacred. If this experiment succeeds, it can open the way to a far more peaceful world in the next century.

I have heard the occasional Westerner maintain that long-term Gandhian struggles employing nonviolent passive resistance do not suit everybody and that such courses of action are more natural in the East. Because Westerners are active, they tend to seek immediate results in all situations, even at the cost of their lives. This approach, I believe, is not always beneficial. But surely the practice of nonviolence suits us all. It simply calls for determination. Even though the freedom movements of Eastern Europe reached their goals quickly, nonviolent protest by its very nature usually requires patience.

In this regard, I pray that despite the brutality of their suppression and the difficulty of the struggle they face, those involved in China's democracy movement will always remain peaceful. I am confident they will. Although the majority of the young Chinese students involved were born and raised under an especially harsh form of communism, during the spring of 1989 they spontaneously practiced Mahatma Gandhi's strategy of passive resistance. This is remarkable and clearly shows that ultimately all human beings want to pursue the path of peace, no matter how much they have been indoctrinated.

The reality of war
Of course, war and the large military establishments are the greatest sources of violence in the world. Whether their purpose is defensive or offensive, these vast powerful organizations exist solely to kill human beings. We should think carefully about the reality of war. Most of us have been conditioned to regard military combat as exciting and glamorous -- an opportunity for men to prove their competence and courage. Since armies are legal, we feel that war is acceptable; in general, nobody feels that war is criminal or that accepting it is a criminal attitude. In fact, we have been brainwashed. War is neither glamorous nor attractive. It is monstrous. Its very nature is one of tragedy and suffering.

War is like a fire in the human community, one whose fuel is living beings. I find this analogy especially appropriate and useful. Modern warfare is waged primarily with different forms of fire, but we are so conditioned to see it as thrilling that we talk about this or that marvelous weapon as a remarkable piece of technology without remembering that, if it is actually used, it will burn living people. War also strongly resembles a fire in the way it spreads. If one area gets weak, the commanding officer sends in reinforcements. This is like throwing live people onto a fire. But because we have been brainwashed to think this way, we do not consider the suffering of individual soldiers. No soldier wants to be wounded or die; none of his loved ones wants any harm to come to him. If one soldier is killed, or maimed for life, at least another five or ten people -- his relatives and friends suffer as well. We should all be horrified by the extent of this tragedy, but we are too confused.

Frankly, as a child, I too was attracted to the military. Their uniforms looked so smart and beautiful. But that is exactly how the seduction begins. Children start playing games that will one day lead them into trouble. There are plenty of exciting games to play and costumes to wear other than those based on the killing of human beings. Again, if we as adults were not so fascinated by war, we would clearly see that to allow our children to become habituated to war games is extremely unfortunate. Some former soldiers have told me that when they shot their first person they felt uncomfortable but as they continued to kill it began to feel quite normal. In time, we can get used to anything.

It is not only during times of war that military establishments are destructive By their very design, they are the single greatest violators of human rights, and it is the soldiers themselves who suffer most consistently from their abuse. After the officers in charge have given beautiful explanations about the importance of the army, its discipline and the need to conquer the enemy, the rights of the great mass of soldiers are almost entirely taken away. They are then compelled to forfeit their individual will, and, in the end, to sacrifice their lives. Moreover, once an army has become a powerful force, there is every risk that it will destroy the happiness of its own country.

There are people with destructive intentions in every society, and the temptation to gain command over an organization capable of fulfilling their desires can become overwhelming. But no matter how malevolent or evil are the many murderous dictators who currently oppress their nations and cause international problems, it is obvious that they cannot harm others or destroy countless human lives if they don't have a military organization accepted and condoned by society. As long as there are powerful armies there will always be the danger of dictatorship. If we really believe dictatorship to be a despicable and destructive form of government, then we must recognize that the existence of a powerful military establishment is one of its main causes.

Militarism is also very expensive. Pursuing peace through military strength places a tremendously wasteful burden on society. Governments spend vast sums on increasingly intricate weapons when, in fact, nobody really wants to use them. Not only money but also valuable energy and human intelligence are squandered, while all that increases is fear.

I want to make it clear, however, that although I am deeply opposed to war, I am not advocating appeasement. It is often necessary to take a strong stand to counter unjust aggression. For instance, it is plain to all of us that the Second World War was entirely justified. It "saved civilization" from the tyranny of Nazi Germany, as Winston Churchill so aptly put it. In my view, the Korean War was also just, since it gave South Korea the chance of gradually developing a democracy. But we can only judge whether or not a conflict was vindicated on moral grounds with hindsight. For example, we can now see that during the Cold War, the principle of nuclear deterrence had a certain value. Nevertheless, it is very difficult to assess all such matters with any degree of accuracy. War is violence and violence is unpredictable. Therefore, it is far better to avoid it if possible, and never to presume that we know beforehand whether the outcome of a particular war will be beneficial or not.

For instance, in the case of the Cold War, though deterrence may have helped promote stability, it did not create genuine peace. The last forty years in Europe have seen merely the absence of war, which has not been real peace but a facsimile founded on fear. At best, building arms to maintain peace serves only as a temporary measure. As long as adversaries do not trust each other, any number of factors can upset the balance of power. Lasting peace can be secured only on the basis of genuine trust.

Disarmament for world peace

Throughout history, mankind has pursued peace one way or another. Is it too optimistic to imagine that world peace may finally be within our grasp? I do not believe that there has been an increase in the amount of people's hatred, only in their ability to manifest it in vastly destructive weapons. On the other hand, bearing witness to the tragic evidence of the mass slaughter caused by such weapons in our century has given us the opportunity to control war. To do so, it is clear we must disarm.

Disarmament can occur only within the context of new political and economic relationships. Before we consider this issue in detail, it is worth imagining the kind of peace process from which we would benefit most. This is fairly self-evident. First we should work on eliminating nuclear weapons, next, biological and chemical ones, then offensive arms, and, finally, defensive ones. At the same time, to safeguard the peace, we should start developing in one or more global regions an international police force made up of an equal number of members from each nation under a collective command. Eventually this force would cover the whole world.

Because the dual process of disarmament and development of a joint force would be both multilateral and democratic, the right of the majority to criticize or even intervene in the event of one nation violating the basic rules would be ensured. Moreover, with all large armies eliminated and all conflicts such as border disputes subject to the control of the joint international force, large and small nations would be truly equal. Such reforms would result in a stable international environment.

Of course, the immense financial dividend reaped from the cessation of arms production would also provide a fantastic windfall for global development. Today the nations of the world spend trillions of dollars annually on upkeep of the military. Can you imagine how many hospital beds, schools and homes this money could fund? In addition, as I mentioned above, the awesome proportion of scarce resources squandered on military development not only prevents the elimination of poverty, illiteracy and disease, but also requires the sacrifice of precious human intelligence. Our scientists are extremely bright. Why should their brilliance be wasted on such dreadful endeavors when it could be used for positive global development?

The great deserts of the world such as the Sahara and the Gobi could be cultivated to increase food production and ease overcrowding. Many countries now face years of severe drought. New, less expensive methods of desalinization could be developed to render sea water suitable for human consumption and other uses. There are many pressing issues in the fields of energy and health to which our scientists could more usefully address themselves. Since the world economy would grow more rapidly as a result of their efforts, they could even be paid more! Our planet is blessed with vast natural treasures. If we use them properly, beginning with the elimination of militarism and war, truly every human being will be able to live a wealthy well-cared for life.

Naturally global peace cannot occur all at once. Since conditions around the world are so varied, its spread will have to be incremental. But there is no reason why it cannot begin in one region and then spread gradually from one continent to another.

I would like to propose that regional communities like the European Community be established as an integral part of the more peaceful world we are trying to create. Looking at the post-Cold War environment objectively, such communities are plainly the most natural and desirable components of a new world order. As we can see, the almost gravitational pull of our growing interdependence necessitates new, more cooperative structures. The European Community is pioneering the way in this endeavor, negotiating the delicate balance between economic, military and political collectivity on the one hand and the sovereign rights of member states on the other. I am greatly inspired by this work. I also believe that the new Commonwealth of Independent States is grappling with similar issues and that the seeds of such a community are already present in the minds of many of its constituent republics. In this context, I would briefly like to talk about the future of both my own country, Tibet, and China.

Like the former Soviet Union, Communist China is a multinational state, artificially constructed under the impetus of an expansionist ideology and up to now administered by force in colonial fashion. A peaceful, prosperous and above all politically stable future for China lies in its successfully fulfilling not only its own people's wishes for a more open, democratic system, but also those of its eighty million so-called "national minorities" who want to

regain their freedom. For real happiness to return to the heart of Asia --
home to one-fifth of the human race -- a pluralistic, democratic, mutually
cooperative community of sovereign states must replace what is currently
called the People's Republic of China. Of course, such a community need not
be limited to those presently under Chinese Communist domination, such as
Tibetans, Mongols and Urghurs. The people of Hong Kong, those seeking an
independent Taiwan, and even those suffering under other communist governments in North Korea, Vietnam, Laos and Cambodia might also be interested in building an Asian Community. However, it is especially urgent that
those ruled by the Chinese Communists consider doing so. Properly pursued,
it could help save China from violent dissolution, regionalism and a return to
the chaotic turmoil that has so afflicted this great nation throughout the
twentieth century. Currently China's political life is so polarized that there is
every reason to fear an early recurrence of bloodshed and tragedy. Each of
us -- every member of the world community -- has a moral responsibility to
help avert the immense suffering that civil strife would bring to China's vast
population.

I believe that the very process of dialogue, moderation and compromise
involved in building a community of Asian states would itself give real hope
of peaceful evolution to a new order in China. From the very start, the member states of such a community might agree to decide its defense and international relations policies together. There would be many opportunities for
cooperation. The critical point is that we find a peaceful, nonviolent way for
the forces of freedom, democracy and moderation to emerge successfully
from the current atmosphere of unjust repression.

Zones of peace

I see Tibet's role in such an Asian Community as what I have previously
called a "Zone of Peace": a neutral, demilitarized sanctuary where weapons
are forbidden and the people live in harmony with nature. This is not merely
a dream -- it is precisely the way Tibetans tried to live for over a thousand
years before our country was invaded. As everybody knows, in Tibet all
forms of wildlife were strictly protected in accordance with Buddhist principles. Also, for at least the last three hundred years, we had no proper army.
Tibet gave up the waging of war as an instrument of national policy in the
sixth and seventh centuries, after the reign of our three great religious kings.

Returning to the relationship between developing regional communities
and the task of disarmament, I would like to suggest that the "heart" of each
community could be one or more nations that have decided to become zones
of peace, areas from which military forces are prohibited. This, again, is not
just a dream. Four decades ago, in December 1948, Costa Rica disbanded its
army. Recently, 37 percent of the Swiss population voted to disband their
military. The new government of Czechoslovakia has decided to stop the
manufacture and export of all weapons. If its people so choose, a nation can

take radical steps to change its very nature.

Zones of peace within regional communities would serve as oases of stability. While paying their fair share of the costs of any collective force created by the community as a whole, these zones of peace would be the forerunners and beacons of an entirely peaceful world and would be exempt from engaging in any conflict. If regional communities do develop in Asia, South America and Africa and disarmament progresses so that an international force from all regions is created, these zones of peace will be able to expand, spreading tranquility as they grow.

We do not need to think that we are planning for the far distant future when we consider this or any other proposal for a new, more politically, economically and militarily cooperative world. For instance, the newly invigorated forty-eight member Conference on Security and Cooperation in Europe has already laid the foundation for an alliance between not only the nations of Eastern and Western Europe but also between the nations of the Commonwealth of Independent States and the United States. These remarkable events have virtually eliminated the danger of a major war between these two superpowers.

I have not included the United Nations in this discussion of the present era because both its critical role in helping create a better world and its great potential for doing so are so well known. By definition, the United Nations must be in the very middle of whatever major changes occur. However, it may need to amend its structure for the future. I have always had the greatest hopes for the United Nations, and with no criticism intended, I would like simply to point out that the post-World War II climate under which its charter was conceived has changed. With that change has come the opportunity to further democratize the UN, especially the somewhat exclusive Security Council with its five permanent members, which should be made more representative.

In conclusion

I would like to conclude by stating that, in general, I feel optimistic about the future. Some recent trends portend our great potential for a better world. As late as the fifties and sixties, people believed that war was an inevitable condition of mankind. The Cold War, in particular, reinforced the notion that opposing political systems could only clash, not compete or even collaborate. Few now hold this view. Today, people all over the planet are genuinely concerned about world peace. They are far less interested in propounding ideology and far more committed to coexistence. These are very positive developments.

Also, for thousands of years people believed that only an authoritarian organization employing rigid disciplinary methods could govern human society. However, people have an innate desire for freedom and democracy, and these two forces have been in conflict. Today, it is clear which has won.

The emergence of non violent "people's power" movements have shown indisputably that the human race can neither tolerate nor function properly under the rule of tyranny. This recognition represents remarkable progress.

Another hopeful development is the growing compatibility between science and religion. Throughout the nineteenth century and for much of our own, people have been profoundly confused by the conflict between these apparently contradictory world views. Today, physics, biology and psychology have reached such sophisticated levels that many researchers are starting to ask the most profound questions about the ultimate nature of the universe and life, the same questions that are of prime interest to religions. Thus there is real potential for a more unified view. In particular, it seems that a new concept of mind and matter is emerging. The East has been more concerned with understanding the mind, the West with understanding matter. Now that the two have met, these spiritual and material views of life may become more harmonized.

The rapid changes in our attitude towards the earth are also a source of hope. As recently as ten or fifteen years ago, we thoughtlessly consumed its resources, as if there was no end to them. Now, not only individuals but governments as well are seeking a new ecological order. I often joke that the moon and stars look beautiful, but if any of us tried to live on them, we would be miserable. This blue planet of ours is the most delightful habitat we know. Its life is our life; its future, our future. And though I do not believe that the Earth itself is a sentient being, it does indeed act as our mother, and, like children, we are dependent upon her. Now mother nature is telling us to cooperate. In the face of such global problems as the greenhouse effect and the deterioration of the ozone layer, individual organizations and single nations are helpless. Unless we all work together, no solution will be found. Our mother is teaching us a lesson in universal responsibility.

I think we can say that, because of the lessons we have begun to learn, the next century will be friendlier, more harmonious, and less harmful. Compassion, the seed of peace, will be able to flourish. I am very hopeful. At the same time, I believe that every individual has a responsibility to help guide our global family in the right direction. Good wishes alone are not enough; we have to assume responsibility. Large human movements spring from individual human initiatives. If you feel that you cannot have much of an effect, the next person may also become discouraged and a great opportunity will have been lost. On the other hand, each of us can inspire others simply by working to develop our own altruistic motivation.

I am sure that many honest, sincere people all over the world already hold the views that I have mentioned here. Unfortunately, nobody listens to them. Although my voice may go unheeded as well, I thought that I should try to speak on their behalf. Of course, some people may feel that it is very presumptuous for the Dalai Lama to write in this way. But, since I received the Nobel Peace Prize, I feel I have a responsibility to do so. If I just took the Nobel money and spent it however I liked, it would look as if the only reason I had spoken all those nice words in the past was to get this prize! However, now that I have received it, I must repay the honor by continuing to advocate the views that I have always expressed.

I, for one, truly believe that individuals can make a difference in society. Since periods of great change such as the present one come so rarely in human history, it is up to each of us to make the best use of our time to help create a happier world.

*   *   *

One of the religions which are very actively participating in the interfaith dialogue movement is the Baha'i Faith Community, of which I give you hereafter only the main principles. Other data you can find on their websites.

Principles of the Baha'i Faith

The *Baha'i World Faith* is the youngest of the world's main religions. It was founded in Iran during the mid 19th century by Siyyid 'Ali-Muhammad (1819-1850 CE). He assumed the title Bab (*"the Gate"*) and prophesized the future arrival of *"One greater than Himself."* One of the Bab's followers, Mirza Husayn-'Ali-i-Nuri (1817-1892), announced that he was the Manifestation predicted by the Bab. He assumed the title Baha'u'llah (*"glory of God"*). His teachings on world peace, democracy, civil rights, equal rights for women, the acceptance of scientific discoveries, etc. were decades ahead of his time.

Bahá'ís believe in a single God who has repeatedly sent prophets into the world through whom he has revealed the *"Word of God."* Prophets include Adam, Krishna, Buddha, Yeshua of Nazareth (Jesus), Mohammed, The Bab and Baha'u'llah. The Bahá'í faith is still looked upon by many Muslims as a breakaway sect of Islam. Baha'ís are heavily persecuted in some countries, particularly Iran. Some 3 million people are adherents of the Baha'i community.

Their principles of belief are worth to be studied and to be better known by a much larger audience:

(1) Independent investigation of the truth;

(2) The essential harmony of science and religion;

(3) Recognition of the divine foundation of all religions;

(4) Universal compulsory education;

(5) The equality of all men and women;

(6) The spiritual solution of economic problems;

(7) The need for a universal auxiliary language;

(8) Universal peace based upon a world federation of nations;

(9) The elimination of all prejudice;

(10) Recognition of the essential unity of mankind.

"Unification of the whole of mankind is the hall-mark of the stage which human society is now approaching. Unity of family, of tribe, of city-state, and nation have been successively attempted and fully established. World unity is the goal towards which a harassed humanity is striving. Nation building has come to an end. The anarchy inherent in state sovereignty is moving towards a climax. A world, growing to maturity, must abandon this fetish, recognize the oneness and wholeness of human relationships, and establish once for all the machinery that can best incarnate this fundamental principle of its life."   Shoghi Effendi, successor of Baha'u'llah.

The present interreligious dialogue movement would not be what it is now without the permanent support for so many years of Reverend Marcus Braybrooke. See his CV on page vi. His overview of the interfaith dialogue movement in the 20th century present a most interesting reading.

15. The Interfaith Movement in the 20th Century,

by Marcus Braybrooke

I) Shaping the Present Reality

Hans Küng ends his book *Global Responsibility* with these words:

> "No human life together without a world ethic for the nations.
> No peace among the nations without peace among the religions."
> No peace among the religions without dialogue among the religions."

--Global Responsibility, Continuum and SCM Press 1991, p.138

One hundred years ago, Charles Bonney, who presided at the World's Parliament of Religions in Chicago, ended his closing address like this: "Henceforth the religions of the world will make war, not on each other, but on the giant evils that afflict mankind." Sadly, religions have failed to fulfill that hope. Yet this century, for all its catastrophic wars and acts of genocide, has also seen the growth of a worldwide interfaith movement. Before trying to discern the path ahead, it is worth pausing to see what has been achieved.

The World's Parliament of Religions, Chicago, 1893

The World's Parliament of Religions was held as part of the World Fair or Columbian Exposition, which marked the four hundredth anniversary of Columbus' "discovery" of America. The word "Parliament" was chosen to emphasize that participants of all religions were equal, but, in fact, the body had no executive or legislative authority. It reflected the optimism and self-confidence characteristic of the USA towards the end of the nineteenth century. Most of the participants were Christian from a wide spectrum of denominations.

Their presuppositions permeated the gathering. Yet the contribution made by those of other faiths, although their number was small, was very significant.

The World's Parliament of Religions gave much attention to the contribution of religion to peace and social issues. Women were encouraged to play quite a part at the Parliament—more so than at most subsequent interfaith gatherings.

The Study of World Religions

The World's Parliament of Religions gave an impetus to the emerging study of world religions. While such study is an academic discipline in its own right, it has greatly increased awareness of the teachings and practices of world religions at every level. This century has seen an enormous increase in knowledge about world religions. Books, films, and videos are widely available. This study has helped to provide accurate information about the religions of the world. Even so, much ignorance and prejudice still exists.

Initially the study was confined to university departments devoted to the Science of Religions or the Comparative Study of Religions—although such departments were very unevenly spread across the world. Slowly, in some countries, the teaching of world religions has spread to schools, although the situation and law in every country is different. For some time many scholars of the subject stood apart from the interfaith movement partly because they felt that their study should be objective or neutral and partly because they concentrated on the study of the texts and the history of religions. Now, in part because there is more interest in the faith and practice of believers, far more scholars take part in interfaith discussions; their participation has enriched the interfaith movement.

Knowledge may not of itself create sympathy. Opportunities for personal meeting and friendship are important to dispel prejudice and to encourage real understanding. Many interfaith groups attach much importance to providing opportunities for young people to meet. Often they discover that they face similar problems and that in every society many young people are questioning all religions. They may also discover how much people of all faiths can do together to work for a better world.

Organizations for Interfaith Understanding

No continuing organization emerged from the 1893 World's Parliament of Religions. At first slowly and recently more rapidly, interfaith groups have been established in many places. Some are quite small, meeting in a home. Members get to know each other and learn about each other's beliefs and practices. Sometimes members pray together or share in social or peace work. Other interfaith organizations are national bodies and some are international, seeking to coordinate global interfaith concern. By 1993, the established international interfaith organizations were the International Association for Religious Freedom, the World Congress of Faiths, the Temple of Understanding, and the World Conference on Religion and Peace.

Those who take part in interfaith bodies seek for a bond between religious believers, despite the differences of belief and practice between and within the great religions. The interfaith organizations all reject *syncretism*, which implies an artificial mixing of religions, and *indifferentism*, which suggests that it does not matter what you believe. None of these organizations are trying to create one new world religion, although some other groups have that hope.

The interfaith organizations accept that most of their members will be loyal and committed members of a particular faith community. Respect for the integrity of other peoples' faith commitment and religious practices is essential. A few members of interfaith organizations may have no specific allegiance and describe themselves as seekers. While aware of the distinctiveness of the world religions, members of interfaith organizations hope that some basis of unity exists or may be discovered, although the nature of the relationship of religions to each other is still much debated. For some people the unity rests upon our common humanity; for others there is an essential agreement between religions on moral values; for others there is a mystical unity, by which they mean that religious experience is ultimately the same and that differences are a matter of culture and language; others hope that through dialogue religions will come closer together and grow in their understanding of the Truth; others stress the need of religious people to work together for peace and justice and the relief of human suffering; for some, it is enough that there should be tolerance and respect, without bothering about questions of truth. All these shades of opinion and many more are reflected within interfaith organizations, which have generally avoided trying to define the relationship of religions. For them, the search for understanding and cooperation is urgent in itself.

In their early years the international interfaith organizations tended to stress what united religious believers. Now, with greater trust and knowledge, equal emphasis is given to appreciating the distinctive contribution each faith—and the various traditions within each faith—make to human awareness of the Divine. Increasingly, those who occupy leadership roles in the various religious communities have begun to take an active part in interfaith organizations, whereas at first the initiative lay with inspired individuals. It has taken a long time to erode the traditional suspicion and competition between religions—and it still persists, especially in the problems created by aggressive missionary work. The main brake on the growth of interfaith understanding has been the conservatism of religious communities. Happily, now, those at the leadership level in many religious traditions recognize the vital importance of inter-religious cooperation.

Peace through Religion

While all efforts for interfaith understanding promote a climate of peace, some interfaith organizations, especially the World Conference on Religion and Peace, have concentrated on encouraging religious people to be active in peace work. Attempts to bring together people of different religions to promote peace date back to the early part of this century. Even so, the first Assembly of the World Conference on Religion and Peace did not meet until 1970. It is hard to assess the impact that religious people can have on political processes, especially as politicians seldom acknowledge those who have influenced them. Modern communications have given added weight to popular opinion.

Religious leaders may play an important role in forming public opinion by insisting on the relevance of spiritual and moral considerations. They have helped to maintain public alarm at the enormous stockpile of nuclear weapons and other means of mass destruction. They have voiced public outrage at the starvation of millions of people due to war, injustice, and unfair patterns of international trade. They have upheld human dignity and protested against torture and racism. They have underpinned efforts to develop internationally agreed standards of human rights and have helped to monitor their application. Interreligious conferences have been among the first to warn of threats to the environment. In local areas of conflict, religious people have often maintained contact across boundaries and divisions. Yet often, too, religious people have used religious loyalties to enflame conflict and have allowed particular interests to outweigh common human and religious moral values. Some extremists stir up religious passions to gain support for their own agendas.

It is even more difficult to evaluate the power of prayer, but certainly remarkable changes have recently taken place in the world scene, especially since the first World Day of Prayer for Peace at Assisi in 1986. Each year some people of all religions join in The Week of Prayer for World Peace. Special days of prayer are held to mark human rights anniversaries and for particular areas of conflict. Many people regularly repeat the Universal Prayer for Peace:

> "Lead me from death to life, from falsehood to truth.
> Lead me from despair to hope, from fear to trust;
> Lead me from hate to love, from war to peace.
> Let peace fill our heart, our world, our universe."

Religious Institutions Engage in Dialogue
Often those who have pioneered the search for good relations between religions have faced misunderstanding and even hostility in their own faith community. They have been accused of compromising or watering-down the distinctive beliefs of their own religion. In fact, however, most pioneers witness that learning about other religions has helped them appreciate their own more deeply.

Slowly the value of interfaith dialogue has become more widely recognized. In the Christian world, in 1966, The Second Vatican Council's decree *Nostra Aetate* transformed the Catholic Church's attitude to people of other religions. A Secretariat for non-Christians was established, which is now called The Pontifical Council for Inter-Religious Dialogue. At much the same time, The World Council of Churches established a Unit for Dialogue with People of Living Faiths (now the Office on Inter-Religious Relations), which has arranged various consultations and has encouraged Protestant and Orthodox churches to rethink their theological approach to other religions. Some other religions now have agencies to encourage dialogue; these include the International Jewish Committee on Inter-Religious Consultations and the World Muslim League's office for inter-religious affairs.

Clearly, official dialogue has a character of its own. Participants have some representative role. Much of the work is to remove misunderstanding and build up good relations, as well as encouraging practical cooperation on moral issues and social concerns. More speculative discussion about questions of "truth" may be inappropriate. Further, while most organizations fully respect the freedom of all who participate in consultations, the host organization may have its own agenda. This means that official inter-religious discussions need to be distinguished from interfaith organizations, where ultimate control rests with a board or executive which is itself inter-faith in composition and where funding comes from several religious communities. The growth of discussions between representatives of religious communities is, however, a sign that the importance of harmony between religions is now seen as urgent by the leaders and members of religious communities themselves. This is in part due to the pioneering work of interfaith organizations.

Bilateral Conversations

As in a family, there are times when the whole family wishes to be together and times when two members of the family want to talk by themselves, so there are times when members of just two religions wish to engage in dialogue. A particular example of this is Jewish-Christian dialogue. A major international organization, The International Council of Christians and Jews, was formed in 1975 to foster good relations between the two religions. Other examples are the growing Christian-Muslim dialogue, some Muslim-Jewish dialogue and considerable Christian-Buddhist dialogue both in North America and in Japan. There are now many study and conference centers in different parts of the world which promote dialogue between members of two or three religions.

The Practical Importance of Interfaith Understanding

The Gulf War, the Salman Rushdie affair, and the conflicts in former Yugoslavia have emphasized the practical importance and urgency of interfaith understanding. No longer can anyone dismiss religion as obsolete or irrelevant to world affairs. But many wonder whether the future belongs to the interfaith movement or whether we are likely to see increasing religious rivalry. Some indeed have an apocalyptic vision of the next century being dominated by renewed conflict between Christendom and the world of Islam. The interfaith movement has serious problems to overcome if it is to achieve its goals.

In all religions there is an increase of extremism, which also alienates others from any religious allegiance. Missionary groups in some religions make exclusive claims that theirs is the only way to truth and salvation. Elsewhere religious differences enflame political and economic divisions and sometimes religion is exploited by the powerful as an instrument of social control. Even India, of whose tolerance Swami Vivekananda boasted at the World's Parliament of Religions one hundred years ago, has seen the increase of "communalism," or rivalry between different religious and ethnic groups.

In Eastern Europe, the renewed nationalism is often closely linked to religious identity and has been accompanied by anti-Semitism and discrimination against religious minorities. It is easy to deplore intolerance - especially in others.

It is harder to understand its causes, which may be psychological or related to a group that is feeling politically, culturally, or economically marginalized. Intolerance may be caused by fear or ignorance or it may be based on exclusive claims to truth.

Even dialogue itself may be misused. As it becomes more popular, it may be "hi-jacked" for ideological purposes—that is to say, people may have hidden agendas such as wanting to change the views of their dialogue partners or seeking to gain their support for a political cause.

Much to Be Done

Despite all the problems, the interfaith movement has made progress, especially in recent years. Even so, it is still very weak. The initiative was often with "marginal" groups—to whom all credit is due. Gradually liberal members of the major religions began to take part. Now, many religious leaders are committed to this work; even so, the religious communities are still reluctant to fund interfaith work, most of which is semi-voluntary. Cooperation between interfaith organizations is still only on an ad hoc basis. Adequate structures for greater coordination and cooperation are required. There is an urgent need, too, for centers of information about worldwide interfaith work. There is also much popular ignorance. The Year of Interreligious Understanding and Cooperation declared by several interfaith organizations in 1993 was intended to increase public awareness of the need for interfaith cooperation and to encourage those involved to assess their progress and to determine priorities for future work.

The educational task is still far from complete. The growth of comparative religious studies has helped to dispel ignorance about the world religions, but ignorance is still widespread. Theologians have helped their communities rethink traditional attitudes to other faiths, yet exclusive attitudes are still common. All religions claim insights into *Truth*. There needs, therefore, to be continuing dialogue so that religions may share their insights and together come to a deeper understanding of Ultimate Reality. This dialogue includes both intellectual discussion and efforts to appreciate each other's patterns of prayer and meditation. Yet in many cases the thinkers are quite remote from religious leaders. Meanwhile, religious rivalries destroy lives. Religious people are reluctant to make clear that their commitment to the search for truth and the defense of human rights is stronger than their group loyalty—costly as this may be.

The interfaith movement is becoming increasingly more practical with a new emphasis on ways of cooperating to face urgent problems and to seek a "global ethic" or consensus on moral values. The discovery of those who attended the first meeting of the World Conference on Religion and Peace in Kyoto, Japan, in 1970, was that "the things which unite us are more important than the things which divide us." The interfaith organizations have shown that people of many religions can agree on the importance of peace and justice and on action to relieve suffering and to save the planet's eco-system. The events and publicity during 1993, The Year of Interreligious Understanding and Cooperation, provided a chance to make the vital importance of interfaith work far more widely known, not only in combating extremism and communalism but in harnessing the energies of all people of faith and of good will to tackle the urgent problems of the world. Only by working together will the dreams of 1893 be realized. Only by standing together will prejudice and discrimination be removed, violence and injustice ended, poverty relieved, and the planet preserved.

II) A New Agenda

Since 1993, there has been rapid growth of interfaith activity throughout the world, with increasing emphasis on its practical importance. The number of local interfaith groups has also increased in several countries. Indeed, I see 1993 as a milestone in the growth of the interfaith movement. The focus has changed from trying to get people of different religions together to discovering what people of faith can do together for our world. Paul Knitter, for example, argues in his recent *One Earth, Many Religions* that "concern for the widespread suffering that grips humanity and threatens the planet can and must be the 'common cause' for all religions." Hans Küng, in his *A Global Ethic for Global Politics and Economics*, seeks to show how moral principles can and should be applied to the affairs of the world. For myself, during the Year of Inter-religious Understanding and Cooperation in 1993, I came to see that we were not just talking about cooperation between religious people, but about cooperation within national societies and between nations as essential for our life together.

Despite the very practical efforts of some groups, up until 1993 much of the energy in the interfaith movement had to go into persuading people of different faiths to meet. There was first of all ignorance and quite often hostility to overcome. People of one faith knew little about another faith and what they knew was often erroneous. A second task was encouraging people of different faiths to get to know each other, to relax in each other's company, to talk and perhaps to become friends. As prejudices were dispelled and friendship grew, many people found they had to rethink their attitudes toward the members and theologies of other religions.

Now, however, many people long for the religions to be "the moral conscience of humanity," as Pope John Paul II expressed it to the Assisi World Day of Prayer for Peace. This new agenda reflects the fact that the great problems that threaten human life and the environment concern us all, just because of our common humanity. Since 1993, several international interfaith bodies have focused on practical questions. [These activities are described in more detail in Chapter 21. Ed.]

The question now is what effect does all this work have. Indeed, the subject of two of the conferences of the International Interfaith Centre at Oxford have been "How effective is interfaith activity in halting and healing conflict?". To have an even greater impact, the interfaith movement must address a number of concerns.

Widening the Circle of Dialogue
1. Traditionalists are welcome.
The dangers that threaten our world society may be the basis on which traditional members of the faiths may be encouraged to engage more fully in interfaith activity. Yet they are often put off by what they suppose to be the "liberal presuppositions" of the interfaith movement. There are those who reject any meeting with members of another faith tradition. Although these are often labeled "extremists" or "fundamentalists," the cause of their suspicion of and hostility to others may be primarily because of political and economic divisions. Many others who perhaps are best described as "traditionalists" do not wish to give religious legitimacy to another faith tradition. Quite possibly, they have not thought much about the matter, but do recognize that people of different faiths have to live together and therefore need to understand some basic things about each other: for example, what foods should not be served at a civic reception in a religiously plural city?

A pluralist society requires respect for those of other persuasions. Even societies where one religion is dominant may have to take account of significant religious minorities. Teddy Kollek, for example, while Mayor of Jerusalem, tried to be sensitive to the religious concerns of Muslim and Christian minorities. Many Islamic states have to make allowance for significant minorities of other faiths.

I doubt if we can reach widespread agreement on the philosophical or theological basis for interfaith work, at least in the immediate future. Perhaps rather than assuming that theological pluralism is the basis for interfaith dialogue, we should acknowledge a pluralism of dialogue. Probably within each religion one can find those to whom the labels "exclusivist," "inclusivist," and "pluralist" can be applied. Perhaps the need is to discover the contribution each group can make to interfaith dialogue.

For instance, the exclusivist stresses commitment, and this is a welcome reminder that interfaith activity should not evade questions of truth. The inclusivist speaks as a member of a particular faith community and can help that tradition reinterpret its theology so that while affirming its central witness it need not deny the witness of others. The pluralist affirms that the richness of the Divine Mystery cannot be contained in one tradition.

I wonder if even as individuals most of us operate within only one model. I recognize that in part I could fit under all the categories. I have a personal commitment as a disciple of Christ; in my theological thinking I seek as a Christian to see God's purpose in the whole religious life of humanity; and as a student of religion and as an interfaith activist, I do not presume that any faith has a privileged position.

2. Listening to Minority Voices.
Practical cooperation is not without its difficulties. Is it genuinely inter-religious and international or are certain groups recruiting support for their own agenda? Marc Ellis, in *his Unholy Alliance,* reminds us that Palestinians feel that Christian-Jewish dialogue has added to their sufferings, while the Dalits in India feel this about Hindu-Christian dialogue. In some places, women feel they have been excluded from the dialogue.

Does the emphasis on religious consensus allow space for the voices of religious minorities and of those who have no formal religious commitment? A consensus document may be a threat to minorities, especially to those whose religious identity is resented by the mainstream.

3. Listening to Spiritual Movements.
We have also to recognize that spiritual wisdom is not the monopoly of religious officials. The Spirit, like the wind, "bloweth where it listeth." I believe that the Chicago Parliament did us all a good turn by opening its doors to all who wanted to come; on the whole, few religions have been in the vanguard of progress. Some groups did withdraw due to the inclusiveness, but that was their choice. It may well be that religious and denomina-

tional organizations and hierarchical leadership will become less significant in the next millennium.

4. Listening to Other Disciplines.
Equally, we need the wisdom of the experts in many particular disciplines, especially those who are people of faith. Dialogue needs to be multi-disciplinary as well as multi-faith. Experts in a whole range of disciplines may themselves be committed members of a faith. This was made clear to me when I spoke to the Retired Generals for Peace about the Global Ethic and the role of the military in peace-keeping. Many of those high-ranking officers were committed members of a faith.

If interfaith dialogue is to deal with the vital issues that face human society, it should not be confined to religious specialists or religious leaders. It needs to engage those with expertise in all the relevant disciplines. Particularly, there should be an attempt to involve in this debate those with political and economic power as well as those who control the media. They, however, will perhaps not be interested until there has been far wider public education about the vital importance of interfaith cooperation. Change will begin to happen only as the politically aware public demands that nations act in the interest of the world society and seek to shape that society according to ethical values upheld by the great spiritual traditions as well as by many humanists.

Difficulties to be Addressed
1) Disagreements Within Religions.
We are all aware of the disagreements within religions. At one Christian-Jewish dialogue group, it was suggested after our first session that the Jews go into one room to sort out their differences and that the Christians should go into another and solve their disagreements. The differences may be not only theological, but relate to the great social, ecological, and moral issues which we have been suggesting should be the focus of interfaith activity.

Intra-religious dialogue is very important. But in our concern for the environment, the protection of human rights, and the struggle for economic justice, we may well find ourselves in opposition to some members of our own and other faiths. The more socially engaged the interfaith movement becomes, the less it may be a unifying force amongst all believers.

2) Interfaith Organizations Need To Work Together.
When people hear of another interfaith organization, the reaction may be, "Do we need another interfaith body?" To those on the outside, one interfaith group looks much the same as another, and the motley variety of initials used for the organizations seems designed to confuse.

In fact, there is plenty of work for them all to do. As we have seen, there is a great variety of approaches to interfaith work and each organization has its own particular focus and constituency. Only by working together will the interfaith movement be listened to by the media and by those who control economic and political power.

There have been suggestions that what is needed is a World Council of Faiths, which could perhaps be formed by the merging together of the various international interfaith organizations. It is questionable whether one super Organization would be more effective or just more bureaucratic. What seems to me important is a sense of partnership between the organizations and awareness of belonging to a movement that is bigger than any of us. I have hoped that there could be some world-wide coordinating body, rather like the International Council of Christians and Jews, for those engaged in Christian-Jewish dialogue, or the Society for Buddhist-Christian Studies.

The International Interfaith Centre (IIC) at Oxford, which has been set up by the International Association for Religious Freedom, the World Congress of Faiths, and Westminster College, Oxford, has as its purpose to encourage education about interfaith activity and to facilitate cooperation amongst all those engaged in this work. The Centre aims to hold information about interfaith work across the world, to keep those involved in touch with each other, while being a source of information to the media; it also aims to encourage research on questions of concern to many people involved in interfaith work, regardless of their particular organization.

As mentioned above, a particular concern at IIC conferences has been to examine how interfaith work can be more effective in areas of conflict, such as Sri Lanka, Northern Ireland, former Yugoslavia, and the Middle East. The center is also developing electronic communication capabilities. Nonetheless, hospitality to visitors to the Centre and the many individual contacts and introductions made by the Centre remain at the heart of its work to create a sense of spiritual fellowship amongst all engaged in what has been called a "Pilgrimage of Hope."

Wishful Thinking?

If the interfaith movement is to be effective in helping to rebuild our world on spiritual and moral principles, there is a great deal of work to be done. In many societies, religions are peripheral to the centers of economic and political power. Perhaps the greatest task is to argue that this is a moral and spiritual world.

Is that hope, as Hans Küng asks in his Preface to *A Global Ethic* (1993), a "sheer illusion"? In answer, he points "the eternal skeptic" to the world-wide change of awareness about economics and ecology, about world peace and disarmament, and about the partnership between men and women. Perhaps one special contribution of faith is to inspire hope that change is possible. Such a conviction is based on our inner life. Although I have stressed the needs of the world as our common agenda, the hope and energy to address this will come from the inner life of prayer and meditation. The source of practical action is our spirituality. Inner and outer belong together. The activist will be exhausted without an inner life and the true mystic longs for the world's renewal.

My hopes for interfaith work are graphically expressed in a passage at the end of Choan-Seng Song's *The Compassionate God*. There he described an African's dream of the world:

A giant snake, enormously powerful, was coiling itself around the globe. The globe seemed too weak to withstand the pressure. I could see the first cracks in it. Then I saw a light at the center of the world. Enter into this light, I was told, but I resisted... But the light was irresistible. I went towards it and, as I did so, I saw many others moving towards it, too. And the snake's grip gradually began to loosen.

Choan-Seng Song comments on the dream:

The world has in fact begun to crack. We seem destined for destruction at our own hands. But behold, miracle of miracles, out of the cracks a light shines... We all need that light, for that light is our only hope—we, the poor and the rich, the oppressed and the oppressors, the theists and the atheists, Christians, Muslims, Jews, Buddhists, and Hindus. We must all get to that light, for it is the light of love and life, the light of hope and the future. The movement of persons toward that light must have constituted a formidable power, for the snake, the demon, begins to loosen its grip on the globe. (The Compassionate God, SCM Press 1982, pp. 259-60)

There is abundant spiritual energy and hope to release our world from the fears and dangers that threaten to crush us, if only we can harness that energy effectively.

*   *   *

Here I wish to say something more concrete about how many of the global changes have first been started inside the Catholic Church and gradually been followed by the other Christian and non-Christian Faith Communities the world over. The changes, or maybe better to call them an evolution, from old past interpretations into new post-modern interpretations are still being worked out on a way of no return and will find hopefully their expression in a re-translating and a re-wording of the liturgical ceremonies of the church. Next to the recent growing interest a bit all over the world in a searching for more spiritual interpretations of the meaning of life itself and of the meaning of man/woman, these changes will create the basis for a renewed interest of younger and elder people in the Churches also as necessary and non-replaceable institutes.

16. Liturgical Vision and the Evolution in the Catholic Church

Remarkable changes in the Catholic Faith Community

These extraordinary changes which I described above in "Global Changes in the Faith Communities" and which are now finding their way at least all over the western world have their origin in the new postmodern vision of Catholic and Protestant theologians as Edward Schillebeeckx, Dominican, Jacques Dupuis, Jesuit, Hans Küng, Theologian, Roger Leenaers. Jesuit, the Anglican theologian John Hick, and many others, and last but not least the writings of the theologians of the liberation theology in particular in South-America.

I quote from the review in Roger Lenaers'book: "Nebuchadnezzar's Dream or The End of a Medieval Church" (see Biblopgraphy):

Lenaers contends that the Catholic Church in the West is declining because of a cultural mutation that started in Europe in the seventeenth and eighteenth centuries with the rise of modern science. Phenomena that had previously been ascribed to supernatural powers appear to have natural causes independent of the divine world. As a result, the divine world has become less visible and plays a less obvious role. Nonetheless, Catholicism, and most of Christianity, have remained attached to the language and images of the Middle Ages. This attachment makes the church a foreign object in the modern world. Its message has become incomprehensible for modern people.

The church, Lenaers suggests, is badly in need of a new language, starting with a new way of speaking about God. The image of God residing in a different world must give way to one of God as the deepest ground of the cosmos. This cosmos is not an ultimate, final creation, but God's progressive self-expression. This new interpretation has far-reaching consequences for the entire Catholic doctrine of faith. Lenaers attempts to show new ways for the modern Church to speak about God, hierarchy, the person of Jesus, afterlife, sacraments, sin, redemption, sacrifice, supplicating prayer and other central topics. His study seeks to be a faithful translation, advanced by modernity, of the same message that was previously transmitted in traditional medieval language.

Repercussion of all these changes on the liturgical celebrations.
There are signs of a growing conviction that there is need for a re-wording of many texts and words in the liturgy and in the administration of the sacraments, which are not endorsable anymore by the common people and in particular by the young. Especially the wording of the Confession of Faith and many of the descriptive words about the Jesus figure and the Eucharist should be rephrased to make them understandable and endorsable by our post-modern people.

a) Restoration of the mystery-filled presence of God in the church building and in the celebration of the Eucharist.
As already exposed in 1994 in my "Interreligious Dialogue Guidelines", it has become my personal opinion that one of the negative side effects of the new liturgy since Vatican II is the disappearance in the church building of the mystery and the sacral which surround the Divine. This mystery of the Divine Presence in our former church buildings was expressed and sustained by the central place of the head altar, the crucifix, the Eucharist bread kept in the head altar and the red twinkling light of the sanctuary lamp.

In the temples and prayer buildings of the old Egypt, in Judaism and in the Eastern religions we always find in the depth of the temples a celebration room with the images and representations of the gods or saints, a place which is immersed in semi-darkness and where only the celebrants have access to. More and more it is now being accepted that even in the Egyptian way of believing (1) and in the Eastern religions like Hinduism and Buddhism (2) the so-called 'gods' or 'saints' (Bodhisattva's in Buddhism) can be considered as representations of the One Ultimate Spiritual Reality, objects of veneration but not of adoration. What is adored, consciously or unconsciously, is not the image but the Divine hidden behind the image(s).

As another good result of Vatican II, the Bible has now also in Catholic churches been placed in a place of honour, which however is seemingly not enough to create a feeling of the mystery of the Divine. The aim of bringing the Eucharist nearer to the faithful has surely been attained because instead of the former small minority, the great majority of the attendants now go to communion

The putting of the main altar nearer to the attending congregation has brought with it the current keeping of the Eucharist in the tabernacle often in the tabernacle of a side-altar with also in many places a disappearance of the sanctuary lamp.

In the Roman Catholic, Anglican and some Protestant Faith Communities, and this in particular since Vatican II, the Eucharist has however been defrocked of its sacredness and its mystery-filled image, first of all by removing the tabernacle with the Eucharist away from the main altar, but also by the current handling of the Eucharist by non-consecrated ministers and other assistants of the celebrant.

A re-evaluation of the former main altar by keeping the Eucharist in the tabernacle of the former main altar would be perfectly in line with the centuries old tradition of the "holy of holies" in the depth of the sanctuary and would be also a re-creation of a feeling of the 'sacred' presence of the Divine in the church building. While it is fully acceptable that the distribution of the Eucharist is also done by lay people, the taking out from and the replacing in the tabernacle should be reserved exclusively for the celebrant.

Testimonies from different countries on the location of the Tabernacle on the head-altar of the church building:

Belgium:
In the Catholic Flemish weekly "Kerk+Leven" of February 18, 2004 we read on p. 3 in the article "Geen zondagsviering meer" (No more Sunday celebration)" (A/N translation):

"The Anglican Church is thinking of not concentrating any more its church celebrations on Sundays. This was reported in the Australian newspaper 'The West Australian'. With this radical new regulations the church leadership wishes to jump on the bandwagon of the changes in society."

In the same above mentioned weekly of March 7, 2007 is this taken up again in an article "Minder eucharistie"(Less Eucharist) by Erik de Smet who says: *In different places in the Flemish country it is the policy of the Church to promote strong liturgical times (Ash Wednesday, Christmas night, Holy Week). This offers more possibilities to come to a more carefully carried out liturgy with a choir, lectors, acolytes...What's more, a filled church makes the participants enthusiast and offers them a stronger church community experience.*

As "strong liturgical times" I would prefer to name the high days of the liturgical year, Christmas, Easter with the Holy Week, Pentecost, All Saints/All Souls Day (as one feast .day).

United Kingdom: On occasion of one of the latest synods of the Church of England, a report lay on the table in which some remarkable recommendations. It states a/o that the average believer has barely time on his weekends to participate in the Eucharist celebration. Sunday is no more considered as a church day, but as a family day, an entertainment day or a sport day. The Church is no more on the list of priorities of modern families who stand more and more under time pressure.

Australia: According to the Australian Anglican bishop Murray is the situation in his country not much different from that in Great Britain. He is convinced that the Churches have to look for new ways to get people involved in Church life, They have therefore to anticipate on the needs of the faithful and dare to break with old formulas, although the parishes, in his view, continue to play an essential role in the faith perception of the common church goer. "We must sell ourselves better" is how he expresses himself "Within a quarter of a century the situation will be completely different, and I can imagine that then there will be no more Sunday celebrations."

USA

In 2003, in a series of essays on the liturgy in the Catholic Reflections & Reports (TCRNews) under the title The Tabernacle and Catholic Worship: Simplicity vs. False Minimalism, Deacon Keith A. Fournier states in his article "Bring the Tabernacle Back into the Sanctuary", as follows:

"I have become convinced that the move of the Tabernacle out of the center of the sanctuary was an over-reaction against a privatized piety that some worried was distracting from the experience of the community nature of Eucharistic worship. Well, having now seen its bad fruit, I have joined the ranks of many, traditionalists included, in concluding that it has been an abysmal failure. The cure was worse than the perceived problem.

. . . Well, I have come to a conclusion; bring Jesus back into the sanctuary. Bring the Tabernacle back into the sanctuary."

Stephan Hand, editor TCRNews, in his article "Where the Eternal Light is Burning" puts it as follows:

". . . .The ongoing neo-modernist reduction of theology and philosophy to "spirituality" promised to triumph by the time the post-conciliar "spirit of Vatican II" began to trumpet itself to the world. The immediate and most dramatic impact of the revolution was in the liturgy. When, despite Sacrosanctum Concilium, the Constitution on the Sacred Liturgy promulgated by Paul VI at the Second Vatican Council, the Tabernacle which housed the Blessed Sacrament from ancient times was later theologically displaced from the altar (even if not intrinsically wrong dogmatically), it was an eloquent, if pernicious, metaphor of the theological and spiritual shift which had taken place first in minds of not a few liturgists. Liberals preferred to see God "everywhere" without the most important distinctions. That Tabernacle, which by solemn decree and Tradition held "the most distinguished and honorable place in the Church", and the altar were always considered inseparable "by origin and [by their very] nature". ......

.Thus the increasingly exaggerated tearing asunder of that which belonged together, which violated that primal unity without justification from the Second Vatican Council, threatened to go directly to the very Heart of Catholic Eucharistic theology! Thankfully, we are seeing some improvements and reversals of this aberration. Note that we are not saying the Tabernacle must necessarily be physically located directly on the altar---which was a late development in the Church---but that theologically and spiritually they cannot be separated. Even in terms of physical location the locus of the

Tabernacle should generally be "central," near the altar. Adoration and the Eucharist, as Cardinal Ratzinger noted again recently, are inseparable."

b) The bodily position of the celebrant or acting minister

It is also in line with the tradition practised in the major world religions that the role of the consecrated celebrant is of great importance. A replacement by lay ministers can be accepted as a temporary transitional period with as reason the lack of priests as it is the case now in Europe and the USA. The efforts towards a more active part of lay people and even women in the Eucharist celebration and in the administration of the Sacraments mean a wished for democratisation of the hierarchical church structures and a more democratic vision on the coming in contact with the Divine. The permanently understood and accepted way of this participation by non-consecrated lay people should be that it is carried out under and with the priest or consecrated person as main ministering actor.

A development, which is liable for discussion in the new liturgy, is the bodily position of the celebrant. Up to Vatican II the celebrant was facing the main altar. This has now in a complete turn around been changed in most churches to a position of facing the congregation. The traditions in the Catholic Church as well as in other Christian and non-Christian Faith Communities of facing the main altar or main image in the deep recess of the sanctuary should be taken into full account. While there is no problem in accepting the congregation-directed position of the celebrant for the teaching part of the celebration, let's say up to the confession of faith, the position of the celebrant should be front-directed for the rest of the celebration up to the communion of the faithful and be again congregation directed for the fare-well benediction at the end of the celebration.

This may have another non-negligible consequence that it would create a further link with the Buddhist faith community where the main temple image is cloaked in semi-darkness expressing the mystery and the elusiveness of the Divine presence and where the position of the celebrating priest is always a front-directed position.

Many are trying to understand the background for the ever-increasing interest of the Christian world in the various forms of Buddhism and Hinduism. It is my impression that this trend has a lot to do with a renewed accent on the ungraspable mystery of the Divine, of the Ultimate Spiritual Reality as it comes into prominence in the Holy Scriptures of the Hindu Veda's and the Buddhist Sutra's and in their liturgical practices. Hindu Yoga and Buddhist Zen meditation are in the centre of attraction for many people in the West. Including more space for silent meditation should be put into practice in the Eucharist celebrations, also as a response to this trend.

c) The offertory

Whatever one may think about sacrificing, it can be said that from ancient times people have found it necessary to offer sacrifices to the Divine in a multiplicity of forms. So, also in the Eucharist celebration a part is dedicated to the offering of the bread and the wine and of the self to the Divine. The financial and maybe other offerings of the attending faithful could and should be included in these offerings. It might be given to the children and the young representing their different youth organizations to bring the bread, wine and water together with the financial offerings into the hands of the celebrant.

d) Re-wording of words and phrases in the liturgical texts.

- **in the Eucharist celebration:** "This is my body, this is my blood" might be rephrased in something like: "Herein the presence of our Lord".

- **the Ten Commandments:** should be re-phrased in consonance with the Global Ethic (3) as it has been presented since 1993 by the Catholic theologian Hans Küng and accepted as a valuable basis for human conduct by a majority of the 7.000 participants of the world Faith Communities on occasion of the interfaith dialogue congress in Chicago in 1993. This global ethic can be considered as being equal to the Golden Rule "In everything, do to others as you would have them do to you; for this is the law and the prophets." (Matthew 7), which is being accepted as a common rule of life by all major world religions.

- The Credo or Faith Confession:

The Nicene-Constantinopolitan Creed has been re-worded into our present Credo of the Apostles as hereunder. And ...there is room for re-wording the words in italics in the graphic hereunder.

The Credo text is a Profession of Faith that was approved by the Council of Nicea in 381 and is known as the Nicene Creed. It was added officially to the Ordinary of the Mass in the 11th century by Pope Benedict VIII.

When the Nicene Creed was drawn up, the chief enemy was Arianism, which denied that Jesus was fully God. Arius (256- circa 336) was a presbyter (=priest = elder) in Alexandria in Egypt.

When the Apostles' Creed was drawn up (4th to 5th century), the chief enemy was Gnosticism, which denied that Jesus was truly Man; and the emphases of the Apostles' Creed reflect a concern with repudiating this error.

Table 16.1

Nicene Creed	Trente Creed
(1) We believe in one God, the Father, the Almighty, maker of heaven and earth, of all that is, seen and unseen.	(1) I believe in God the Father Almighty, Creator of Heaven and earth
(2) We believe in one Lord, Jesus Christ, the *only* son of God, eternally begotten of the Father,	(2) And in Jesus Christ, His *only* Son, our Lord;
(3) For us and for our salvation he came down from heaven: by the power of the Holy Spirit he became incarnate from the *Virgin* Mary, and was made man.	(3) Who was conceived by the Holy Ghost, born of the *Virgin* Mary,
(4) For our sake he was crucified under Pontius Pilate; he suffered death and was buried.	(4) Suffered under Pontius Pilate, was crucified, dead, and buried;
(5) On the third day he rose again in accordance with the Scriptures;	(5) *He descended into hell*; the third day He rose again from the dead;
(6) He ascended into heaven and is seated at the right hand of the Father.	(6) He ascended into Heaven, sitteth at the right hand of God the Father Almighty
(7) He will come again in glory to judge the living and the dead, and his kingdom will have no end.	(7) From thence He shall come to judge the living and the dead
(8) We believe in the Holy Spirit, the Lord, the giver of life, who proceeds from the Father [and the Son]. With the Father and the Son he is worshipped and glorified. He has spoken through the Prophets.	(8) I believe in the Holy Ghost
(9) We believe in one holy catholic and apostolic Church.	(9) in the Holy Catholic Church, the communion of saints
(10) We acknowledge one baptism for the forgiveness of sins.	(10) in the forgiveness of sins,
(11) We look for the resurrection of the dead,	(11) in the *resurrection of the body*, and
(12) and the life of the world to come. AMEN.	(12) in life everlasting. AMEN

It is obvious that this re-wording is a process which will take place over a quite long period of time and has to be worked out by theologians and other bible and linguistic specialists.

Roger Lenaers in his book Nebuchadnezzar's Dream gives an inspiring example of a re-wording of the Apostles'Creed:

I believe *in* God, endless Love,
Primeval Wonder that expresses Itself in an amazing way
in the evolution of the cosmos and the human.
And I believe *in* Jesus Christ, our Messiah,
God's unique human image,
born from human parents,
yet entirely the fruit of God's initiative of salvation.
Who has accepted suffering and death,
was crucified by order of Pontius Pilate, died and was buried,
but nevertheless fully lives, because he merged into God,
and thus became an all-healing force,
that will lead the entire humanity to completion.
I believe in the inspiring activity of God's holy breath of life,
And in the worldwide community in which Jesus Christ lives on,
and in God's offer to heal us and transform us into real human beings.
And in the divine future of humankind, a future of life.
Amen.

Sense of Community and solidarity

What people in first contacts with new charismatic movements in the Catholic Church such as Opus Dei, Focolare and others, and non-catholic movements such a the Brahma Kumaris and some new religions in Japan, the Risshō Kōsei-Kai and the Sōka Gakkai, strikes most is the feeling of solidarity, of oneness and fellowship, of belonging to a living community. This kind of feeling is greatly lacking or at least not coming sufficiently into expression in liturgical gatherings, and surely in daily life where e.g. only a limited number of people say hallo to unknown persons. The consciousness of being all brothers and sisters is not alive and surely not practised in daily life and not sufficiently in the liturgical ceremonies. The decreasing attendance to Sunday Mass in the West does of course also not help towards a feeling of belonging to a great community. Most of the now too large church buildings have become oppressive by their emptiness.

As a means to revaluate the Church as a living community and to promote this feeling of solidarity with each other, more attention should be paid to the major feast days such as Easter, Christmas and All Saints/All Souls day, and maybe some others, which are the only days in the year when churches still have plenty of attendants. More attention should be paid to the preparation and the styling of these high days of the ecclesiastical year. All parish organizations and surely the young should take part in the preparation and in an active participation in the Eucharist gathering. Those are the feast days on which the faithful could be invited to participate in Eucharist gatherings on a deaconate level around their deacon in the "mother church" as the Belgian Cardinal Godfried Danneels calls it, and even on a diocesan level in the cathedral around their bishop. Such mass gatherings could be enlivened with songs and dances, sociable dining and shopping, which would create among the participants the feeling of joyful and valuable belonging to a living community in solidarity with each other. This could also lead to a renewed faith and to a renewed revaluation of the church community to which they all belong.

As another way of concentrate the attention more on Eucharist celebrations on feast days, might this also not be the time to re-think the meaning of the everyday mass obligation for priests, also when nobody or maybe only a solitary servant is present? Although it may have become a tradition, one may ask whether its practice has not   become obsolete in our post-modern times. The least which could be done presently is the lifting of this obligation by the Vatican authorities. The same can be said about the dayly breviary obligation.

Notes:
(1) Marleen Reynders, Onder het oog van de zonnegod, Het Spectrum, Davidsfonds/Leuven, 2003
(2) See my website "Buddhism and Hinduism monotheistic?"
(3) See my website "Global Ethic Draft Text".
(4) See my website   "Declaration of the Human Responsibilities"

*   *   *

As stated above, the world has seen, or better has not seen yet because it is still unknown by the common people and even by most people involved in the interfaith dialogue movement, the creation of 4 councils of religious leaders. I consider it to be worthwhile to give hereunder a rather detailed description of the four, because these initiatives could be so many steps towards the creation of a "United Faith Communities Organisation" as described further on: From the mentioned participants, globally acceptable representatives of the different world faith communities might come forward or selected as members of the aimed at United Faith Communities Organization

17. Councils of Religious Leaders

Since 2001 the world has seen the creation of three councils of world religious leaders and one continental European council. I could replace in the text below the word 'World Council of Religious Leaders' by 'United Faith Communities Organisation' which name I would prefer as a partner of the United Nations Organization.

1. World Council of Religious Leaders (WCRL)

(Millennium Peace Summit 2000 New York, 2002 Bangkok)
Rationale and Concept
Inaugural Meeting of the Steering Council October 22-24, 2001

Background
Over the years, many leaders, both religious and secular, have recognized the need to create an entity that would address critical world issues from the perspective of the faith traditions. By bringing together the leaders from the Buddhist, Christian, Hindu, Jewish, Islamic and Indigenous traditions, the human community can begin to draw upon the collective wisdom and universal moral and spiritual principles that are the bedrock of all the great religions.

Over the past few decades, interreligious dialogue and relations have advanced to the point where such an entity is no longer an ideal but a concept whose time has come. It took two world wars to give birth to the United Nations. During the last few decades, it has taken numerous conflicts involving religion to make concrete the need for a World Council of Religious and Spiritual Leaders.

The creation of this World Council was one of the fundamental purposes for organizing the Millennium World Peace Summit of Religious and Spiritual Leaders at the United Nations in August 2000. The goal has been to create a body of religious leaders that would work in close coordination with the United Nations, to bring the spiritual repository of the human community to the solving of critical world problems. United Nations Secretary-General Kofi Annan fully recognizes and appreciates the value religious leaders bring to the political equation. Indeed, there growing acknowledgment that there will not be peace in this world without the leadership and cooperation of the religions, which cross national boundaries and have far greater reach than most political bodies.

The tragedy of September 11, 2001 has created a new urgency as the world faces the danger of realignment along religious lines. As diversity grows in communities around the world, so too does intolerance of differences. These threats are also hastening the opposite – the emergence of a reinforced commitment to find the common voice within religion – the central universal values that would form the basis for a new global vision. The need for a World Council of Religious and Spiritual Leaders is clearer today than it was one year ago. The challenge now is to move from concept to reality.

The Current Crisis

On September 11th, 2001, a tragedy of massive proportion changed the world. Religion moved to center stage in a way few could have envisioned. Religious fundamentalism, a small but vocal presence in all faith traditions, seeks to divide the world along religious lines. The dangers posed by these extremes within the religious tradition are now known to be a grave threat to the human community. Only the world's respected religious leadership can truly counter this threat.

What could a World Council do to abate the dangers of religious extremism and the consequent terrorist activities? Throughout history, religion has been a force for bringing destruction as well as benefit to humankind. Can a World Council steer religious fervor and commitment toward the common good? Can a World Council strengthen our shared values and help transform ignorance and the fear of difference into respect and appreciation?

September 11th made clear how fragile still is the ability of the religions to honor each other. It also made clear the degree to which we have become a global community, unable any longer to avoid knowing and respecting each other. Ironically, the events of September 11th set the stage for religious leaders to come forward in a new way, their audience no longer just their own constituents, but rather the entire global community.

Mission

During a recent conference call, the Archbishop of Canterbury told us that religions now need to redefine their theologies for modernity. If we are to address the most critical problems, the religions need to act in concert, rather than seek to fulfill their own, sometimes opposing, ends.

This redefining of the theologies can help find the common purpose of religion – to relieve suffering, foster harmony, promote the dignity of all life. In the same conference call, the Chief Rabbi of England spoke about creating a world culture that recognizes the dignity of difference and finds unity in diversity.

The mission of the World Council of Religious and Spiritual Leaders is to create dialogue among the most senior leaders of all the major faith traditions. The purpose is not to discuss theology or matters that pertain to the organization or foundation of any individual faith tradition, but rather to find a means of working together to address critical social issues – poverty, conflict, intolerance, environment degradation, terrorism, etc. Just as the United Nations requires nation states to dialogue with each other, this Council would necessitate exchange among the religions, where currently there is no formal body for such engagement on world issues.

Structure

Each of the major religious traditions has its own internal dynamic and organizational structure. Most of the religions are nonhierarchical and do not speak with a singular voice. The Catholic Church is the exception. Where there is a hierarchy, this structure would determine representation on the Council. Where there is none, eminent leaders from a religious tradition who have the respect and recognition of their community globally could represent the faith. The Council will evolve from a group of members who are committed to the concept and to working together to address global problems through the wisdom of the faith traditions.

Purpose of the Steering Council

The inaugural meeting of the Steering Council took place on October 22-24, 2001 at the Rockefeller Brothers Conference Center in Pocantico Hills, New York. The Steering Council will define the mission and purpose of the Council. Leaders from the religious traditions and will explore how the World Council could function from the perspective of their faith tradition, and how their tradition could be represented.

Specific subjects to be discussed:

Organization and structure of the World Council

Representation: by religion, region, gender, race

The mandate: responding to a world crisis

Relationship to United Nations and other international organizations, such as the World Bank

Where and when to meet

Funding

Implementation of decisions

Process for creation of the World Council

If critical social problems are to be successfully addressed, an integrated framework of religion, government and business must be created. Just as the United Nations has invited members of civil society to work with government on global issues, the World Council must actively engage with business and government so that all major sectors of society will become part of the process of creating social transformation. Thus initiatives launched by the World Council could be carried out with the help of governments and businesses around the world.

This inaugural meeting of the Steering Council for the World Council of Religious and Spiritual Leaders has been made possible through a grant from the UN Foundation/Better World Fund.

New York–[August 29, 2000]– Participants of the Millennium Peace Summit of Religious and Spiritual Leaders took the historic step of presenting a Commitment to Global Peace to UN Secretary-General Kofi A. Annan that outlines key areas in which religious leaders can play an active role in reducing conflict and addressing the critical needs of humankind.

Table 17.1

Headquarters	Secretariat	India (+91)
Empire State Building		Country Director
350 Fifth Avenue, Suite 5403	5A Nai Lert Tower, 2/4 Wireless Road,	E-165Greater Kailash I New Delhi 110048,
New York, NY 10118,	Patumwan,	India
USA	Bangkok 10330,	Mobile. 98 1000 7273
Tel. +1 (212) 967 2891	Thailand	Tel. (11) 2621 3141
Fax. +1 (212) 967 2898	Tel. +66 2 252 1748	Fax. (11) 2644 9797
Mr. Bawa Jain, secretary	Fax. +66 2 655 0382	Mr. Praveen Saini,
b.jain@wcorl.org &	Email.	p.saini@wcorl.org &
hq@wcorl.org	secretariat@wcorl.org	india@wcorl.org

Co-Chairs
His Holiness Somdet Phra Buddhacharya, Acting Supreme Patriarch of the Kingdom of Thailand
Sephardic Chief Rabbi Shelomo Amar, Chief Rabbi of Israel
Askenazi, Chief Rabbi Israel Meir Lau, Chief Rabbi of Israel
His Holiness. Jayendra Saraswati, The Shankaracharya of Kanchipuram, India
His Excellency Ayatollah Mahmoud Mohammadi Araghi, President of the Islamic Culture and Relationship Organization of the Islamic Republic of Iran.
His Excellency Dr. Aabdullah Abdul Muhsin Al-Turki, Secretary General of the World Muslim League.
Venerable Min Zhiting, President of the China Taoist Association
Board
Reverend Joan Brown Campbell, Director Department of Religion Chautauqua Institution.
Chief Oren Lyons, Chief Onandoga Nation.

H.E. Kamel AL-Sharif, Secretary General International Islamic Council For Daw'a and Relief.

Rt. Rev Riah Abu Al-Assal, Bishop of the Episcopal Anglican Diocese Jerusalem and the Middle East.

His Eminence Gregorios Theocharous, Archbishop of Thyateira and Great Britain.

His Holiness Swami Dayananda Saraswati, Chairman All India Movement for Seva.

Rabbi Arthur Schneier, Founder and President Appeal of Conscience Foundation.

Most Venerable Master Sheng Yen, Founder Dharma Drum Mountain Buddhist Association.

Venerable Phra Thepsophon, Rector University Mahachulalong -kornrajavidyalaya.

Bawa Jain, Secretary General, World Council of Religious Leaders (b.jain@wcorl.org)

Advisors

Senior Advisor:

His Excellency Mr. Budimir Loncar, Former Minister of Foreign Affairs of Yugoslavia.

Advisors:

Hiroshi Matsumoto, President Inner Trip Reiyūkai International.

Jane Goodall, PhD, CBE, UN Messenger of Peace & Founder   - The Jane Goodall Institute.

Ms. Setsuko Nakanishi, Honorary WCRL Member Spiritual Leader, Founder ITRI.

International Experts Group

Dr. Doudou Diene, UNESCO.

Professor Dr. Ervin Lazlo, Founder and President The Club of Budapest.

His Excellency Dr. L.M. Singhvi, M.P, Senior Advocate Supreme Court of India.

Professor Seyyed Hossein Nasr, Department of Islamic Studies, George Washington University.

His Excellency Dr. Karan Singh, Member of Parliament, India.

Reverend Dr. C. Welton Gaddy, Executive Director Interfaith Alliance Foundation.

Honorable Leticia Ramos Shahani, Presidential Adviser on Culture Office of the President of the   Philippines.

Reverend Joan Brown Campbell, Director Department of Religion Chautauqua Institution.

His Excellency Ambassador Onur Gokce, Ministry of Foreign Affairs of the Republic of Turkey.

His Excellency Mr. Kenneth Kaunda, Former President of the Republic of

Zambia.

His Excellency Mr. Budimir Loncar, Former Minister of Foreign Affairs of Yugoslavia.

The secretariat for The Millennium World Peace Summit will oversee the administrative functioning of the world council, to be based in New York.

The problem here is that since the creation of this council in 2001, as far as I know, there has been no news at all on the carrying out of their above-mentioned Mission and Subjects to be discussed, nor about any concrete positive activities of the world council, up to this year of 2008.

2. Board of World Religious Leaders

The Eliyah Interfaith Institute
First meeting: December 14-17 2003, Seville, Spain
"Religion, Democratic Society and the Other:
Hostility, Hospitality and the Hope of Human Flourishing"
Second meeting: November 2005, Wu Lai, Taiwan
"Crisis of the Holy »

Attended by 45 religious leaders of 5 of the main world religions from 20 different countries:

10 Buddhist Leaders
H.H. the Dalai Lama, India
Ven. Zoketsu Norman Fisher, USA
Blanche Zenkei Hartman, USA
Dharma Master Hsin Tao, Taiwan,
Ven Bhikkhuni Kusuma, Sri Lanka,
Ven. Jinwol Lee, Korea,
Venerable Ashin Nyanissara, Myanmar,
Venerable Phra Thepsophon, Thailand,
Ven. Karma Lekshe Tsomo, USA,
Venerable Khandro Rinpoche, India,
10 Christian Leaders
Ecumenical Patriarch Bartholomew I, Turkey,
Sr. Isabelle Flye Sainte Marie, Israel,
Rev. Frank Griswold, Presiding Bishop, USA,
Archnishop Karl Gustav Hammar, Sweden,
Cardinal Theodore Edgar McCarrick, USA,
Patriarch Mesrob II, Turkey,
Archbishop Butros Muallem, Israel,

Bishop Vincentiu Ploisteneau, Romania,
Abbot Dr. Notker Wolf OSB, Italy,
Rev. Bishop Baerbel Wartenberg-Potter, Germany,
6 Hindu Leaders
Sudhamani Mata Amritananda Mayi (Amma), India,
Guruji Sri Rishi Prabhakar, India,
Sri Ravi Shankar, India,
His Holiness Sri Sri Sugunendra Theertha Swamiji, India,
Dadi Janki, India,
Bhai Mohinder Singh, Engeland,
9 Jewish Leaders
Chief Rabbi Eliyahu Bakshi-Doron, Israel,
Chief Rabbi Shear Yashuv Cohen, Israel,
Rabbi Menachem HaCohen, Rumenia,
The International Jewish Committee on Interreligious Consultations (IJCIC),
USA,
Chief Rabbi Berel Lazar, Russia,
Rabbi Michael Melchior, Jeruzalem,
Rabbi David Rosen, Israel,
Chief Rabbi Jonathan Sackis, Engeland,
Chief Rabbi Shmuel René Sirat, France,
10 Muslim Leaders
Sheick Muhammad Nur Abdallah, USA,
Sayyed Jawad al-Khoei, Engeland,
Dr. Y. Mossa Basha, USA,
Sheik Muhammad Husham Kabbani, USA,
Dr. Wahidudin Khan, USA,
Imam W. Dean Mohammad, USA,
As-Sayyid Shaykh Muhammad Nazim Adil al-Qubrusi al-Haqqani, Cyprus,
Dr. Adamou Ndam Njoya, Cameroon,
Dr. Abdurrahman Wahid, Indonesia,
Additional Participants / Observers at the Meeting of 2003 include:
Cardinal Carlos Amigo Vallejo O.F.M., Spain
Sister Therese Andreron, Beatitudes Community
Bishop Stephen W. Sykes, Durham University, UK
Prof. Vincent J. Cornell, University of Arkansas
Maria Reis Habito, Museum of Religions, Taiwan

Resolution of the Eliyah Academy Think-tank,
Proposed for consideration and adoption by the assembled board of world
religious leaders, Sevilla, December 2003.
Whereas current tensions among religious communities around the world cry
out for attention, making us painfully aware of the hostility generated by

human behavior and by the ways religion contributes to it; and Whereas we seek to establish alternative models and provide such resources that will encourage hospitality and collaboration between world religions; and Whereas we recognize the important role that religious intellectuals and scholars play in the shaping of their tradition and in aiding the course of its growth; and Whereas with these goals in mind, the Elijah Think-tank was formed, bringing together men and women, learned scholars of Buddhism, Christianity, Hinduism, Islam and Judaism, who hail from Canada, Great Britain, India, Israel and the United States; and Whereas these scholars have devoted extensive time over the past two years to meet in Arkansas and in Great Britain, and to engage in their various locales in the study of the attitude to the other, as expressed in their religions; and Whereas our cooperative study has brought us to realize that all our traditions express the highest spiritual vision possible for humanity, as well as noble means of treating those outside our own traditions, but also more human elements that, under the impact of various historical circumstances and a range of human reactions to them, have cultivated less noble attitudes to the other, It is our sincere recommendation:

That all of our religions engage in a process of self examination that will allow them to draw forth and develop the loftiest values about human life and dignity, hospitality to the other, and the ultimate vision for human flourishing, as these are contained within the traditions, in order to overcome any historical situations that have led to hatred of the other, ultimately leading to war and bloodshed.

That all of our religions empower their scholarly representatives to undertake such study in a sustained and considered way.

That such study and reflection be carried out not only in the privacy of each religion's study houses but also in the company of experts representing other religions, following our experience of how such collaborative work can have an enriching and transforming effect, encourage the best in our traditions to surface, permit extensive mutual enrichment and enable the kind of constructive reflection that can aid our traditions in conversation with one another in contemporary society.

That a permanent institution be established with the goal of advancing the kind of collaborative research and reflection that we have experienced, providing a symbol of collaboration for world religions and allowing them to face together, in their diversity, the broad range of challenges presented by contemporary reality.

That all participants in the Sevilla meeting on "Religion, Society and the Other" endorse this statement and continue to support and collaborate in the development of collaborative group studies and the development of educational materials to be carried out by scholars of all world religions in the framework of the Elijah Interfaith Institute.

3. Leaders of World and Traditional Religions

The First Congress of the Leaders of World and Traditional Religions took place on 23-24 September, 2003 in the City of Astana, capital of the Republic of Kazakhstan –under the chairmanship of President Nursultan Nazarbayev. The purpose was to develop a constructive dialogue between different confessions.

This Congress was the first representative religious forum held under the patronage of a Head of State. The leaders of the largest confessional bodies from 17 countries of Europe, Asia, Middle East and America participated in this event. Pope John Paul II, Patriarch Alexis II of Moscow and all Russia, the Archbishop of Canterbury, and the Ecumenical Patriarch sent welcoming addresses to the participants of the Congress.

Special envoys with messages from the King of Saudi Arabia and President of Egypt attended the Congress. The United Nations Secretary General, the Presidents of the USA, Russia, France, and Iran; the Prime Ministers of the United Kingdom and Italy, and other distinguished political leaders sent their congratulations.

Within the framework of the Congress, its participants had an open exchange of thoughts on the role of the religion in the contemporary world and the humane character of the values of many religions. The religious leaders adopted the final Declaration of the First Congress, in which it was stated that "the religions must aspire towards greater co-operation, recognising tolerance and mutual acceptance as essential instruments in the peaceful co-existence of all peoples." The Declaration expresses the readiness of the Congress participants not to tolerate the use of religious differences as the means of fuelling hatred and discord and to save humanity from the global conflict of religions and cultures.

The success of this event led to the Resolution of the First Congress to convene this inter-religious forum at least every three years. This resolution shows the timeliness of the idea of maintaining the constant dialogue between the religions in the sake of the peace and accord.

The Resolution also honoured Kazakhstan in inviting that country to host the Second Congress of World and Traditional Religions in Astana in 2006.

Aims and objectives of the Congress

The purpose of the Second Congress is to create the instruments to enable good relations between different confessions, based on inter-religious tolerance, mutual respect and peaceful coexistence.

In reaching this aim the participants of the Second Congress should accomplish the following tasks:

- to elaborate and adopt the general document setting out the principles of the dialogue between the religious leaders and organisations with state, public and political institutions. This document will mark the agreement to set up a mechanism to prevent conflicts on religious grounds, to provide ways of resolving possible religious conflicts, abstaining from making any appeals or actions directed against other religions, and establishing behavioural norms for believers in relation to non-believers;

- to ensure the functioning of the Congress of the Leaders of World and Traditional Religions as a standing international forum by adopting the Provision on the Congress Secretariat, establishing the procedure of its formation and financing;
- to define the ways the Congress will interact with the United Nations, United Nations Educational, Scientific and Cultural Organisation, Organisation for Security and Cooperation in Europe and other international organisations in the sphere of maintaining peace and security;
- to extend the format of the Congress participants to involve scientists, political and public representatives, to enable the discussion of issues of the dialogue development between civilizations on a wider basis;
- to consider the possibility of extending the Joint Appeal of the Second Congress participants to the world community to undertake radical measures to fight poverty, disease, and social injustice as the grounds for religious extremism;
- to adopt special resolutions with an appeal for reconciliation to the Heads of States and organizations opposing each other in conflicts in various regions of the world;
- to provide a wide distribution of the Congress's ideas and resolutions.

Attended by:

Representatives of Islam: 7 personalities from Saudi Arabia, 2 from Egypt, Iran, Pakistan, India, Libya and Kazakhstan.

Representatives of Christianity: 7 from Turkey, Armenia, Russia, Vatican, USA, Switzerland, UK.

Representatives of Buddhism: 4 from Korea, China, Taiwan, Thailand.

Representatives of Judaism: 2 from Israel.

Representative of Shinto: 1 from Japan

Representatives of Taoism: 1 from China

Representative of Hinduism: 1 from India

Representatives of international religious organizations: two Protestant leaders, one from USA, one from Switzerland,.

Guests of honour

13 political leaders from Malaysia, Switzerland, UNESCO, France (2), Korea, Belgium (2), UAE, USA, OSCE Austria.

Principles of Inter-Religious Dialogue
1. Dialogue shall be based upon honesty, tolerance, humility and mutual respect. It requires effective listening and learning, producing genuine engagement.
2. Dialogue must assume equality of partners and create the space for free expression of opinions, perspectives and beliefs, allowing for the integrity of each culture, language and tradition.
3. Dialogue must not aim at the conversion or defamation of the interlocutor, nor may it aim at demonstrating the superiority of one's own religion over that of others. It should not aim at eliminating differences, but rather at knowing and respecting them. It should enable participants to explain their faith honestly and clearly.
4. Dialogue aims at avoiding prejudice and misrepresentation of the faith of the other, thus encouraging better knowledge and understanding of the other. It helps prevent conflict and the use of violence as a means of reducing tension and resolving disputes.
5. Dialogue offers a way towards the peaceful coexistence and fruitful cooperation of peoples. It encourages better education, may also help towards a greater understanding of the importance of dialogue by the mass media and minimise the risk of religious extremism.
6. Inter-religious dialogue can serve as an example for other kinds of dialogue, especially social and political dialogue for the good of societies.
7. Dialogue conducted in a spirit of tolerance emphasizes that all people inhabit the same earth. This assumes certain shared values such as the sacredness of life, the dignity of all human beings and the integrity of creation and nature.
8. Dialogue assumes that religion plays a vital and constructive role in society. It promotes the common good, recognises the important role of good relationships between people and respects the specific role of the state in society.
9. Dialogue is fundamentally important for future generations to benefit from better relations between people of different religions and cultures.

The Second Congress of World and Traditional Religions seems to have taken place in the City of Astana, capital of the Republic of Kazakhstan in September 2006 and lasted 3 days.

There is however no news at all about this Second Congress, nor about whatever follow-up activity since the foundation in 2003 and nobody seems to be reachable for comment.

4. European Council of Religious Leaders (ECRL)

On 12 March 2002, Senior European religious leaders announced the launching of the first pan European religious leaders council, the WCRP/Europe Religious Leaders Council. The Council consists of thirty members representing Western and Eastern European States, including the members of the Commonwealth of Independent States and Turkey.

Summarizing the discussions of the Executive Committee, Rabbi Sirat noted major changes in Europe including: increasing cultural and religious pluralism; the rapid movement of information, commerce and labor across national boarders; the transformation of the social and political legacies of the wars of the last century; and the new and still fluid forms of political, military, and economic alliances. H.E. Cardinal Danneels noted that Europe is challenged to exercise a major role in the world in establishing international security, as well as economic and political orders that are consistent with its religious and civilizational values. H.E. Metropolitan Kirill noted the growing gap between the deep legacy of religiously inspired values that once offered a basis for moral consensus in Europe and the increasing dominance of other values more related to technical modes of thought and driven by economic efficiency.

European Council of Religious Leaders (ECRL) is a body of senior religious leaders of Europe's historic religions including Christianity, Judaism, and Islam, with Buddhists, Hindus, Sikhs and Zoroastrians in Europe who have committed themselves to cooperating for conflict prevention, peaceful co-existence and reconciliation. ECRL is a participating body of the World Conference of Religions for Peace.

                 http://www.religionsforpeace.net/Europe/ECRL.html

Executive Committee meetings:
November 11-12, 2002: inaugural meeting in Oslo, Norway.
September 29 - October 1, 2003: in Sarajevo, Bosnia-Herzegovina
February 6, 2006: in Oslo, Norway.
Members
Three co-Moderators:
Bishop Gunnar Stälsett, Lutheran Bishop of Oslo and a member of the Nobel Peace Prize Committee.
Grand Rabbi René-Samuel Sirat, Vice President of the Council of European Rabbis.
H.E. Dr. Mustafa Ceric, is the Raisu-I-Ulama (Supreme Head) of the Islamic Community in Bosnia and Herzegovina, Grand Mufti of Bosnia since 1993. He is also the Grand Mufti of Sanjak, Croatia and Slovenia. He served as an imam in Chicago and Croatia and as a professor in Bosnia, Malaysia, and the U.S.

Additional members of the Executive Committee :
H.E. Godfried Cardinal Daneels, Archbishop of Mechelen-Brussels.
H.E. Metropolitan Kirill, Metropolitan of Smolensk.
Mr. Jehangir Sarosh, Moderator of the WCRP/Europe Governing Board.

H.E. Bishop Stålsett, speaking for the Executive Committee, stated that these new realities present Pan-European challenges that extend beyond the boarders of any single European State, and, thus, require Pan-European multireligious responses. Bishop Stålsett noted that the WCRP/European Religious Leaders Council would engage relevant European social and political bodies regarding major social challenges confronting Europe and would help to establish multireligious action projects when appropriate. Bishop Stålsett announced that the Council would meet in Oslo, Norway, 11-12 November 2002.

Dr. Mustafa Ceric, citing the positive value of the Interreligious Council of Bosnia-Hercegovina in the aftermath of the war there, noted that the WCRP/European Religious Leaders Council would complement and assist the national chapters of WCRP. The new Council should provide support for helpful forms of collaboration among the religious communities of different states in Europe. Mr. Sarosh noted the new Council and the existing WCRP national chapters would provide complementary and reinforcing approaches to multireligious cooperation.

The WCRP/European Religious Leaders Council is part of the World Conference on Religion and Peace (WCRP), a worldwide multireligious coalition of believers that is organized on an international, regional, and national basis, on every continent. WCRP national chapters already exist in many States in Europe. WCRP is based upon the principle of acknowledging and respecting differences in religious belief and worship, and it is solely dedicated to multireligious cooperation for peace based on those moral concerns that are deeply held and widely shared among the world's religious communities.

*   *   *

In the current development of our world, still troubled by the many conflicts and problems which we all know too well, a start could and should be made on the international level to let these four councils propose qualified personalities on a tentative basis and as an intermediate phase, but who in a later stage could be accepted as full representatives. In this way a preparatory world forum could be created as a stepping stone to a formal United Faith Communities Organization.

18. A United Faith Communities Organization (UFCO)

Historical evolution

The 20th century has been a turbulent period in the history of our world, with many changes in the ways of life especially in Western countries. This century will be remembered because of the remarkable growth in world unity by the creation of more than ten international organizations in the political, financial and commercial sectors, towards the end of the 20th century the creation of the European Union, and the changing of a mentality of confrontation into a mentality of collaboration with the word "dialogue" becoming most commonly and universally used in all sectors of public life. (see in my website my texts World Forum of the Faith Communities and Global Changes in the Faith Communities)

The Catholic Church went through an upheaval of substantial changes which started with a new more scientifically based Bible interpretation in the 40-ties, followed by the second Vatican Council in 1962-1965 with as consequences the conversion in the liturgical language from Latin to the vernacular languages, the declaration of respect for other religions and cultures.

In the same period people in the western world changed from a centuries long stable belief in church authorities unto an acceptance of the individual personal conscience and knowledge as a basis for one's behavior. and with as a by-product a growing disobeying of former precepts and prohibitions and a lesser belief in dogmas. These are revolutionary changes which have had their influence on other Christian and even non-Christian religions.

From fundamental atheism with its aim of eradicating religion, communism and nazism brought about an estimated 100 million victims. Our world went also through two brutal world wars with 80 million war victims and all kinds of other conflicts in an age still of confrontation rather than of collaboration and dialogue. This has become an impossibility in the currently 27 united nations of Europe with its 500 million inhabitants.

Current world situation

In our current 21st century, our world is still faced with the problems of an escalating gap between rich and poor, the poverty of 20 percent of the world population, the millions of refugees in refugee camps or on the run from local conflicts, the one million or more Vietnamese children victims of Agent Orange, the globalization process as a way of no return with however its negative side-effects and the worldwide migration flood from the poorer to the richer nations.

The world's political, financial, and industrial leaders acknowledge that something needs to be done. Most of them however reluctantly follow the war on terrorism policy of the US, but neglect to follow the insistent appeal of among many others, Kofi Annan, Secretary-General of the UN, to pay more attention to correcting the roots which are at the origin of terrorist actions.

Action program for the World Faith Communities and the Interfaith Dialogue Movement

The faith communities, in cooperation with non-governmental organizations (NGOs), could speed up the process of dialogue by carrying out the neces-sary role of pressing and pushing the political leaders to arrive at a more efficient collaboration to convert the war on terrorism into a global effort to do something about the harm done to the growing number of refugees and about many of the socio-economic structures which are at the origin of the trend of violence and of most of the problems which our world is still facing today.

The interest in and the attendance at meetings of the Interfaith Dialogue Movement (IDM) in almost all countries have expanded in recent years in such a way that it can now be called a world global movement

The time is getting ripe for the idea of the creation of a global forum of the faith communities (religions as well as other traditions and humanist convictions). In step with the growth of worldwide globalization in the political, commercial and financial world, this project should become an issue of primary importance and could become THE historical event of the 21st century, by the creation of a United Faith Communities Organization as a worthy collaborator with its namesake the **United Nations Organization**. From the 228 world countries in 2006, 192 nations have united in the UNO without having had to change their identities. Why could this not become a reality for the world faith communities?

A United Faith Communities Organization (UFCO)

The above mentioned four councils of religious leaders may be proud of an impressive member list of religious personalities belonging to the main religions of the world and should become the step stones towards the creation of a United Faith Communities Organization as a 'combined force' of the faith communities of the world.

A next step could be the selection of a limited group of religious leaders from the members of these four councils joined by personalities from humanist and other convictions to form the first nucleus of a qualified representative United Faith Communities Organization.

Finally a quotation from Leonard Swidler in his Global Ethic proposition: (his website: http://astro.temple.edu/~dialogue/Swidler/)

"At the same time the world has been slowly, painfully emerging from the millennia-long Age of Monologue into the Age of Dialogue. As noted above, until the beginning of a century or so ago, each religion, and then each ideology--each culture tended to be very certain that it alone had the complete "explanation of the ultimate meaning of life, and how to live accordingly". Then through the series of revolutions in understanding, which began in the West but ultimately spread more and more throughout the whole world, the limitedness of all statements about the meaning of things began to dawn on isolated thinkers, and then increasingly on the middle and even grass-roots levels of humankind: the epistemological revolutions of historicism, pragmatism, sociology of knowledge, language analysis, hermeneutics, and finally dialogue.

Now that it is more and more understood that the Muslim, Christian, Secularist, Buddhist, etc. perception of the meaning of things is necessarily limited, the Muslim, Christian, Secularist, etc. increasingly feels not only no longer driven to replace, or at least dominate, all other religions, ideologies, cultures, but even drawn to enter into dialogue with them, so as to expand, deepen, enrich each of their necessarily limited perceptions of the meaning of things. Thus, often with squinting, blurry eyes, humankind is emerging from the relative darkness of the "Age of Monologue" into the dawning "Age of Dialogue"--dialogue understood as a conversation with someone who differs from us primarily so we can learn, because of course since we now growingly realize that our understanding of the meaning of reality is necessarily limited, we might learn more about reality's meaning through someone else's perception of it."

*   *   *

19. For a more genuine Image of Japan

Because of all the inspiring things I have learned from Japan, and preferring not to advance my own opinion on the subject which seems to be rather rose-colored, I present the reader hereafter first with a text from Doug Struck, Washington Post Service, dated 9 February 2001, which might straighten out a lot of preconceived ideas about Japan, followed by one of my own impressions on occasion of a trip through Japan in 2002.

Japan as it really is can be better understood from this exceptional article, which was published in the International Herald Tribune of Feb. 9. 2001, comparing the societal differences between the U.S.A. and Japan.

Japanese are Perplexed by U.S. Views of Japan

Doug Struck, Washington Post Service

TOKYO – The U.S. Treasury secretary, Paul O'Neill, said recently (begin 2001) that he would urge Japan to improve its economy but that he would not prod. It's more a question of "how do we help the people of Japan achieve a higher standard of living." Mr. O'Neill said.

Although U.S. officials have been urging the Japanese for years to slow their phenomenal savings rate and spend their way back to a boom, the remark has some Japanese chortling behind Guccini gloved hands.

Noriko Hama, a chief economist at Mitsubishi Research Institute in Tokyo, said: "It's a bit bizarre to be talking about raising the living standard of this country. Japan is the largest net creditor in the world and is thus the richest country in the world. This is far from a country that needs its standard of living raised. If anything, because people's standard of living is so high, they are a bit complacent about the economic situation." Noriko Hama added that Mr. O'Neill's view was "about a quarter-century old."

The high living standard is clearly visible on streets crowded with shiny new cars driven by Japanese in expensive suits and dresses going to jobs where they will earn more, on average, than Americans, Japanese have higher incomes, more savings, longer lives and better health than Americans, according to a host of statistical indicators. And they work less to achieve it: The image of Japanese working themselves to death aside, the average workweek among manufacturing workers is five hours shorter than in the United States. American workers on average put in the equivalent of two weeks more work per year than the Japanese, according to the International Labor Organization.

Japanese also pay less of their salary to taxes. Workers give less than 12 percent of their incomes to the government; in the United States, the burden is more than 16 percent, according to the Bank of Japan.

And the Japanese say they get more services. Health care is virtually free; child care is offered at a modest fee for working parents. Every ward in Tokyo has a large public swimming pool, and every neighborhood has several playgrounds.

Japan's public transportation system is probably the most efficient in the world: Tokyo's commuter trains provide 21 million rides a day, and on average Japan's high-speed intercity trains pull in within 18 seconds of their scheduled arrival time.

Proportionately more Japanese take overseas vacations than Americans – and they still manage to save money. While American workers spent more than they earned last year, the average Japanese family put 13 percent of its paycheck in savings. Japanese have banked $6.5 trillion in savings, according to the Bank of Japan.

The government here agrees with Mr. O'Neill's goal of bolstering the Japanese economy, which has been sputtering along with little real growth for a decade. In the third quarter of last year, the economy actually contracted at an annual rate of 2.4 percent, the government said Thursday.

With the U.S. economy slowing, many economists had been hoping that Japan could absorb imports from Asia and elsewhere to keep the global economy humming.

But the usual prescription for that – increased spending by Japanese consumers – may not work here, precisely because the standard of living is so high.

The consumer market is saturated here," Noriko Hama said. "People who want them have three or four cars. When you go around the streets of Japan, where do you find the recession?"

Indeed, Japan's stagnation is largely a phantom – one does not see it here. Japan's unemployment rate is at a record high, but after 10 years of doldrums the rate is 4.7 percent, compared with 4.2 percent in the United States after eight years of roaring boom.

Much of the economic burden is on the books of Japan's corporations, not on the backs of Japanese citizens, Japan's public officials and corporate executives have largely resisted the route so often urged by the United States to cut their losses, cut their work force and let weak companies go bankrupt.

Japan balks at the U.S. model wherein highly paid chief executives rescue a struggling company by throwing thousands of its employees out of work. Instead, workers keep their jobs while the companies limp along. It may be inefficient capitalism, they say, but workers have jobs.

And it shows. If the standard of living is measured by how much people buy, the Japanese are doing well. Walk down a Tokyo street, and one is jostled by a parade of Louis Vuitton handbags; fashion industry estimates say that nearly two thirds of high-end, brand name products in the world are bought by Japanese.

In the countryside, people may be less fashion-conscious than in Tokyo, but not less affluent. Everybody has a color television, and nine in 10 households have a microwave oven, according to the Economic Planning Agency in Japan. Eighty five percent of households have a car – one can get a small but efficient new model for $10,000 or less. More than 40 percent of households have a computer, and 39 percent have a set of golf clubs.

Critics are quick to acknowledge that Japan does have some major problems. The heavy weight of conformity and consensus is a huge brake on social, political and even economic progress. Japan is struggling with ways to sort out solutions to problems ranging from its identity and role in Asia to how to cope with a rapidly aging society.

But even measured by social factors. Japan's living standard fares well. Japanese women have the longest life expectancy in the world, and Japanese men are second only to Swedes, according to the United Nations.

The rate of heart attacks is one third that in the United States. And the Japanese daily diet includes 82 grams of fat, compared with the 146 grams consumed – and ultimately worn – by the average American. Japanese are growing healthier and taller, the typical 11-year-old child is 14 centimeters (51/2 inches) taller than at the end of World War II.

"The average standard of living, and the satisfaction level, is higher here than in the United States," said Naoji Yui, a partner of Accenture, the firm formerly known as Andersen Consulting.

In the United States, the rich guys are very rich, but the poor guys are very poor, In Japan, the rich guys are not so rich, but the poor are not so poor."

Impressions on occasion of a trip through Japan in 2002
Lucien F. Cosijns

Positive Points
- At night, no cars are allowed to park on the streets except on lined off parking places.

- An official document as proof of owning or renting a parking space is requested when buying a new car.
- Metal covers above gas and water sewers are 100% even with the surrounding road surface.
- Car roads all over Japan, in the cities as well as in the countryside, are in perfect state.
- Footpaths, all too few, but where they are, are in perfect state, mostly in asphalt but in the cities now in colourful tiles.
- Protecting bumpers along the roads are most in painted metal, and rust is rarely seen.
- Maximum speed on highways is limited to 100 km/hr, on other ways to 60km/hr.
- Names of villages and towns, and also of all train and metro stations, and most of the road directions are stated in three ways: in Japanese ideograms, in Japanese phonetic scripture and in our Roman alphabet.
- Public transport: trains and busses run on the minute if not on the second. The Shinkansen Superexpress trains run now between Tokyo and Osaka (450km) since 1964 and the lines have since then been expanded to some 4.500km. linking all the main cities. Between Tokyo and Osaka cities, there is now such a train every seven minutes, a local train 'Kodama' with 10, and a more direct train the 'Hikari' with 16 wagons and a thousand seats. The Hikari runs that distance in less than 3 hours, with an average seat occupation of 70%. Not one serious accident has occurred on these lines since 1964. They link a population in and around Tokyo of about 20 million with a population in and around Osaka of some 8 million.
- Announcement of the name of upcoming stops are made by taped radio system on all public transport systems in busses, trains, trams and subways.
- Rice planting and harvesting is done by special tractors replacing completely the hand planting. It has taken the agricultural machinery engineers of Japan till the 80s to develop such machines, which are now being exported and used more and more in all eastern countries.
- The extravagantly high salaries to top managers of big companies are unknown in Japan, except now maybe in some foreign controlled enterprises. The gap between higher and lower salaries is much smaller than in the US or the EU. Taxes on normal income of individuals and on company profits as well as on heritance income are keeping the Japanese population in a rather homogeneous society with a reasonable sharing rate in the common welfare by all. Total company income tax rate including corporate tax, inhabitant taxes, prefectural, municipal, and enterprise tax in 2002 : up to 4 million yen (€ 25.000) 30.80%, up

to 8 million yen 33.10%, over 8 million yen 44.79% (€ 1 = ¥ 163,
¥ 100 = € 0,6 Dec. 2007).

- One of the main characteristics of Japanese society is the giving of
priority to the common good above private interests. During the 'boom'
period of the sixties. Japan knew a lot of strikes in all sectors of society,
while there have been no strikes at all during the so-called 'crisis period' of the eighties up to 2005. Global collaboration to solve the problems is considered by everybody as the responsibility of each citizen
and of each enterprise and organization.
- An almost obsessive care of keeping Japan clean and of bodily clean-
ness: every day a bath is the rule in Japan for everybody. Most homes
have their own bath which is in most cases a typical Japanese sitting
bath, the most expensive in cedar wood, while there are also public bath
facilities in all residential areas in the cities. About 150m people of a
total population of 128m yearly visit Japan's 15,700 *onsen ryokan*
(spa-town inns), not for curing but just for pleasure.
- And last but not least, as a consequence of this way of life, Japan has
had and still has no slums, no beggars, and only a very limited number
of homeless people for which the cities since 5 years ago provide tents
and shelter in the city parks. Homeless people in Tokyo and Osaka
numbered not more than 7.000 in a population of 127 million in 2001,
which number increased in 2005 to some 30.000 due to the economic
crisis period in the 90's and also to an increasing immigration, legally
and illegally of workers from less privileged countries. The rate of
criminality and of possession of weapons is by far the lowest in the
world. The criminality rate for the US stands at 92% and for Japan as by
far the lowest in the world at 21,5 in 1995. Only guns for hunting are
permitted, although the famous Yakuza groups sometimes disturb the
peace by gunfight quarrels among themselves. This limits the criminal
shootings to 230 per year.
- The reader will without doubt expect here a word on the 'Yakuza' gangsters' of Japan. Maybe he has read the book Yakuza, written and supported by seemingly very authoritative American experts on Japan, and
he will then surely believe that the Japanese Yakuza are the same
gun-slinging and drug-handling gangsters we know to be active in the
US and in other parts of the world, and that also Japan is a drug-infested
and gun-infested country. Almost everything I have read in this book is
against what I have seen and experienced during all those long years of
my participating in the life of the Japanese in Japan. To be sure, there
are groups of Yakuza, which are in most cases well organized groups of
construction company workers. I know by personal experience and
contacts that these groups in Tokyo and Osaka efficiently control open

roadside markets and open-air fast-food stands, from which they receive a commission on sales, and that they also operate in the unhealthy and lower sections of the sex-entertainment world. There was also a short period a few years ago when there were internal fights going on between members of two quarrelling groups, with some violence and assassinations as result. I have personally never seen a gun in Japan, and I do not know any Japanese who is in possession of a gun or even a pocket knife. Drug dealing is a very, very limited business, and can in no way be compared even with what is going on in Europe. I have also never seen any violence on Japanese streets in daylight or at night, and know by experience that the Tokyo and Osaka streets are completely safe even for a girl alone at night.

Negative Points
- Almost no bicycle road and very few footpaths. Lack of space (80% of the country is mountainous territory with a population density of 360 per square kilometre) is the main problem of Japan and if there are problems, they can in most cases be understood by this lack of space with which they have learned to live. As an emergency measure, bicycles are allowed since some years to use the footpaths in the cities.
- Electric and telephones cables are overhead, which is a thorn in the eyes of all photographers and which surely does not improve the sight of Japanese towns and cities. Since around 1985 the underground laying of the cables has started in the bigger cities and on the main streets of smaller towns, and is used as a means to improve the footpaths where the poles have been an obstacle for the pedestrians and for car and truck traffic in the smaller towns and villages for so many years. Most footpaths in the cities are bordered with metal bumpers, mainly as security protection for the children on their way to school.
- The density of population (Tokyo and its suburbs, 100 x 50 Km, has a population of about 45 million !) means an unbelievable occupation density on all public traffic systems in the rush hours in cities like Tokyo and Osaka, which looks like an almost unsolvable situation for still many years to come. What would mean revolution in Western countries, is being accepted by the Japanese with a "Shikata ga nai" it can't be helped.
- What is lacking on the side of Japan, as the second economic world power, is a more clearly pronounced striving to uphold to the world at large the basic ideas of its society "harmony in mutual respect", "common good above private interests", and the attitude of "Go and Learn". The action-image of Japan to the outside world should be one for peace and for union in collaboration, first in collaboration with the other eastern governments to upheld and defend their own ways of life, and from that basis come to an enriching dialogue with the countries of the West

and of the African continent. The various Faith Communities of Japan should first of all come to a union in collaboration among themselves in order to enable them to play their appropriate representative role in the religious and in the political world.

*   *   *

20. Buddhism and Hinduism monotheistic

Here I present as closing feature a subject which might still be rather controversial and will have to be studied and tackled by theologians and other experts in this field, asking whether Buddhism and Hinduism could not be conceived as monotheistic religions. In my opinion, accepting this concept would enlarge the scale of the Christian ecumenical movement by including Buddhism and Hinduism as participants in the dialogue meetings of the three up to now so-called monotheistic religions, Christianity, Islam and Judaism.

Buddhism

It can be said of Buddhism that there is an overall acceptance by Buddhist in general of a Spiritual Ultimate Reality as the origin and the final destination of all human beings as well as of all living and all other material things, of which the Buddha has been the main prophet. Just like in Hinduism, the multitude of Saints (gods, bodhisatvas) can be considered as historical representations of deeply religious human beings who are being revered more as Saints than as 'gods'.

According to Buddhism and more in particular to the Zen schools, insight into and understanding of oneself and of the universe by intuition, feeling, direct apprehension, is much more important than reasoning. The Chinese yin-yang relatedness of all things is inherent in the way of looking at the material and spiritual aspects of our world by Buddhist believers. *Prajna* (intuition) in contrast with *Vijnana* (reasoning discrimination) plays a more than primordial role in the philosophical/religious interpretation of the teachings of the old Zen masters in China and in Japan.

A second concept, which is relevant in most interpretation of the teachings of Buddhism, is the relatedness of all things. All is nothing, nothing is all. Emptiness is fullness. Fullness is emptiness. The Divine is no-thing, the Divine is all. This concept of relatedness is expressed, according to our western ways of the reasoning mind, in seemingly contradictory ways of expressions and explanations. A Western Buddhism, since some years in full expansion, will have to find a reasonably acceptable foundation and interpretation for these kind of contradictions.

The main aim of Zen-meditation is to empty the self from all worldly attachments so that the Self can enter. The self is the Self. Never is there any mention of the divine nor does the word God, with our western meaning of a personal being, exist in Buddhism. Buddha himself simply refused to answer questions related to the Ultimate Reality. What however can the "nirvana-enlightenment, which is described as the ultimate of insight and of understanding of Truth, mean if it has nothing to do with complete happiness and with love, as the highest expression of the human life in its fullness and therefore of the Divine Ultimate Reality?

Christians and Jews too must realize that their concept of God, even when God is thought of as a spirit, is only a picturization. According to their picture God is a person, a father, a mother. God is a forgiver, a creator (maker), a king with a kingdom. God is a judge, a rewarder, a punisher, who talks (in revelation), listens (in prayer), is offended (when humans sin). The Holy Trinity is a western concept of the Divine. In any discussion on theism and atheism, Jews and Christians should never forget that their concept of God is thus composed of pictures borrowed from behavioral patterns of human beings, and that its inner content is more complex than they ordinarily take it to be. There is probably no concept more difficult to analyze than that of God. Whitehead is quite right when he says: Today there is but one religious dogma in debate: What do you mean by "God"? In this respect, today is like all yesterdays. This is the fundamental religious dogma, and all other dogmas are subsidiary to it [Whitehead, 68].

Hereby as corroboration of considering Buddhism as a monotheistic religion, just a few indications of this acceptance of a Spiritual Ultimate Reality.

From "Buddhism Made Plain", Antony Fernando, Sanchar Kendra, India, 1985 :

But in the original usage of Gautama, the rabbis, and Yeshua, nirvana and the reign of God are realities that pertain primarily to an individual's life here and now. They designate the fullness of the humanhood that individuals can achieve at this moment. They both describe the state of mind of fully awakened individuals or of persons fully liberated from their personality weaknesses. p.132

Many others who today worship God or gods have concepts of divinity very different from that of the Christian and the Jew. Some concepts found in India, for example, may be mentioned as illustrations.

God can be male (Krishna) or female (Parvati). The idea of a mothergoddess was a very popular belief in ancient India. A god can be married; Vishnu is married to Lakshmi. He may have one wife or several wives; god Katarangama has two wives. A god can be pictured as having several heads and hands (Sivanataraja) or as a human being with some animal features.

The god Ganesha is shown as having an elephant face, and the god Hanuman, a monkey face. God can be a person or an impersonal reality. The At-man-Brahman, or the world-soul of the Hindus, is impersonal.

The Judeo-Christian idea of God may present a more evolved and more refined version of God, but still it remains only one among many ways in which humanity pictures to itself the unseen, unheard transcendental Reality. p.124

Gautama's question is not about whether God exists or not, but whether belief in God has any relevance to the immediate problems of humanity. In that sense he cannot really be called an agnostic. It is true that like the agnostic he ignores the fact of God's existence. Nevertheless, his attitude toward God differs from that of the ordinary agnostic. The agnostic adopts an attitude of indifference, but Gautama is neither indifferent nor unconcerned. He is very concerned, but the object of his concern is humanity and its liberation, not God. Had he seen any recognizable link between human liberation and the concept of God, Gautama would have been the first to include the worship of God in his system of liberation. p.120

There is thus a conspicuous difference between Gautama's objections to belief in God and those of the traditional atheist and agnostic. His argument against God is not leveled against religion. On the contrary, it is in the very name of religion, and as an attempt to save religion, that he omits the concept of God. Differently expressed, Gautama tells the believer in God: let us avoid the confusing and controversial concept of God, of divinity, and let us immediately work toward the divinization of humanity. p.120

In examining the critical attitude of the prophets and Yeshua, and many of his fellow Jews, there is revealed a common bond between Gautama on the one hand, and the prophets and Yeshua on the other, in the stand each of them took against the theism of their day. Unanimously, they condemned the false theism that prevailed in the societies to which they belonged. The prophets, Yeshua, and his fellow Jews, of course, did not go so far as Gautama in completely rejecting the idea of God, but all were at one in their conviction that there is an utterly meaningless form of theism that is destructive to the personality. They were at one in affirming that the best and the most needed form of the worship of God is that expressed by sublimity of character or a life of goodness. p.120

From "Studies in Zen", by the world-famous Dr. D.T. Suzuki, The Anchor Press, UK., 1955, 1957. one of the many books trying to interpret Zen and Zen-meditation :

Each unit is associated with another unit singly and with all other units collectively in a net-like fashion.(p.121)

There must be something of subject in object, and something of object in subject, which makes their separation as well as their relationship possible.

p.93-94
When a blade of grass is lifted, the whole universe is revealed there; in every pore of the skin there pulsates the life of the triple world, and this is intuited by prajna, not by way of reasoning but "immediately". p.94
But as our minds always demand an interpretation, we may say this: not unity in multiplicity, not multiplicity in unity; but unity is multiplicity and multiplicity is unity. In other words, prajna (intuition) is vjnana (reasoning, discrimination) and vijnana is prajna, immediately apprehended. p.95
Prajna vision includes the totality of things, not as a limited continuum, but as going beyond the boundlessness of space and the endlessness of time. Prajna is a unifying principle. p.122
To trace the tracelessness of the Zen mater's life is to have an "unknown knowledge" of the ultimate reality. p.151
In reply to a question from a monk "What do we have after the mirror is polished", the reply is "The ancient mirror". Dr. Suzuki explains: The ancient mirror is the ultimate reality, the Godhead, the mind, the undifferentiated totality. p.160
...Zen's business is to make us realize that philosophizing does not exhaust the human urge to reach the ultimate. p.189
...scholars were in doubt as to the possibility of the Buddha-nature being present in all beings regardless of their sentiency or consciousness, while the philosopher in question was convinced that every being, man or no-man, was in possession of the Buddha-nature. p.195

From "SHINRAN, An Introduction to his Thought", by Yoshifumi Ueda and Dennis Hirota, Hongwanji International Center, 1989:
Shinran states: The realm of nirvana refers to the place where one overturns the delusion of ignorance and realizes the supreme enlightenment ...and Buddha-nature. Buddha-nature is none other than Tathagata. This Tathagata pervades the countless world; it fills the hearts and minds of the ocean of all beings. p.170
For Shinran however, the Pure Land, like Amida Buddha, is in essence the light of wisdom; it is formless, transcending all conceptions of time and space. Thus to enter the Pure land means to realize enlightenment. p.172

From "Boeddha en zijn leer", Hermann Beckh, Christofoor, 1992 :
p. 13: (Own translation) Buddhism never talks about things as something real; Dharma is the spiritual reality, hidden behind things, as revealed to the spiritual eye (dharmacaksus) of the Buddha or saint, the highest spiritual reality like Buddha has viewed it, and which can be attained by the way of meditation.

From "Buddha", Karen Armstrong, Viking/Penguin 2001. From a very extensive bibliography, Armstrong has compiled a life of the Buddha, which makes easy reading almost as a novel, using vivid descriptions founded on the many data in the Buddhist Holy Scriptures, which give also a historically good insight in the cultural and religious background of the Buddha and his first disciples. (560-483BCE). She says: "All sages of the Axial era (800-200 BCE), the Hebrew Prophets in Judea, Zarathustra (Zoroastrianism) in Persia, Mahavira (Jainism) and Gauthama Siddhartha (the Buddha) in India, Confucius and Lao Tse in China, Socrates, Plato and Aristoteles in Greece, were convinced that there was an absolute reality that transcended the confusions of this world – God, Nirvana, the Tao, Brahman – and sought to integrate it within the conditions of daily life". "The yogins believed that they would at last become one with their true Self, which was Unconditioned, Eternal and Absolute."

Hinduism

From the studies of the Indian 'holy' scriptures, it is now evident that one can find in them a general acceptance of the existence of an Ultimate Spiritual Reality in a kind of Holy Trinity of Brahma, Vishnu and Krishna, and of which the other multitude of Saints (gods) are an expression or emanation of the Ultimate Reality in their different forms and expressions. This means that next to Sikhism, which is already considered as a monotheistic religion, also Hinduism can now be considered not so much as a pantheistic religion but can be brought under the umbrella of monotheistic religions. I quote a text from   "In Search of the Cradle of Civilization" by George Feuerstein, Subbash KAK and David Frawley, The Theosophical Publishing House, 1995, p. 31:   *"Max Müller, (the well known interpreter and translator of Hindu Sanskrit texts - author's note) even coined a new term – henotheism -in order to explain the tendency of the Vedas to ascribe supremacy now to one deity and later to another, as if they were perfectly interchangeable, saw this as a form of religiosity hovering between polytheism and monotheism. However the teaching of many deities who are simultaneously one is the same idea found in later Hinduism, where deities like Brahma, Vishnu, Shiva, and their consorts are all deemed aspects of the same supreme reality, the Godhead."*.

I quote hereunder some corroborative extracts, from Wikipedia, the free encyclopedia.
Hinduism is monotheistic and is inclusive monotheism. All personal forms of God are Saguna Brahman. Hindus worship the personal form of God or Saguna Brahman as Vishnu or Shiva. They are either adherents of Vaishnavism or Shaivaism, which are monotheistic faiths. A common prayer for Hindus and Vaishnavas in particular, is the Vishnu Sahasranama or 1000 names of God. To understand Hinduism, in more detail, which has been so

misunderstood, please see the web site,
  www.hinduism-today.com/archives/2003/10-12/44-49_four_sects.shtml.
Hinduism is confusing to the outsider because there are celestial deities such
as devas, or called gods which are subordinate to Brahman or God.

Hinduism is really considered a broad monotheistic religion by Murli
Nagasundaram, Ph.D., in his *Boise Statesman,* Oct. 8 2001, p.
Local 8 :
If this is accepted, then one should include Hinduism in that set; it is a
religion at least as old as the oldest of the Abrahamic religions and counts
over 800 million persons among its members. Yes, that is correct: Hinduism
is a monotheistic religion. A misconception of the religion has caused it to be
portrayed in much of the West as being polytheistic. It takes a deep under-
standing of the religion – which is based on a completely different paradigm
than that of the Abrahamic religions – to appreciate this fact. While some
Hindus are atheists, and many are agnostic, and others are animists, most
believe in a god, and in fact exactly One God (even the atheists, animists and
agnostics).

From a 15-pages text on Hinduism, by Dr. C.P. Ramaswami Aiyar, Dr.
Nalinaksha Dutt, Prof. A.R. Wadia, Prof. M. Mujeeb, Dr. Dharm Pal and Fr.
Jerome D'Souza, s.j.
Every variety of Hindu philosophy has its source in the Upanisads, the
Brahma Sutras of Badarayana of Vyasa and the Bhagavad-Gita which forms
a part of the Mahabharata. It was as a reaction to the tendencies exhibited by
Buddhism and Jainism that the orthodox schools of Indian philosophy had
their origin and the Bhagavad-Gita is their epitome.
    This work contains the essence of Indian teaching about the duties of life
as well as spiritual obligations. Everyone has his allotted duties of various
kinds. Sin arises not from the nature of the work itself but from the disposition
with which the work is performed. When it is performed without attachment
to the result, it cannot tarnish the soul and impede its quest. True Yoga
consists in the acquisition of experience and the passage through life in
harmony with the ultimate laws of equanimity, non-attachment to the fruits of
action, and faith in the pervasiveness of the Supreme Spirit. Absorption in
that Spirit can be attained along several paths; and no paths to be preferred
exclusively and none to be disdained. P.5
    Later followers of Ramanuja included a number of scholars who
sustained his philosophic system through the centuries. While accepting the
set rituals of initiation and worship, they admitted Jains, Buddhists, Sudras
and Harijans into their fold. A celebrated successor of Ramanuja was
Nimbarka, who lived about the same time as Madhvacarya. P.9
    According to his philosophy, which is a type of Bhedabhedavada, that is,

the theory of the Absolute as Unity-in-difference, Brahman or the Absolute has transformed itself into the world of matter and spirit. As the Life-force, Prana manifests itself in the various cognitive sense functions, and yet keeps its own independence, integrity and difference, so the Brahman also manifests itself through the numberless spirits and matter, without losing itself in them. As the spider spins its web out of itself and yet remains independent of the web, so the Brahman splits itself up into numberless spirits and matter but retains its fullness and purity.

One of the important Saivite sects known as Virasaiva was founded by a Brahmin named Basava, who was for some time the minister of a ruler in Kalyan. The Basava Purana outlines Basava's life. This, as also Basava's own writings in Kannada, describes the fundamentals of a doctrine based on rigid monotheism, Shiva being regarded as the supreme, limitless and transcendent entity. Brahmana is the identity of "being", "bliss" and consciousness, and devoid of any form of differentiation. It is limitless and beyond all ways of knowledge. It is self-luminous and absolutely without any barrier of knowledge, passion or power. It is in Him that the whole world of the conscious and the unconscious remains, in a potential form untraceable by our senses, and it is from Him that the whole world becomes expressed or manifest of itself, without the operation of any other instrument. P.11

The great saints of Maharashtra and Bengal created a wonderful literature of Bhakti based on the worship of Rama or of Krishna. Vallabhacarya, in particular, attacked Sankara's Advaita doctrine. He preached that by God's grace alone can man obtain release. Caitanya, a contemporary of Vallabha, and his followers called Goswamis, were itinerant preachers whose sincerity of religious experience brought about a reformation in Bengal. The common features in Bhakti cults have been pointed out by D. S. Sarma in his Renaissance of Hinduism, in ten characteristics of which here the first three:

1. *Belief in one supreme God of Love and Grace.*
2. *Belief in the individuality of every soul, which is nevertheless part of the Divine Soul.*
3. *Belief in salvation through Bhakti.*

From Ven. Vivekananda's speech on occasion of the Interfaith Dialogue Conference of the Parliament of World's Religions, September 11-28, 1893. At the Parliament of Religions meeting in Chicago, Sept. 11-28, 1893, Ven. Swami Vivekananda struck a note of universal toleration based on the Hindu belief that all religions lead to the same God. He also declared in Chicago that the religion of the Hindus is centered on selfrealisation; idols, temples, churches and books are aids and nothing more.

He is everywhere the pure and formless one. The Almighty and the All-merciful. "Thou art our father, thou art our mother; thou art our beloved friend; thou art the source of all strength; give us strength. Thou art he that bearest the burdens of the universe: help me bear the little burden of this life." Thus sang the Rishis of the Veda; and how to worship him – through love. "He is to be worshiped as the one beloved," "dearer than everything in this and the next life."

This is the doctrine of love preached by the Vedas, and let us see how it is fully developed and preached by Krishna, whom the Hindus believe to have been God incarnate on earth. ....

..... On the very outset, I may tell you that there is no polytheism in India. In every temple, if one stands and listens, he will find the worshipers, applying all the attributes of God, including omnipresence, to these images. It is not polytheism, neither would the name henotheism answer our question.

..... The Hindu man is not traveling from error to truth, but from truth to truth, from lower to higher truth. To him all the religions from the lowest fetichism to the highest absolutism mean so many attempts of the human soul to grasp and realize the Infinite, determined by the conditions of its birth and association, and each of these mark a stage of progress, and every soul is a child eagle soaring higher and higher; gathering more and more strength till it reaches the glorious sun.

....Thus it is that the Vedas proclaim not a dreadful combination of unforgiving laws, not an endless prison of cause and effect, but that at the head of all these laws, in and through every particle of matter and force, stands One, "by whose command the wind blows, the fire burns, the clouds rain and death stalks upon the earth." And what is His nature?

He is everywhere, the pure and formless One, the Almighty and the All-merciful. "Thou art our father, Thou art our mother, Thou art our beloved friend, Thou art the source of all strength; give us strength. Thou art He that beareth the burdens of the universe; help me bear the little burden of this life." Thus sang the Rishis of the Veda. And how to worship Him? Through love. "He is to be worshiped as the one beloved, dearer than everything in this and the next life." This is the doctrine of love declared in the Vedas, and let us see how it is fully developed and taught by Krishna whom the Hindus believe to have been God incarnate on earth.

He taught that a man ought to live in this world like a lotus leaf, which grows in water but is never moistened by water; so a man ought to live in the world – his heart to God and his hands to work. It is good to love God for hope of reward in this or the next world, but it is better to love God for love's sake; and the prayer goes: "Lord, I do not want wealth nor children nor learning. If it be Thy will, I shall go from birth to birth; but grant me this, that I may love Thee without the hope of reward – love unselfishly for love's sake." One of the disciples of Krishna, the then Emperor of India, was driven from his kingdom by his enemies and had to take shelter with his queen, in a forest in the Himalayas and there one day the queen asked how it was that he, the most virtuous of men, should suffer so much misery. Yudhishthira answered, "Behold, my queen, the Himalayas, how grand and beautiful they are; I love them. They do not give me any- thing but my nature is to love the grand, the beautiful, therefore I love them. Similarly, I love the Lord. He is the source of all beauty, of all sublimity. He is the only object to beloved; my nature is to love Him, and therefore I love. I do not pray for any-thing; I do not ask for anything. Let Him place me wherever He likes. I must love Him for love's sake. I cannot trade in love." The Vedas teach that the soul is divine, only held in the bondage of matter; perfection will be reached when this bond will burst, and the word they use for it is, therefore, Mukti – freedom, freedom from the bonds of imperfection, freedom from death and misery...the Christian is not to become a Hindu or a Buddhist, nor a Hindu or a Buddhist to become a Christian. But each must assimilate the spirit of the others and yet preserve his individuality and grow according to his own law of growth.

And last but no least, in his essay "A Hindu Perspective" on Sharing Wisdom, on occasion of the Elijah Board of World Religious Leaders Meeting in Amritsar, India, November 26-30, 2007, Prof. Anantanand Rambachan says about Hinduism: *Although the infinite God is the true end of all human longing, the fullness of being that all seek, the tradition has admitted consistently that God transcends all limited human efforts at definition and description. The Taittiriya Upanishad (2.9.1) speaks of the Infinite as "that from which all words, along with the mind, turn back, having failed to grasp." The Kena Upanishad (2:3) expresses the impossibility of comprehending the infinite as one does a limited object by delighting in the language of paradox:It is a central Hindu conviction that our words are inadequate and that the One is always more than we could define, describe or understand with our finite minds. A God whose nature and essence could be fully revealed in our words or who could be contained within the boundaries of our minds would not be the One proclaimed in our traditions. The often quoted Rg Veda (1.64.46) text: "The One Being the wise call by many names.*

*   *   *

The long way we have come in the evolution of our world of today and in particular in the religious world, as described in most of the above texts, can be understood by looking at some statements uttered, one century ago in 1893 on occasion of the first international dialogue meeting of the Parliament of World's Religions on September 11-28, 1893 in Chicago:
1) from the speech "The Ultimate Religion", by the Rev. John Joseph Keane, Catholic:
... In the first place, this comparison of all the principal religions of the

world has demonstrated that the only worthy and admissible idea of God is that of monotheism. It has shown that polytheism in all its forms is only a rude degeneration. It has proved that pantheism in all its modifications, obliterating as it does the personality both of God and of man, is no religion at all, and therefore inadmissible as such; that it cannot now be admitted as a philosophy, since its every first postulates are metaphysical contradictions. Hence the basis of all Religion is belief in the one living God....

His concluding sentence: *Jesus Christ is the ultimate center of Religion. He has declared that his one organic church is equally ultimate. Because I believe him, here must be my stand forever.*

2) from the speech of Rev. George Dana Boardman, Baptist, "Christ the Unifier of Mankind":

.... Thus the Son of Man, by his own incarnation, by his own teachings, by his own death, by his own immortality, is most surely unifying mankind. And the Son of Man is the sole unifier of mankind. Buddha was in many respects a very noble character; no Buddhist can offer him heartier reverence than myself. But Buddha and his religion are Asiatic; what has Buddha done for the unity of mankind? Why are we not holding our sessions in fragrant Ceylon? Mohammed taught some very noble truths; but Mohammedanism is fragmental and antithetic; why have not his followers invited us to meet at Mecca? But Jesus Christ is the universal man and therefore it is that the first Parliament of Religions is meeting in a Christian land, under Christian auspices, Jesus Christ is the sole bond of the human race .....

*   *   *

We are privileged too live in the dawn of a new era in our world's history where confrontation is withdrawing and gradually being replaced by collaboration. Our 21st century is witness to the birth of a new age where the first signs of a new moral global concept are budding. The world village will have the Golden Rule as the global ethic for the common people with as forerunners the world faith communities. This century will also witness the creation of a world forum of the Faith Communities as a most valuable meeting partner to the United Nations, bringing religion and politics on the way of collaboration. May this booklet be a small contribution to this historical process.

ANNEX 1 Main Interfaith Dialogue Organizations in the World

Table: Annex I

Addresses	Tel Fax E-mail
EUROPE	
BELGIUM (country tel. nr. +32, omitting the first '0')	
ARCHDIOCESE MECHELEN-BRUSSELS Wollemarkt 15, 2800 MECHELEN Luk Van Hilst, secretary	015 216.501 015 209.485 aartsbisdom@kerknet.be
AVICENNE GROUP Rue des Coteaux 221, 1030 BRUXELLES Rev. Jean-Matthieu Lochten s.j..	02 216 9901 02 216 9287 jlochten@ulb.ac.be
BAHA'I GEMEENSCHAP Troonstraat 205, 1050 BRUSSELS Guido Cooreman	02 648 5360 02 646 2177 centrebahai@brutele.be
ESPACES BRUSSEL Murillostr. 6, B-1040 BRUSSEL Rev. Jean Claude Lavigne op.	02 733 8458 02 736 9957 espace.s@club.innet.be
EUROPEAN CENTER FOR ETHICS Deberiotstraat 26, 3000 LEUVEN Prof. John A. Dick	016 324.558 016 323.788 john.dick@oce..kuleuven.ac.be
INTERNATIONAL ECUMENICAL FELLOWSHIP Tiensestraat 112, 3000 LEUVEN Prof. A. Denaux, president	016 326 393 016 323 793
SINT-ANDRIESABDIJ Zevenkerken 4, 8200 BRUGGE	050 380.136

Rev. Fernand Van Heuverswijn osb

SINT-EGIDIUSGEMEENSCHAP
Lombardenstr. 28,
2000 ANTWERPEN
Hendrik Hoet, president,
Jan De Volder

03 226 0737
03 231 4837
santegidio@online.be
www.santegidio.org

URI-EUROPE
Coteauxstr. 221
1030 Brussel
Rev. Jean-Matthieu Lochten s.j..

02 2169901
02 2169287
jlochten@ulb.ac.be

WCRP BELGIUM Asrl
2 Avenue Boileau,
1040 Bruxelles
Joseph Agie de Selsaten, president

02 735 0433
02 735 0433
excoser.j.agie@skynet.be

KERKWERK   MULTICULTUREEL
SAMENLEVEN
Pastorijstraat 37, 2050 ANTWERPEN
Didier Vanderslycke

03 235.6482
kms@broederlijkdelen.be

INTERRELIGIEUZE DIALOOG
Lianne De Oude, Dominee
Hasseltse Beverzakstr 240, 3500
Hasselt

011-81 2 3 81
lianne.deoude@vpkb.be

WERKGROEP   INTERRELIGIEUZE
DIALOOG ANTWERPEN
Philippedreef 9, 2970
s' GRAVENWEZEL

03 383.0433

HUMANISTS

EUROPEAN HUMANIST
FEDERATION
Campud de la Plaine
ULB, CP237
B-1050 BRUSSELS
Mr. Claude Wachtelaer, pres.

02 6276890
02 6276801
fhe@ulb.ac.be

ISLAM

EXECUTIEVE VAN DE MOSLIMS IN
BELGIE
Rouppeplein 16, 1000 Brussels
Dr. D.Beyens, president,
Mr. Mohammed Yamouchi

02 648 35 60
02 203 2321
faridelmachaoud@hotmail.com

MOSKEE BRUSSELS

02 735.2173

Jubelpark 14, 1000 BRUSSELS   02 770.9840 (private)
Mr. Dr Omar Van den Broeck

ISLAMITISCH DIALOOG- EN
INFORMATIECE.NTRUM   011 455056
Mr. K. Bahattin   Mobile: 0477420896
Beverlosestwg 444,   islamdialoog@hotmail.com
3582 BERINGEN

TURKS ISLAMITISCHE CULTURELE
VERENIGING GENT, VZW.
Kazemattenstr. 80, 9000 Gent   09-225 1778
Mr. Cemal Gawdarle   09 225 3542
Warandestraat 45, 9000 GENT

UNIE VAN TURKSE
VERENIGINGEN VZW.   03 2899113
Dendermondestr. 36   03 2897710
2018 ANTWERPEN   utvtdb@pandora.be
Aydin Resat, voorzitter

THE NETHERLANDS (+31)

STICHTING TEILHARD DE
CHARDIN
Quarterly : GAMMA   72 533 2690
Op de Wieken 5, 1852 BS HEILOO,   sttdc@worldonline.nl
NEDERLAND   http://home.wprldonline.nl/-sttdc
Mr. Henk Hogeboom van Buggenum,
Chairman

INTERRELIGIEUS BERAAD   70 3648407 / 6   12530887
Amaliastraat 10, 2514 JC   Den Haag   henniedepous@iofc.nl
Hennie de Pous-de Jonge   www.interreligieus.nl

WERKGROEP   INTERRELIGIEUZE
SAMENWERKING   70-364 4590
Anna Paulownastraat 78, NL-2518 BJ -3614846
DEN HAAG   eml:jehms@globalxs.nl
Dhr. Wite L.W.Carp

URI-BELGIUM-NETHERLANDS
REGIONAL COMMITTEE   40-2125984
Van der Lansstraat 2, NL-5644 TA 40-2125984
EINDHOVEN   imbensan@worldacCE.ss.nl
Mrs Annie Imbens

DIOCESAAN
MISSIESECRETARIAAT BREDA   76-561 4916
Fatimastraat 5, NL-4834 XT BREDA   76-560 1983

Dhr. Eric Joris

Rev. Hamva Zeid-Kalaini (Imam)	-2948471
Dickenslaan 16-2, NL-3533 UTRECHT	-2948471

FRANCE (+33)

EUROPEAN PEACE. UNIVERSITY
51, Bois Chatton,   5042-7306
F-01210 VERSONNEX   5042-7506
Prof. Johan Galtung

FRATERNITE D'ABRAHAM
18, rue des Graviers,
F-92200 NEUILLY/SEINE   14747 4057
Mr. Emile Moatti (also WCRP)

INSTITUT DES SCIENCES ET
THEOLOGIE DES RELIGIONS (ISTR)   49-030373
(Revue: Chemins de Dialogue)   491 411692 ?
38, rue Paul Coxe,   49-030375
F-13015 MARSEILLE
Rev. Jean Marc Aveline

ORGANIZATION DES TRADITIONS
UNIES   47925-5490
7808 Hameau St. Hugon, 73110   47925-7573
ARVILLARD   karmaling@karmaling.org
Rev. Lama Denis Teundroup (Institut
Karma Ling)

UNITED TRADITIONS   47608-4724
ORGANIZATION   uto@unitedtraditions.org
7808 Hameau St. Hugon,   jeanchristian@wanadoo.fr
F-73110 ARVILLARD   www.unitedtraditions.org
Jean Christian Gunsett, gen.secr.

GERMANY (+49)

A CENTRE FOR THE WORLD
RELIGIONS e.V,   7764 93970
Saegestr. 37   7764 939739
D-79737 HERRISCHIED   steea@t-online.de
Mrs. Anke Kreutzer

CHRISTLICH-ISLAMISCHE
GESELLSCHAFT e.V. (CIG)   221-781411
(Christian-Islamic Society)   221-781411
Im Wichemshof 36,   chrislages@aol.com
D-50769 KÖLN

Klaus Schuenemann, gen.secr.

DEUTSCHE MUSLIM LIGA Bonn e.V.
(German Muslim-League Bonn)   228-330915
15, Hans-Boeckler Allee,   228- 330915
D-53177 BONN   dmlbonn@aol.com
Sheik Bashir Ahmad Dultz, Pres.

Co-founder of the German Muslim-League
Hamburg and of the Ce.ntral Coucil of
Muslims in Germany;   http://members.aol.com/dmlbo
Muslim Team-Leader of the JCM   nn/welcome.html
Ammerdown,UK; member of the WCRP,
URI-European Exec. Committee,WPR; a/o.

EUROPEAN BUDDHIST UNION
Buddha House, Uttenbühl, D-87433 OY 14568-4800
MITTELBERG   14568-5588
Mr. Heinz Roiger

GLOBAL ETHIC FOUNDATION   7071-62646
Prof. Dr. Hans Küng, president,   7071-610140
Prof.Dr. Karl-Josef Kuschel,   office@stiftung-weltethos.
vice-president.   uni-tuebingen.de
Waldhäuser Str. 33,   www.uni-tuebingen.de/stiftung-welte
D-72076 TÜBINGEN   thos

ITALY (+39)

CE.NTRO FRANCE.SCANO
INTERNAZIONALE   75-815193
Circonvallazione Aurelia 50, I-06081 75-815197
ASSISI
Rev. Maximilian Mizzi

PONTIFICAL COUNCIL FOR
DIALOGUE BETWEEN THE
RELIGIONS   6689-84321
Via dell'Erba, 1, 00193   ROMA   6689-84494
President Cardinal Paul Poupard   pcid-office@interelg.va
Msgr. Pier Luigi Celata, secretary

ROMANIA (+40)

CENTRUL INT'L ECUM.PENTRU
DIALOGUE SPIRITUAL   1-8158377
Calea Calarasiloc 83, RO-BUCARESTI 3 1-3127432
Rev. Stan   Alexandru   (Orthodox)

HUNGARY (+36)

MANREZA CONFERENCE. CE.NTER
Feny Utca 1,   26-347681
HU-2099 DOBOGOKO   26-347633
Rev. Szabolcs Sajgo, s.j..

SWITZERLAND (+41)

BAHA'I INTERNATIONAL COMMUNITY   22-7985400
United Nations OffiCE., Route des Morillons 22-7986577
15,   bic@geneva.bic.org
CH-1218 Grand-Saconnex (Geneva)

PAX ROMANA   37-227482
Rue des Alpes, 7 BP 1062,   37-227483
Mr. Mauricio Molina

WORLD COUNCIL OF CHURCHES
150 Route de Ferney
POB2100, H-GENEVA 2   22-791611
Rev. Dr Samuel Kobia, Gen. Secretary   22-7910361
Rev. Hans Ucko, editor of the quarterly   hu@wcc-coe.org
Current Dialogue.

UNITED KINGDOM (+44)

BRAHMA KUMARIS UK   181-4591400
Global Co-operation House   181-451648
65 Pound Lane, UK-LONDON NW 102HH   bk@bkwsugch.demoCEo.uk
Sister Maureen Goodman

INTERNATIONAL INTERFAITH
CENTRE(IIC)   1865-202745
2 Market Street, UK-OXFORD OX1 3EF   1865-202746
Dr. Joy Barrow   iic@interfaith-CE.nter.org

INTERNATIONAL ASSOC. FOR   1865-202744
RELIGIOUS FREEDOM (IARF)   1865-202746
2 Market Street, UK-OXFORD OX1 3EF   iarf@interfaith-CE.nter.org
Mr. ......, Chair

THE INTER FAITH NETWORK FOR THE
UK   20 79317766
8A Lower Gosvenor Place,   1865-877968
London SW1W 0DN   ifnet@interfaith.org.uk
Mr. Brian Pearce

THE ISLAMIC FOUNDATION   1530-244944
Markfield Conference Centre   1530-244946
Ratby Lane, Markfield, UK-LE67 9RN

LEICESTERSHIRE
Prof. Ataoullah Siddiqui

UNITED RELIGIONS INITIATIVE EUROPE 31 Kirk Close, UK-OXFORD OX2 8JL Josef Boehle, European Coordinator	1865-433918 1865-433918 jboehle@compuserve.com
WESTMINSTER INTERFAITH ORGANIZATION 2 Church Avenue, Southhall, UK-MIDDX.UB2 4DH	181-8340690 181-8340690
THE MULTIFAITH CENTRE University of Derby, Kendleston Road, Derby, DE22 1GB Dr. Paul Trafford	1332-591285 1332 622772 paul@chezpaul.org.uk www.multifaithnet.org
THREE FAITHS FORUM - for Muslim -Christian-Jewish Dialogue. . Star House, 104 Grafton Road, London NW5 4BD Mr Sidney L. Shipton OBE	020 7485 2538 (Ext 5) 020 7485 4512 threefaiths@sternberg-foundation. co.uk www.threefaithsforum.org.uk
WORLD CONGRESS OF FAITHS (WCF) 125 Salusbury Road, London, NW6 6RG, UK Chair: Rabbi J Tabick Quarterly: Interreligious INSIGHT	1865-202751 1865-244096 info@worldfaiths.org r.boeke@virgin.net www.worldfaiths.org
UNITED RELIGIONS INITIATIVE UK Eskdale Vicarage, Boot UK-CUMBRIA CA19 1TF Malcolm Stonestreet	19467 23242 870 0205577 19467 23142 judith@mconf.edi.co.uk
WORLD FAITHS DEVELOPMENT DIALOGUE (WFDD) c/o The International Study Centre , The Precincts, Canterbury Kent CT1 2EH	wfdd@btinternet.com www.wfdd.org.uk
EUROPEAN COUNCIL OF RELIGIOUS LEADERS (ECRL) C/O WCRP, 18/20 Vale Road, Herts, Bushey, WD2 2HE, UK Jehangir Sarosh,	(0)1923 211168 1923 211169 wcrp@mrj.co.uk
Minorities of Europe Legacy House, 29 Walsgrave Road, Coventry, CV2 4HE, UK.	24 7622 5764. 247622 5764 deepak@gnaik.freeserve.co.uk

www.moe-online.com/

AMERICA (+1)

USA

INTERFAITH CENTER OF NEW YORK
20 East 79th Street
New York, N.Y. 10021
Rev. James Parks Morton

INTER-RELIGIOUS   FEDERATION   FOR
WORLD PEACE.(IRFWP)
4 West 43rd Street,   irfwp@pipeline.com
USA-NEW YORK, NY10036   Newsletter twiCE. a year
Dr. Thomas G. Walsh (exec.dir. Int'l Religious
Foundation)

INTERNATIONAL RELIGIONS
FOUNDATION   502-6357983
3121 Teal Avenue, Louisville, USA-Kentucky 502-5345671
40213   dhyr17a@prodigy.com
Thomas G. Walsh, Executive Director

MULTIFAITH RESOURCES
POB128, WOFFORD HEIGHTS, CA93285
Rev. Charles White

NORTH AMERICAN INTERFAITH
NETWORK
512 Bedford Road, Armonk, NY 10504 USA
Dr. Peter Laurence., Chair

PARLIAMENT OF THE WORLD'S
RELIGIONS(PWR)   312-6292990
70E. Lake, Suite 205   312-6292991
Illinois, Chicago   60601   program@cpwr.org
Mr. Dirk Ficca , director (Succeeded Jim   www.cpwr.org
Kenney)

UNITED RELIGIONS INITIATIVE (URI)
Presidio Bldg., 1009 POB 29242   415-5612300
SAN FRANCISCO CA 94129-0242   415-5612313
Rev. Bishop William E. Swing, Episcopal office@united-religions.org
California Diocese   www.united-religions.org
Rev. Charles Gibbs, exec.director

THE TEMPLE OF
UNDERSTANDING(TOU)   212 573-9224
211 East 43rd Street, Suite 1600   212 5739225

New York, NY 10017
Sr. Joan Kirby

jkirby@templeofunderstanding
.org

INTERNATIONAL COMMITTEE FOR THE
PEACE COUNCIL
2702 International Lane, Suite 108
Madison, Wisconsin 53704 USA

608 241-2200
608 241-2209
icpc@peacecouncil.org
http://www.peacecouncil.org/

IINTERNATIONAL COUNCIL OF
CENTRAL NEW YORK
3049 E. Genesee Street Syracuse NY 13224
Mr. Bob Hanson, exec.dir.,

315-4493552
315-4493103
bhanson@powerfcu.net

INTERNATIONAL COUNCIL OF
CHRISTIANS AND JEWS
Martin Buber House
P.O. Box 11 29, 64629 Heppenheim,
Germany
Head office in the USA
Gen. Secr.: Fr. Prof. John Pawlikowski,
O.S.M., USA

6252.93120
6252.68331
info@iccj-buberhouse.de

MILLENNIUM WORLD PEACE SUMMIT
OF RELIGIOUS AND SPIRITUAL
LEADERS
Empire State Building
350 Fifth Avenue, Suite 5403
New York, NY 10118, USA
Mr. Bawa Jain

212 967 2891
212 967 2898
info@millenniumpeacesummit.
org
b.jain@wcorl.org
www.millenniumpeacesummit.
org

WORLD CONFERENCE. OF RELIGIONS
FOR PEACE.(WCRP)
777 United Nations Plaza, New York, NY
10017
Dr. William Vendley

212-6872163
212-983-0566
wcrp@wrj.co.uic (?)

SOUTH AMERICA

United Nations Spiritual Forum for World
Peace Initiative
Via Verde 9440, (Lo Curro) Vitacura,
Santiago, Chile,

SOUTHEAST-ASIA

BANGLADESH (+880)

INTER-RELIGIOUS COUNCIL FOR
PEACE. & JUSTICE.
14/20, Iqbal Road,

2 9141410
2 8122010
bicpaj@bigjoy.net

DHAKA 1207
Brother Jarlath D'Souza, CSC

INDIA (+91)

NATIONAL COUNCIL OF CHURCHES
IN INDIA
Christian Council Campus,
Civil Lines, POB 205
NAGPUR 440 001 (M.S.)INDIA
Rev.Dr.Joseph Ipe, gen.secr.

712-531312
712-520554
ncciindia@bom4.vsnl.net.in

MADURAI KAMARAJ UNIVERSITY
Department of Interreligious Relations
3, Vallabai Road,
MADURAI 625 002
Prof. Dr. A. Pushparajan

452-537542
Priv.-481056
452-566630/
452-481056
pura@eth.net

THE HENRY MARTYN INSTITUTE OF
ISLAMIC STUDIES
5-8-660/1/B/1, Chirag AliLane,
HYDERABAD 500 001 POB153
Dr. Andreas D'Souza

40-201134
40-203954
hmiis@hd1.vsnl.net.in

Rev.Dr. Rosario Gomez, s.j..
168 Janaki Nagar
CHENNAI 600 087

442 2777

gltc@vsnl.com

NATIONAL INST. OF
VALUE-EDUCATION FOR PEACE.
(DHARMA BHARATHI)
P.B No.150, 35-Saket Nagar,
Indore 452001, M.P.
Rev. Varghese Alengaden

731-564211
731-524339
dharma@sancharnet.in

http://www.dharmabharathi.o
rg

DR.ALEXANDER MAR THOMA
CE.NTRE FOR DIALOGUE
S-55, J.P.Nagar, Railway Station
P.O.,Tiruvalla, Kerala 689111
Prof.Dr. Abraham Karickam

473 601118
474 454087

SRI LANKA (+94)

INTER-CULTURAL RESEARCH
CENTRE
21G4 Peramura Mawata,
Edeniya-Kadawatha
Prof. Antony Fernando

1 925359
1 925359
inculture@eureka.lk

INTER RELIGIOUS PEACE. FOUNDATION Sri Isipathanaramaya, 180/34 Grandpass Rd. SRI LANKA 575987 COLOMBO Ven. Madampagama Assagi Nayako Thero	1 440387 1 446672 nad@sit.lk
CENTRE FOR SOCIETY AND RELIGION 281 Deans rd., Rev. Dr. Oswald Firth, omi Rev. Tissa Balauriya, omi	1 695925 1 688690 csrlibra@slt.lk

INDONESIA (+62)

INDONESIAN COMMITTEE ON RELIGION AND PEACE. Jalan Sukabumi 11 JAKARTA 10310, INDONESIA Lukman Harun, secretary general	21-31555219 21-31552343
INSTITUTE FOR INTERFAITH DIALOGUE IN INDONESIA (DIAN) Banteng Utama 59, Perum Banteng Baru Yogyakarta 55581, Indonesia Mr. A. Sarapung	274 880149 274 880149 dianinterfidei@yahoo.com www.interfidei.or.id

KOREA (R.O.K.) (+82)

SOCIETY FOR INTER-RELIGIOUS DIALOGUE Jl. Imam Bonjol 39, 10310 Jakarta, Indonesia Abdurrahman Wahid, President	21 327478 21 3918529 cutmutiah@dnet.net.id

KOREA (R.O.K.) (+82)

WON BUDDHISM HEADQUARTERS 344-2 Shin Young-Dong CHON BUK, KOREA 570-754 Rev. Kim Sang Ho, Dept. Intl.Affairs	653 503270 653 503270
Rev. Jinwol, Zen Master (Young Ho Lee, Ph.D., URI) Samsobang, Uwon Villa 402 193-120 Changchung-dong 2ga, Ching-ku, SEOUL,	2264 8261 2264 8261 jinwol@cakra.dongguk.ac.kr http://seos.dongguk.ac.kr/uri-korea

KOREA-100-392

THAILAND (+66)

FEDERATION OF ASIAN BISHOPS' CONFERENCES Rev. Brother Edmund Chia, Exec.Secr. 122/6-7 Soi Naaksuwan 10120, THAILAND	2681 5421 2681 5422 edchia@pc.jaring.my
THAI INTER-RELIGIOUS COMMISSION FOR DEVELOPMENT Rev. Sulak Sivaraksa 124 Soi Wat Thongnopakhun, BANGKOK 10600 THAILAND	2 223 4915 2 225 9640 atc@bkk.a-net.net.th sop@ffc.or.th
INTERNAT. NETWORK FOR ENGAGED BUDDHISM (INEB) Rev. Sulak Sivaraksa, managing director P.O.B. 19 Mahadthai Post OffiCE., BANGKOK 10200 THAILAND	2 433 7169 2 433 7169 ineb@Loxinfo.co.th www..bfp.org/ineb.html/
DHAMMA METTA SANTI Rev. Santikaro Bhikkhu C/O Suam Mokkh, Ampoe Chaiya, SURAT THANI 84110 THAILAND	77 431597 santikaro@suanmokkh.org

JAPAN (+81)

HONGWANJI INTERNATIONAL CENTER (Jôdô Shinshû Buddhist Church) Higashi-Nakasuji, Rokujô-sagaru, KYOTO 600, JAPAN Rev. Yasuaki Hayashi, exec.dir.	75 371-5547 -4070
KOMAZAWA UNIVERSITY (Sôtô Buddhist Community) 1-23-1 Komazawa, Setagaya-ku, TOKYO 154, JAPAN Rev. Dr. Yasuaki Nara, president emeritus	3-3418 9002 3-3418 9026
MYÔSHINJI, RINZAI BUDDHIST COMMUNITY (40 temples complex) REI-UN-IN TEMPLE 398 Hanazono, Myôshinjicho, Ukyô-ku, KYOTO 616, JAPAN	75 462 4648 75 4624648

Rev. Shunan Noritake, headpriest

SÔGENJI, RINZAI BUDDHIST COMMUNITY	862 778226
Maruyama 1069	862 766181
OKAYAMA city, Okayama Pref., JAPAN	sogenji@po.harenet.ne.jp
Rev. Shôdo Harada	

THE KONKO CHURCH OF IZUO
3-8-21 Sangenya-Nishi, Taisho-ku,   6-551 0035
OSAKA 551, JAPAN Rev. Yoshinobu 6-553 7073
Miyake, exec.director.

THE OHMOTO FOUNDATION   771-225561
Kameoka city, Kyoto-fu 621-8686, Japan   771-250061
Rev. Mitsuo Yamazaki, Exec.Director   yamazaki@oomoto.or.jp

KUROZUMIKYO (Shinto)
Shintozan Onoue, OKAYAMA,   86 2842121
JAPAN 701-1292   86 2847173
Rev. Munemichi Kurozumi   michi@po.harenet.ne.jp

SHINJI SHUMEIKAI, Fukuoka Ctr.
Fukushige 1-6-7, Nishi-ku,   aac41070@pop17.odn.ne,jp
FUKUOKA-shi, JAPAN

NEAR-EASTERN COUNTRIES

ISRAEL

Elijah Interfaith Institute   +1 (214) 360.9669
10 Caspi St., Talpiot,   +972 (2) 673-3465
Jerusalem   93554   admin@elijah.org.il
Rev. Rabbi Alon Goshen-Gottstein   http://www.elijahinterfaith.or
g

THE ISRAEL INTERFAITH
ASSOCIATION
P.O.B.7739, JERUSALEM   msyuda@mscc.huji.ac.il
Yehuda Stolov, director

JORDAN (+962)

ROYAL INSTITUTE FOR INTER-FAITH   6 618051
STUDIES (RIIFS)   6 618053
P.O. Box 830 562,   wocmes2@riifs.org
Amman 11183, JORDAN
Mr. Baker al-Hiyari,   Secretary General

6 5539471

THE ROYAL ACADEMY FOR ISLAMIC   6 5526471
CIVILAZATION RESEARCH
(Al Albait Foundation)
Albait Jo, Amman 11195, JORDAN
Dr. Nassir El-Din El-Assad, President

IRAN (+98)
INSTITUTE FOR INTERRELIGIOUS
DIALOGUE
No. 38, Tahery St., POBox 15875/5934
Valieasr Ave. Tehran, IRAN
Mr. Arezoo Khosravi
Mr. Seyed Mohammad Ali Abtahi

khosravi@iid.org.ir
iid@iid.org.ir
info@iid.org.ir

22040340021-

Aim of this list is the promotion of exchange of mutual knowledge and of collaboration on a national and supranational level between the organizations active in interfaith dialogue. All readers are kindly invited to complete these lists informing the author, and to fill in the missing coordinates especially in the case of India where there are seemingly more than a hundred of such organizations.

A list of related magazines and/or news letters would also be another step towards the aimed at mutual knowledge and collaboration and to the creation of national and international newsletters. Kindly invited to also supply information on such editions.

PS: on request, copies in A4 size of chapters of this book
will be e-mailed by the author as e-mail attachment.

Buddhism, Baha'i, Indigenous Traditions, Christianity, Hinduism, Islam, Jainism, Judaism, Shintō, Zoroastrianism, Taoism, Sikhism.

Lucien F. Cosijns   Pr. Poppestraat 44, 2640 Mortsel, Belgium
T. +32 3 455.6880   F. +32 2 706 5883   lucien.cosijns@telenet.be
www.interfaithdialoguebasics.be

ANNEX 2 International Interfaith Conferences since 1893

Table: Annex 2

'No human life without a world ethic for the nations;
No peace among the nations without peace among the religions;
No peace among the religions without dialogue among the religions.
(Hans Küng, Global Ethics)

1893.09.	Parliament of the World's Religions**(PWR)**, first world conference in Chicago.
1899.05.18.	International Peace Conference, The Hague, Netherlands.
1900	Foundation of the International Association for Religious Freedom **(IARF)**, UK. Regular conferences have been held all through the century.
1919	Foundation of the International Fellowship of Reconciliation, The Hague, Netherlands.
1921-1926:	"Conversations de Malines", Belgium, between Catholics and Anglicans.
1936	Foundation of World Congress of Faiths **(WCF)**, UK
1945	Creation of the United Nations Organization **(UNO)**, NY, USA.
1948	Foundation of the World Council of Churches (Christian churches: Protestant, Anglican, and Orthodox)**(WCC)**. Switzerland.
1948.10.12.	Universal Declaration of Human Rights
1957	First Indian Interreligious meeting at New Delhi.

1960	Creation of The Temple of Understanding **(TOU)** NY, USA.
1966	The Second Vatican Council's decree "Nostra Aetate", meant a substantial change in attitude of the Catholic Church to other religions, resulting in the erection of a 'Pontifical Council for Inter-Religious Dialogue'.
1968	January : New Delhi International Interfaith Symposium by the Ghandi Peace Foundation. In his introductory speech Dr. Zakir Husain said: 'When the spirit of the Mountain Sermon, the compassion (karuna) of Buddha's wisdom, the Hindu concept of non-violence (ahimsa) and the passion of the Islam for obedience to the will of God can go together, then we shall see what strong powers can be created for peace in the world.'
From 1968 on:	**Interreligious conferences and congresses were organized on a regular basis** by the mentioned organisations, IARF, WCF, WCC, TOU, WCRP.
1970	Kyoto, Japan: foundation of World Conference on Religion and Peace **(WCRP)**. 500 participants, with as speakers Dom Helder Camara, Dr. Eugene Carson Blake for the World Council of Churches, Dr. Nikkyo Niwano for Rissho Kosei Kai, Japan, Thich Nhat Hanh (Tibetan Buddhism). Followed by WCRP world conferences 1974 in Leuven, Belgium; 1979 in Princetown(USA); 1984 in Nairobi with 600 participants from all world religions; 1989 in Melbourne, Australia.
1974	The International Conference for the Encounter of Jews, Christians and Muslims in Europe **(JCM)**, founded in 1972, started their yearly conferences, every year twice for a whole week, in the Hedwig-Dransfeld-Haus at Bendorf, near Koblenz, Germany.
1981.09.10.	Universal Islamic Human Rights Declaration, Islamic World Congress, Dr. Jinnamullah Khan, secretary general.
1983	Universal Peace Conference by the Brahma Kumaris

	(BK) World Spiritual University, India, with declaration of a Charter for Universal peace, followed by five more peace conferences held on Mount Abu, the BK headquarters in India.
1983	The 1983 Ammerdown meeting was convened by the World Congress of Faiths and The Temple of Understanding to seek ways of collaboration between international interfaith organisations.
1985	Ammerdown Conference by WCF and TOU plans to commemorate the 1893 meeting.
1985	The Promise of World Peace, by the Baha'i Universal House of Justice. The "Peace Messenger" award was granted by the UNO in 1987.
1986	Foundation of the North American Interfaith Network **(NAIN)**, USA.
1986.10.27.	Assisi (Italy) prayermeeting on invitation by Pope John Paul II with representatives of all world religions.
1986.11.17-19.	First Muslim-Christian Consultation, organized by the Al-Albait Foundation, Amman, Jordan, followed by another similar consultation in 1987, 1988, 1989, 1993, 1994,1996 and from 1989 followed also by yearly Muslim-Christian symposia with the Pontifical Council for Interreligious dialogue (The Vatican).
1987.03.	Establishment of The Inter Faith Network for the United Kingdom**(IFNUK)**, linking 70 organisations.
1987.08.03-04.	Prayermeeting on Mount Hiei, Kyoto, on invitation by the Buddhist Tendai church, with participation of leaders of the world religions, which meeting has been repeated each year since then.
1988	2nd Ammerdown Conference, in cooperation with IARF, TOU, WCF, and WCRP.
1989	The Christian-Muslim Pentecost Conference (CMPC) started their yearly conferences, sponsored by the Hedwig-Dransfeld-Haus, Bendorf, and the

German Muslim-League Bonn e.V. (DMLBonn), Bonn, Germany.

1989

The Dialogue-Conference Christianity-Islam, organised by the German Muslim-League, Bonn e.V. and the Evangelische Erwachsenbildung im Kirchenkreis an Sieg und Rhein, Siegburg, started their yearly conferences in Maltheserhof, König-swinter-Römlinghoven (near Bonn).

1990

IARF Congress in Hamburg.

1991

Won Buddhist Interreligious meeting in cooperation with IARF, Rep. of Korea,
centenary celebration of the Won Buddhist religion, Founder Sot'aesan.

1991

World Fellowship of Interreligious Councils : Conference in Cochin, India.

1992.09.13-15

Europe, Religions and Peace, at Leuven and Brus-sels, Belgium, organized by Sant-Egidio and the Catholic Diocese of Mechelen-Brussels.

1992

Delhi Conference : Sikhs religion in cooperation with the Council of World's Religions, Unification Church.

1992

Interreligious Conference in Berkeley, San Fran-cisco, by the North American Interfaith Network (NAIN).

1993.08.18-22

Bangalore Conference "Sharing Visions for the Next Century"., Sarva Dharma Sammelana. Organised by the International Interfaith Organizations Coordinat-ing Committee in a unique first global collaboration with four of the main western interfaith organisa-tions: WCF, IARF, IIC and WCRP gathering of 600 people actively engaged in inter-faith work in 28 countries.

1993.08.

World Fellowship of Interreligious Councils : Kanyakumari, India.

1993.08.28-09.05.

On occasion of the Parliament of World's Religions 1993, almost unanimous acceptance by the delegates of the Global Ethic as proposed by Prof. Hans Küng, Tübingen, Germany.

1993.12.	Foundation of the International Interfaith Centre (IIC), UK.
1994	World Conference WCRP in Riva di Garcia, Italy.
1994.12.12-18.	"The Contribution by Religions to the Culture of Peace", Barcelona, Spain, organized by UNESCO, attended by 57 personalities of the main world religions. 'Declaration on the Role of religion in the Promotion of a Culture of Peace'.
1995.07.	Creation of the United Religions Initiative (URI), by the Episcopal Bishop William Swing, Grace Cathedral, San Francisco, USA., as a world project to create a United Religions Organization, besides the UNO., in which all world religions and spiritual movements should be represented. Charter and establishment of the United Religions Organization planned for the year 2000.
1997.04.26.	Creation of the "United Traditions Organization"(UTO), Karma Ling Institute, Lama Denys, Hameau St Hugon, 73110 Arvillard, France.
1997.06.20-22.	"Roads of Faiths" - The Malta Declaration, organized by UNESCO, attended by 25 personalities of the Jewish (6), Christian (10), Muslim (7), Buddhist (1) and Sikh (1) faiths, and 5 of the organizers.
1997.09.	'Universal Declaration of Human Responsibilities' by the InterActive Council, Tokyo, Japan.
1998.03.28-30.	International Interfaith Conference(IIC)annual conference, Westminster College, Oxford.
1998.06.20-26.	United Religions Initiative Global Summit III, Stanford University, near San Francisco.
1999	World Conference WCRP in Amman, Jordan.
1999.03.27-29	IIC Conference in Oxford, UK , Facing the Past, Freeing the Future.
1999.05.11-15.	World Peace Conference, centennial anniversary of a similar conference in 1899 in The Hague, Netherlands, by Stichting Davidhouse, Spiritueel geboortecentrum, Rotterdam, Netherlands.

1999.06.20-26.	United Religions Initiative Global Summit IV, Stanford University, near San Francisco.
1999.06.21-30.	Int'l Coordinating Council in Israel, In the Footsteps of Abraham - a spiritual pilgrimage.
1999.07.29-08.03.	Sorrento Retreat Centre with IIC in Canada. Healing of the Nations: Religious Communities Contributing to Peace and Wholeness.
1999.07.29-08.03.	IARF Congress, Creating an Earth Community: a Religious Imperative, Vancouver, Canada.
1999.10.	Vatican convoked: International Interreligious Assembly "On the Eve of the Third Millennium. Collaboration among the Different Religions". 200 Participants from 20 different religious traditions from 21 different countries.
1999.11.10-14.	Anuvrat Global Organization 4th International Conference on Peace & Nonviolent Action, New Delhi, India
1999.11.25-30.	WCRP Assembly in Amman, Jordan. Global Action for Common Living: Religion in the Next Millennium.
1999.12.01-08.	Council of the Parliament of World's Religions in Capetown, South Africa. A New Day Dawning: Spiritual yearnings and Sacred Possibilities. IIC/CPWR Symposium: Interfaith in Action in a Global Context.
1999.12.31-2000.01.02.	72 Hours of Interfaith Peacebuilding, United Religions Initiative, World-wide events.
2000.01.22-26	World Fellowship of Inter-Religious Councils in Cochin, Kerala, India: "Hope in Harmony". More than 200 participants of all faith communities in India.
2000.03.01-02	Ecumenical Interfaith Conference 2000 at Beltville, USA. The High Priestess: Women & Ministry.
2000.04.08-09.	IIC Conference : Education for Peaceful Living.
2000.06.	Worldwide signing of the United Religions Charter, supported by walking pilgrimages all over the world. 19.11.2000: First European signature at the Unesco

	House, Paris
2000.08.25-28	National Convention on Communal Harmony & Peace Trust, Kanyakumari, India. 200 delegates representing 11 Indian States
2000.09.24-26	"Oceans of Peace", Religions and Cultures in Dialogue, 13th International Meeting, Lissabon, Portugal. Organized by the Saint-Egidio Community. www.santegidio.org/uer/lisbona2000
2001.03.18-20	International Interfaith Network meeting of 14 international interfaith organizations in Oxford, UK.
2001.04.24-25	International Inter-Faith Consultation on Peace, Security & Reconciliation, Freetown, Siera Leone.
2001.09.02-04	"Frontiers of Dialogue. Religions and Civilizations in the new millennium". 400 Religious leaders from the main faith communities, with conferences, open to the public, attended by thousands, Barcelona, Spain, organized by Sant'Egidio.
2002.02.03-07	Interfaith Pilgrimage-Conference at Coimbatore. India, World Fellowship of Inter-Religious Councils (WFIRC), Upasana, + Divyodaya, Coimbatore. Theme: Promises and Challenges of Inter-Religious Dialogue. Contact: upasana_dr@satyam.net.in
2002.06.12-14	Founding Meeting of the World Council of Religious Leaders at Buddhonthon Main Hall, Nakhon Pathom and The United Nations Conference Centre, Bangkok, Thailand. More than 100 religious leaders from around the world representing 13 religions attended. A direct outcome of the Millennium World Peace Summit of Religious and Spiritual Leaders in 2000 in New York.
2002.06.24-28	Asian Conference on Religion and Peace, Yogyakarta, Indonesia. Theme: Asia, The Reconciler, 300 attendants from 20 countries, belonging to the main world religions.:
2002.07.28-08.02	31st World Congress, IARF, Budapest, Hungary. Theme: Religious Freedom: Europe's Story for Today's World.
2002.09.01-03	Sant-Egidio yearly meeting in Palermo, Sicily, Italy.

"Religions and Cultures between Conflict and Dialogue", 465 religious (7 Cardinals, Orthodox Patriarchs, Muslim and Judaic representatives) and political (President of Burundy Pierre Buyoya, Queen Paula of Belgium) personalities, 4000 participants.

2003.04.25-30   St. Petersburg, Russia.Dr. Kamran Mofid, UK. An Interfaith Perspective on Globalisation, Ethics, Spirituality and Religions.

2003.07.27-08.02   Conference under the theme "Religion and Globalization" organized by the Payap University and Payap University's Institute for the Study of Religion and Culture, Chiang Mai, Thailand, co-sponsored by the International Network of Engaged Buddhists and many other organizations from around the world and within Thailand.

2003.12.14-17   Interfaith meeting "Religion, Society and the Other: Hospitality, Hostility and the Hope of Human Flourishing" in Cordoba, Spain, of over 40 religious leaders and scholars from around the world.

2004.07.07-13   Barcelona, Spain, Council for a Parliament of the World's Religions, Theme:
Pathways to Peace: The Wisdom of Listening, The Power of Commitment

2004.07.22   WCPR Symposium "Peace Building in Iraq : the Role of Multi-Religious Cooperation" held in Kyoto, Japan, attended by 180 religious delegates from Japan, Iraq and other countries.

2004.09.04-07   World Prayer Day for Peace, by Sant'Egidio. 15.000 participants among whom 400 representatives from more than ten faith communities.

2004.09.13-17   Africa's Contribution to the Religious and Spiritual Heritage of the World, meeting in Addis Ababa, Ethiopia. 40 Participants from 10 different countries, Christians, Muslims, African traditional religions and spirituality, followers of Candomblé, Orixas and Santeria. Organized by the WCC's Office on Interreligious Relations in cooperation with the Pontifical Council for Interreligious Dialogue.

	World Alliance of Reformed Churches (1875), 24th
2004.0730-08.13	General Council, at Accra, capital of Ghana., attended by 400 delegates from 218 reformed faith communities. The previous General Council took place in 1997 at Debrecen, Hungary, with follow-up events in 1999, 2003 and 2004. See the statement on their website.
2004.12.06-07	Dialogue on Interfaith Cooperation, attended by 124 delegates from different religious traditions from 13 countries including 9 ASEAN members, organized by the Dept. of Foreign Affairs of the Republic of Indonesia and the Dept. of Foreign Affairs and Trade of Australia, in cooperation with the Islamic Central Committee of Muhammadiyah of Singapore.
2005.01.21-25	The World Forum on Theology and Liberation in Porto Alegre, Brazil, attended by180 theologians from all parts of the world (just before the 26-31 January World Social Forum (WSF), organized by ecumenical organizations in Latin America, and supported by international ecumenical bodies including the World Council of Churches (WCC),
2005.06.22	Conference on interfaith Cooperation for Peace United Nations Headquarters This ground-breaking conference was held at the United Nations that brought together government representatives, members of the United Nations system, and religious NGOs. There they discussed the need for strengthened interfaith dialogue and its importance for peacebuilding. The Conference aimed to enhance interfaith cooperation among governments, civil society and the United Nations system, including the promotion of the culture of peace and dialogue among civilizations, and the translation of shared values into action, to achieve sustainable peace in the twenty-first century. This conference was organized by the tripartite convening group composed of Governments: Argentina, Bangladesh, Gambia, Germany, Indonesia, Iran, Kazakhstan, Morocco, Pakistan, Philippines, Senegal, Spain and Tunisia; UN System

organizations: UNESCO, UN/DESA and the World Bank; and Civil Society led by the Committee of Religious NGOs at the UN, with the Baha'i International Community, Temple of Understanding, United Methodist Church, United Religions Initiative, and World Peace Prayer Society.

2005.06.07-09   CRITICAL MOMENT IN INTERRELIGIOUS DIALOGUE CONFERENCE, organized by the WCC at the Ecumenical Centre, 150 route de Ferney, Switzerland, with 130 participants from more than 10 different faith communities.

2006.02.14-23   Invited by the National Council of Christian Churches (CONIC) (Evangelical Church of Lutheran Confession in Brazil (IECLB), the Anglican Episcopal, Reformed, Methodist, United Presbyterian, Syrian Orthodox and Roman Catholic Churches), the 9th assembly of the World Council of Churches (WCC) will be held in Porto Alegre, Brazil, from 14-23 February 2006. Its theme is a prayer: *"God, in your grace, transform the world"*. The first WCC assembly of the 21st century, it will gather up to 3,000 church leaders and ecumenical representatives from nearly every Christian tradition around the world. As such, it will be one of the broadest global gatherings of its kind.

2007.01.20-25   Over 75,000 participants gathered in Nairobi during the 7th edition of the World Social Forum under the clarion *"People's Struggle's, People's Alternatives"* . It placed social justice, international solidarity, gender equality, peace and defence of the environment on the agenda of the world's peoples.

2007.11.26-30   Elijah Board of World Religious Leaders' meeting in India. The theme for the meeting is: *"Sharing Wisdom: The Case of Love and Forgiveness"*.

ANNEX 3 Declaration of Human Responsibilities

As proposed by the InterAction Council, Tokyo, Japan, 1 September 1997

Introductory Comment

It is time to talk about human responsibilities. Globalization of the world economy is matched by global problems, and global problems demand global solutions on the basis of ideas, values and norms respected by all cultures and societies. Recognition of the equal and inalienable rights of all the people requires a foundation of freedom, justice and peace - but this also demands that rights and responsibilities be given equal importance to establish an ethical base so that all men and women can live peacefully together and fulfill their potential. A better social order both nationally and internationally cannot be achieved by laws, prescriptions and conventions alone, but needs a global ethic. Human aspirations for progress can only be realized by agreed values and standards applying to all people and institutions at all times.

Next year will be the 50th anniversary of the Universal Declaration of Human Rights adopted by the United Nations. The anniversary would be an opportune time to adopt a Universal Declaration of Human Responsibilities, which would complement the Human Rights Declaration and strengthen it and help lead to a better world.

The following draft of human responsibilities seeks to bring freedom and responsibility into balance and to promote a move from the freedom of indifference to the freedom of involvement. If one person or government seeks to maximize freedom but does it at the expense of others, a larger number of people will suffer. If human beings maximize their freedom by plundering the natural resources of the earth, then future generations will suffer.

The initiative to draft a Universal Declaration of Human Responsibilities is not only a way of balancing freedom with responsibility, but also a means of reconciling ideologies, beliefs and political views that were deemed antagonistic in the past. The proposed declaration points out that the exclusive insistence on rights can lead to endless dispute and conflict, that religious groups in pressing for their own freedom have a duty to respect the freedom of others. The basic premise should be to aim at the greatest amount of freedom possible, but also to develop the fullest sense of responsibility that will allow that freedom itself to grow.

The InterAction Council has been working to draft a set of human ethical standards since 1987. But its work builds on the wisdom of religious leaders and sages down the ages who have warned that freedom without acceptance of responsibility can destroy the freedom itself, whereas when rights and responsibilities are balanced, then freedom is enhanced and a better world can be created. The InterAction Council commends the following draft Declaration for your examination and support.

Universal Declaration of Human Responsibilities

Preamble
Whereas recognition of the inherent dignity and of the equal and inalienable rights of all members of the human family is the foundation of freedom, justice and peace in the world and implies obligations or responsibilities,

whereas the exclusive insistence on rights can result in conflict, division, and endless dispute, and the neglect of human responsibilities can lead to lawlessness and chaos,

whereas the rule of law and the promotion of human rights depend on the readiness of men and women to act justly,

whereas global problems demand global solutions which can only be achieved through ideas, values, and norms respected by all cultures and societies,

whereas all people, to the best of their knowledge and ability, have a responsibility to foster a better social order, both at home and globally, a goal which cannot be achieved by laws, prescriptions, and conventions alone,

whereas human aspirations for progress and improvement can only be realized by agreed values and standards applying to all people and institutions at all times,

Now, therefore, the General Assembly proclaims this Universal Declaration of Human Responsibilities as a common standard for all peoples and all nations, to the end that every individual and every organ of society, keeping this Declaration constantly in mind, shall contribute to the advancement of communities and to the enlightenment of all their members. We, the peoples of the world thus renew and reinforce commitments already proclaimed in the Universal Declaration of Human Rights: namely, the full acceptance of the dignity of all people; their inalienable freedom and equality, and their solidarity with one another. Awareness and acceptance of these responsibilities should be taught and promoted throughout the world.

Fundamental Principles for Humanity:

Article 1: Every person, regardless of gender, ethnic origin, social status, political opinion, language, age, nationality, or religion, has a responsibility to treat all people in a humane way.

Article 2: No person should lend support to any form of inhumane behavior, but all people have a responsibility to strive for the dignity and self-esteem of all others.

Article 3: No person, no group or organization, no state, no army or police stands above good and evil; all are subject to ethical standards. Everyone has a responsibility to promote good and to avoid evil in all things.

Article 4: All people, endowed with reason and conscience, must accept a responsibility to each and all, to families and communities, to races, nations, and religions in a spirit of solidarity: What you do not wish to be done to yourself, do not do to others.

Non-Violence and Respect for Life

Article 5: Every person has a responsibility to respect life. No one has the right to injure, to torture or to kill another human person. This does not exclude the right of justified self-defense of individuals or communities.

Article 6: Disputes between states, groups or individuals should be resolved without violence. No government should tolerate or participate in acts of genocide or terrorism, nor should it abuse women, children, or any other civilians as instruments of war. Every citizen and public official has a responsibility to act in a peaceful, non-violent way.

Article 7: Every person is infinitely precious and must be protected unconditionally. The animals and the natural environment also demand protection. All people have a responsibility to protect the air, water and soil of the earth for the sake of present inhabitants and future generations.

Justice and Solidarity

Article 8: Every person has a responsibility to behave with integrity, honesty and fairness. No person or group should rob or arbitrarily deprive any other person or group of their property.

Article 9: All people, given the necessary tools, have a responsibility to make serious efforts to overcome poverty, malnutrition, ignorance, and inequality. They should promote sustainable development all over the world in order to assure dignity, freedom, security and justice for all people.

Article 10: All people have a responsibility to develop their talents through diligent endeavor; they should have equal access to education and to meaningful work. Everyone should lend support to the needy, the disadvantaged, the disabled and to the victims of discrimination.

Article 11: All property and wealth must be used responsibly in accordance with justice and for the advancement of the human race. Economic and political power must not be handled as an instrument of domination, but in the service of economic justice and of the social order.

Truthfulness and Tolerance

Article 12: Every person has a responsibility to speak and act truthfully. No one, however high or mighty, should speak lies. The right to privacy and to personal and professional confidentiality is to be respected. No one is obliged to tell all the truth to everyone all the time.

Article 13: No politicians, public servants, business leaders, scientists, writers or artists are exempt from general ethical standards, nor are physicians, lawyers and other professionals who have special duties to clients. Professional and other codes of ethics should reflect the priority of general standards such as those of truthfulness and fairness.

Article 14: The freedom of the media to inform the public and to criticize institutions of society and governmental actions, which is essential for a just society, must be used with responsibility and discretion. Freedom of the media carries a special responsibility for accurate and truthful reporting. Sensational reporting that degrades the human person or dignity must at all times be avoided.

Article 15: While religious freedom must be guaranteed, the representatives of religions have a special responsibility to avoid expressions of prejudice and acts of discrimination toward those of different beliefs. They should not incite or legitimize hatred, fanaticism and religious wars, but should foster tolerance and mutual respect between all people.

Mutual Respect and Partnership

Article 16: All men and all women have a responsibility to show respect to one another and understanding in their partnership. No one should subject another person to sexual exploitation or dependence. Rather, sexual partners should accept the responsibility of caring for each other well-being.

Article 17: In all its cultural and religious varieties, marriage requires love, loyalty and forgiveness and should aim at guaranteeing security and mutual support.

Article 18: Sensible family planning is the responsibility of every couple. The relationship between parents and children should reflect mutual love, respect, appreciation and concern. No parents or other adults should exploit, abuse or maltreat children.

Conclusion

Article 19: Nothing in this Declaration may be interpreted as implying for any state, group or person any right to engage in any activity or to perform any act aimed at the destruction of any of the responsibilities, rights and freedom set forth in this Declaration and in the Universal Declaration of Human Rights of 1948.

*   *   *

BIBLIOGRAPHY

Books by Marcus Braybrooke,
On Interfaith

Pilgrimage of Hope. One Hundred Years of Global Interfaith Dialogue.
Tells the story of interfaith organizations from 1893 to 1992. Published by
SCM Press. 0-334-02500-1

A Heart for the World: The Interfaith Alternative: A passionate plea for the
religions of the world to work together for peace, to relieve poverty, and to
work for the environment. Special 1 905047 43 6

Stepping Stones to a Global Ethic, A Selection of Documents from interfaith
conferences, Ed by Marcus Braybrooke, published by SCM Press. post free
033401574-X

On Christianity

The Explorer's Guide to Christianity. 'A passionate plea for an open
Christianity and memorable guide to the core of the faith.'
This book is now available online at www.religion-online.org

On Judaism

How to understand Judaism. A straight forward introduction with black and
white pictures. Published by SCM Press 0-334-02614-8

Dialogue with a Difference. Theological reflection by some Jewish and
Christian thinkers. Edited by Tony Bayfield and Marcus Braybrooke.
Published by SCM Press.

Christian-Jewish Dialogue: The next Steps forward. SCM Press.

On Prayer

Learn to Pray: A practical guide to enriching your life through prayer.
Published by Duncan Baird, 1-903296 22 6.

1,000 World Prayers, An Anthology of Prayers from many Traditions, John
Hunt o-books, 1-1903816173.

Meditations for a peaceful Heart and a peaceful World, o-books 1-84181-
2307.

On Islam

What can we learn from Islam, o-books, 1 903816-27-0.

On Hinduism

What can we learn from Hinduism, o-books 1 903816-20-3.

Other Recommendable Reading

Selection of Books

by Küng, Hans, Catholic Theologian:
Christianity and the World Religions: Paths to Dialogue with Islam, Hinduism and Buddhism, Orbis Books, 1986.
Reforming the Church Today: Keeping Hope Alive, Crossroad Pub Co., 1992.
Theology for the Third Millennium: An Ecumenical View, Anchor, 1990.
Judaism: Between Yesterday and Tomorrow, Crossroad, 1992.
Christianity: Essence, History, and Future, Continuum International Publishing Group, 1996.
Global Responsibility: In Search of a New World Ethic, Continuum International Publishing Group, 1993.
Islam: Past, Present and Future, Oneworld Publications, 2007.

by Toffler, Alvin:
Future Shock, Mass Market Paperback, 1971.
The Third Wave, Rh Value Publishing, 1987.
Powershift: Knowledge, Wealth, and Power at the Edge of the 21st Century, 1991.

Others:
Lenaers, Roger s.j., *Nebuchadnezzar's Dream or The End of a Medieval Catholic Church*, Gorgias Press, 2007. Catholicism, and most of Christianity, have remained attached to the language and images of the Middle Ages. This attachment makes the church a foreign object in the modern world. Its message has become incomprehensible for modern people. A re-wording of the language used in the Eucharist and in the Sacraments should be a primary subject of theologians and liturgists.
Fernando, Antony, *Buddhism made Plain, and Christian Path to Mental Maturity*, Intercultural Book Promotors, inculture@eureka.lk (the latter translated into Dutch and edited under the title 'Het Christendom in Evolutie' by the Teilhard de Chardin Foundation, Holland. sttdc@worldonline.nl
Hughes, Richard Seager, *The Dawn of Religions Pluralism, Voices from the World's Parliament of Religions*, 1893Open Court, La Salle, Illinois 6130, USA, 1993.
Beversluis, Joel, *Sourcebook of the World's Religions, An Interfaith Guide to Religion and Spirituality*, Publishers Group West, 1993.
Huxley, Aldous, *The perennial Philosophy*, Flamingo, 1994.

Teilhard de Chardin, Pierre, (1881-1955), (5 livres) *Le Phénomène Humain, L'Apparition de l'Homme, La Vision du Passé, Le Milieu Divin, en L'Avenir de l'Homme*, Editions du Seuil, 1955.

Thich Nhat Hanh, *La Vision Profonde*, Albin Michel, 1998.

Panikkar, Raimon, *A Dwelling Place. for Wisdom*, Westminster/John Knox Press, 1993.

Armstrong, Karen, *A History of God*, Mandarin Paperback, 1993, 1994, 1995. (translated into many languages) and all her other books.

Des Jardins, Arnaud, *Regards Sages sur in Monde fou, Entretiens avec Gilles Farcet*, La Table Ronde, 1997.

Revel, Jean-François & Matthieu Ricard, *Le moine et le philosophe,, Le bouddhisme aujourd'hui*, Nil Editions, 1997.

Mofid, Kamran, *Globalisation for the Common Good*, Shepard-Walweyn, UK, 2002. And other books by this author.

Ozaki, Robert, *Human Capitalism*, Kodansha, 1991.